THE CUBA COMMISSION REPORT

The Cuba Commission Report

A HIDDEN HISTORY OF THE CHINESE IN CUBA

The Original English-Language Text of 1876

no author
pru says

INTRODUCTION BY DENISE HELLY

THE JOHNS HOPKINS UNIVERSITY PRESS

BALTIMORE AND LONDON

© 1993 The Johns Hopkins University Press
All rights reserved
Printed in the United States of America on acid-free paper

Originally published by The Imperial Maritime Customs Press,
Shanghai, 1876. The original edition contained the French-language
version of "Despatch to Yamên" and "Replies to Queries" as well as
the Chinese-language version of "Despatch to Yamên."

Johns Hopkins Paperbacks edition, 1993

The Johns Hopkins University Press
2715 North Charles Street
Baltimore, Maryland 21218-4319
The Johns Hopkins Press Ltd., London

Library of Congress Cataloging-in-Publication Data
The Cuba Commission report : a hidden history of the Chinese in Cuba : introduction by
Denise Helly.
    p.   cm. — (Johns Hopkins studies in Atlantic history and culture)
Originally published: Shanghai : Imperial Maritime Customs Press, 1876.
Includes bibliographical references.
ISBN 0-8018-4641-2 (pbk. : alk. paper)
1. Alien labor, Chinese—Cuba—History.   2. China—Foreign relations—Cuba.   3. Cuba—
Foreign relations—China.   I. China Cuba Commission.   II. Series.
HD8208.5.C5C83   1993
331.6'25107291—dc20   92-38926

A catalog record for this book is available from the British Library.

CONTENTS

A Note to the Reader

In the course of the nineteenth century, many millions of people, most of them coming from poor and populous agrarian societies, left their homes to cross whole oceans in search of a better life. We know a good deal about these migrations, but far less than we would like to know, particularly about the personal experiences of the migrants themselves. What follows is an unusual series of accounts of just such experiences.

Given the immense scale of the migrations, *The Cuba Commission Report*, which deals specifically with the condition of Chinese workers in Cuba, may appear to be only a modest item in migration history. Yet it is an invaluable one, for its substance arose from face-to-face encounters of questioner and respondent occurring under extremely difficult conditions. Rather than being solely history, it is also in its own way oral history—and an unusually early specimen of oral history.

None of the migrants who here "speaks" through interlocutors could have known his or her destiny. Each had left country and family, and though most had hopes of returning eventually to the lands and kinfolk they had left behind, few were able ever to do so. What they said here is essentially the last trace that most of them left in the written record. Yet because this document survives, the migrants live on through their words, through what they witnessed, and through how they judged what they saw.

Thus the reissue of this remarkable inquiry places in the hands of students and others a powerful document in the history of labor in the Americas. Like most primary documents, however, the report of the Cuba Commission does not yield up its richest evidence easily or at first glance. With this in mind, we decided to print the facsimile edition in a workbook format, with soft covers and generous margins, thereby hoping to encourage readers to explore it with pencil in hand, querying, tallying, and underlining as they read.

To dig out its riches, the reader may want to adopt some of the stratagems of a historian or anthropologist returning from fieldwork with a photocopy of a suggestive and puzzling document. Charles Gibson, the historian of colonial Mexico, used to advise his graduate students that, when faced with a dense archival source and uncertain what to do next, they should start to make lists. This seemingly simple technique lay at the heart of Gibson's discoveries about continuities between Aztec and Spanish rule in the Valley of Mexico; it can also be used in examining *The Cuba Commission Report*.

One might, for example, use lists to explore the meanings that the Chinese witnesses gave to their sufferings. The basic notion of labor coercion is not unfamiliar to us, and one's first response is to see this report as relentless evidence of oppression. It is possible to go further, however, noting the specific character and frequency of grievances reported by the laborers. In addition to reports of physical violence, there are detailed testimonies about the shame felt by the workers at being stripped naked and sold like animals, their revulsion at the food they were fed, and their rage at being punished by slave foremen. By identifying different categories of grievance and abuse, and tallying their incidence, one can develop a more complex picture of the character of oppression itself while raising additional questions about the uses of interview data.

Following the methods of an ethnographer, one can also take care to note and query the unfamiliar. Many of the deponents, for example, refer to the indignity of having their hair forcibly cut. One deponent reported: "In the Havana barracoon, for refusing to permit the removal of my queue, I was almost beaten to death." These reports encourage one to inquire into the significance of the queue for a Chinese male in these decades, and also hint at the significance of forced dishonor and humiliation in the process of labor control in a slave society. There is a cultural and historical specificity to dishonor, and this is reflected in the workers' concern both with their hair and with the disposition of their bones after death.

Finally, evidence of resistance to abuse pervades this document. By noting patterns in the form and content of resistance, one can discern the relative importance of the strategies of legal challenge, the accumulation of money for self-purchase, and the organization of collective action. Though essentially unprotected by the law, Chinese workers nonetheless frequently appealed to authority. Laws, even laws that were repeatedly breached, created a space for challenge that indentured laborers were prepared to seize. Like slaves before and after them, they insisted upon the recognition of rights that they may have known would never be willingly respected—and through their insistence, they helped to define freedom for themselves.

Most of the laborers' acts of resistance were met by brute force, and their goals were thwarted. But by presenting their petitions and depositions, more than two thousand Chinese workers voiced their experiences, challenged their oppressors, and thereby helped bring about an abrupt end to the trade that had carried them to Cuba. In the process, they left an indelible record of their ordeal and of their own capacity to make history in the face of overwhelming force.

Rebecca J. Scott
Sidney W. Mintz

The Cuba Commission Report

INTRODUCTION

Denise Helly
Translated by Sidney W. Mintz

The *Cuba Commission Report*, a remarkable document by any measure, is considered by some to be one of the most unusual sources for the history of labor migration ever assembled. Although it deals with events that occurred late in the nineteenth century, the narratives of cruelty and suffering provided by the *Report* remind one of earlier eras in labor history, including the era of New World slavery. This system had by no means been entirely eliminated from the hemisphere when the materials for the *Report* were being collected. In fact, the circumstances the *Report* details were related directly to the economy and politics of a slave-based society, one entangled in the tortuous transition to free labor.

The commission that collected the information for the *Report* was created by imperial decree for purely political reasons, but the *Report* itself was prepared by representatives of a country that lacked the capability of protecting its citizens abroad, either militarily or politically. Hence the *Report* also dramatizes the awful fate of those who, through no fault of their own, had in effect become men without a country; since they were totally unprotected by their homeland while abroad, the migrants were fair game for all who were their hosts. The frustration and rage of such victims, once understood, may also help us grasp the powerful nationalism of people who, bereft of the protection of their homeland, feel doomed to become helpless pawns in the modern world.

The *Report* is an oral history. If it were presented to readers without explanation and without background, the text might seem enigmatic and bizarre. But once that background is provided and the circumstances of the gathering of its text are understood, readers will appreciate the difficulties and dangers that accompanied the *Report*'s preparation. This is, indeed, labor history and migration history—but of a sort rarely narrated in so terrifying a manner. As such, it is a chapter in a lengthy and depressing tale, a tale not yet ended.

The history of international labor migration during the last several centuries has also been a history of the expansion and growth of the domestic and overseas economies of the Western powers. The increases and declines in the global movement of labor clearly mark successive periods in the restructuring of the economies of the West. Such shifts in population are visible signs of unequal employment opportunities, as revealed on an international level.[1] In effect, certain population groups are compelled to exile themselves if they wish to survive economically and to maintain their social status. Others who are slightly better off may actually achieve some upward economic or political mobility by means of migration. Some natives of the host society may be able to maintain or even improve their status as a result of the arrival of foreign workers.

International migration of labor power is governed by two general tendencies. First, increases in the cost of labor in capitalist economies are constant because of inherent structural propensities. Continuous, ongoing capital accumulation requires a steady supply of labor and, as a result, a steady rise in the number of people who must rely upon wage labor to ensure their subsistence. It brings about a reduction in the importance of the economic role of the domestic sphere; a rise in the costs of reproducing the labor force; and the greater possibility of resistance (sometimes in the form of political organizing by wage laborers) aimed at some improvement of work conditions and wage levels. Second, unequal national development and a spatial concentration of capital result in a relative surplus population of workers in less industrialized countries. These workers are then employed by the dominant economies according to their estimates of production risks and their structural needs, as these evolve.[2]

By working backward over the course of two centuries, one can discern four principal periods in migrant labor history. Starting in the mid 1970s, the industrial evolution of the West was affected by the entry into the world market of some newly industrialized Third World countries. These nations were able to compete for themselves in those sectors of production that, for nearly half a century, had experienced substantial employment, but under Western management and control. This internationalization of economic exchange had contributed, for the past dozen or so years, to the growth of a modest capacity to create new jobs in developing countries and, in Western societies, to the local enlargement of the more capitalistic sectors of production. It also engendered a strong demand for a highly qualified and mobile labor pool, resulting in a devaluation of that part of the labor force that was not able to perform up to the new standards. Transfers of this latter, less qualified labor power to the West diminished drastically, and have practically halted in Western Europe. In France, for example, annual entry levels of laborers declined from about 226,000 in 1973 to 39,000 in 1987;[3] and in Canada from 218,000 in 1974 to 84,000 in 1985.[4] In contrast, levels in the United States never declined, but during the 1970s they reached a plateau at about 390,000 entries a year.[5] The numbers rose during the 1980s, but recruitment turned more and more toward highly qualified workers.

A different cycle had taken shape in the twenty-five years following the end of World War II (1945–70). In that period, an increase in productivity coupled with the introduction of mass production and the consolidation of the welfare state brought about important economic growth, an increase in the cost of labor, and new demands for labor power. The use of immigration to provide a reserve of labor typified the industrial nations such as Germany, Great Britain, the Scandinavian countries, France, the United States, and Canada, which had opened up their borders to large numbers of people coming from the Mediterranean countries. When this flow slowed during the 1960s, the countries of the Third World found themselves exporting part of their unemployed on the one hand, but losing some of their most qualified workers on the other. Between 1950 and 1970, 6.4 million Europeans reached the Americas,[6] while another 7.5 million people left Southern Europe to move northward or left Ireland for the United Kingdom.[7] These migrations met the demand for less qualified labor while permitting North America to make use of highly qualified workers who had been trained at the expense of their countries of origin. In 1975, these two types of foreign workers made up 10 percent of the labor supply of the countries of Western Europe (25% in Switzerland, 11% in France, 9% in West Germany, 7% in Austria and Belgium, 6% in Sweden) and, despite the difficulties of estimating their numbers because of illegal immigration, approximately 10 percent in the United States.[8]

Another cycle of decreasing migration could be observed during the twenty years preceding World War II when, as a result of severe economic contractions in the 1920s and the crash of 1929, Western Europe and North America closed their borders to immigrants. This cycle, however, followed one of major immigration, during the era of economic liberalism and rapid industrialization from about 1850 to 1910. The most important cycle in the history of population transfers took place in this period, initiated to satisfy labor needs of the leading economic powers (the United States, France, and Great Britain). From about 1850 until the beginning of World War I, approximately 40 million Europeans of all origins crossed the oceans, the majority destined for North America. At the same time many Eastern and Southern Europeans migrated to France and Belgium, where rapid industrial development had caused a shortage of urban labor. In France, for example, there was a slowing of demographic growth and a feeble movement from the countryside to the city. In North America, the opening of more land to agriculture created immense labor needs in both the United States and Canada.

Yet an even earlier cycle, beginning before the periods outlined above, can be plotted in this graph of labor migration. It involved the movement of many thousands of persons, not toward European and American societies, but toward territories controlled by Western powers. During the nineteenth century, massive intercontinental transfers of population increased the value of agricultural land situated in the colonies of the Western powers. The commerce in Asian workers despatched to the plantations of Southeast Asia, the Philippines, and Indonesia, as well as the Antilles, was a manifestation of this phenomenon, as was the commerce in African slaves for use in the Americas. In terms of the chronology outlined above, this first major movement of Asian "free" workers in the modern era was the result of a radical restructuring of a colonial labor system. It took place on the Spanish colony of Cuba.

THE DECLINE OF THE PEARL OF THE ANTILLES

In the mid-nineteenth century, when white immigrants were penetrating previously unsettled regions of North America and Australia, migrant Chinese laborers were going into the mines of California and British Columbia and other Chinese were being despatched to the plantations of Southeast Asia. In those same years, the Spanish colony of Cuba had reached its zenith as a prosperous plantation colony fueled by slave labor. Cuba had 436,000 slaves in 1843; they constituted more than half of the island's population and made up the majority of its work force. In that same decade, however, the "Pearl of the Antilles," as Cuba was known, faced economic decline.[9]

The growth of the slave-based sugar plantation had been arithmetical, and it rested on several conditions. Extensive land would have to be cleared annually. This land had to be near ports, from which the sugar could be shipped for export. In turn, the sugar mills had to be connected to the ports by rail. To avoid increases in the cost of labor, a supply of enslaved or "enslavable" labor had to remain available on the coasts of Africa for the life and work conditions of the Cuban slaves never allowed for any natural growth of population. In the 1830s, an average minimum life expectancy of five years for slaves in Cuba was viewed as necessary to amortize the investment of capital needed to purchase a "piece of ebony"—the common term used to denote a slave. Finally, the export market for sugar had to be stable, so that sugar prices could be fixed at levels favorable to the planters.

If these conditions were met, the annual average profits of a plantation of 50 hectares with about 100 slaves could reach as high as 8–10 percent of invested capital. Between 1800 and 1840, a high demand for sugar in the international market favored the appearance of enormous estates in Cuba, each with three hundred to four hundred slaves. Above this level, however, profits fell vertiginously, the logic of quantitative growth bringing in its wake a progressive decline in the productivity of each slave added. More important, two international developments contributed to the destruction of the unstable equilibrium of the Creole sugar slave plantation: British opposition to slavery, and the large-scale production of beet sugar in France.

British Imperialism

During the first half of the nineteenth century, the British Isles were consuming about one third of the sugar that reached the world market; part of that sugar was imported from Cuba, the world's leading producer. But in 1807, Great Britain abolished the slave trade in the empire and in 1838 put an end to slavery itself, thereupon providing the colonial slave owners with the consolation of large monetary indemnities. In time, the sugar plantations of the British Antilles came to produce only raw sugar for the metropolitan refining industry. An intensified antagonism arose between Cuban and English interests, and it took the form of British-Spanish rivalry over Cuba. Great Britain desired not only to destroy the slave-based system of sugar production in order to dominate the world sugar market but also to seize Cuba from Spain.

Great Britain sought to protect sugar production in its Indian colonies and on Mauritius, a port of access to Asia it had seized from France. In 1817, and again in 1835, London signed agreements with Madrid aimed at bringing about Spanish suppression of the slave trade; but these treaties did not meet with complete success until 1865. Spain was itself enmeshed in the slave trade, which brought Madrid substantial financial benefits and ensured the political loyalty of the powerful Creole planters, through whom Spain could maintain control over its most lucrative colony. Hence, the struggle over the "Pearl of the Antilles" was a harsh one, and it involved not only the Spanish and the British who did not dare make a direct attack on the island, but the North Americans as well.

Neither Spain nor Britain dared to challenge the Creole oligarchy in Cuba for fear of pushing them into the arms of the United States—a slaveholding country to which many Creole planters actively hoped Cuba might one day be annexed. The Civil War in the United States put an end to this fantasy, leading as it did to the abolition of slavery in that country in 1865. Since both slavery and slave trading had become illegal in the British Empire, however, Britain was able to hamper the activities of the Havana and Seville slave dealers, obliging them to engage in more burdensome clandestine traffic. For instance, slave traders were compelled to buy ever more swift sail to elude pursuit by the Royal Navy. In spite of their efforts, 26,026 enslaved Africans destined for Cuba were seized by the British fleet from 1824 through 1866.[10]

Production Costs

British prosecution of the slave traders dealt a severe blow to the Cuban plantations and led to increases in the price of slave labor. A male adult slave worth 300 to 400 pesos in 1830 was worth 1,000 or more pesos by 1855. Hence, from the 1840s onward, the planters in Cuba envisioned many solutions to the rising cost of labor. One was to encourage more slave births and to raise these children as slaves, but this turned out to be even more difficult than replacing adult slaves at the going market price. The planters attempted to get Great Britain to accept an arrangement for hiring free Africans on contract, but London saw this as a ruse, and refused. They also tried to secure the abolition of a clause in the Spanish slave code of 1842 that regulated the living conditions of slaves and allowed them to purchase their freedom, beginning with a down payment of 50 pesos to their masters. In turn, the planters adopted a policy of *buen trato* (good treatment), which consisted of shortening the hours of slave labor, establishing infirmaries on each plantation, distributing better food, and providing a weekly period of rest. In effect, the principle of maximum profit was replaced by that of minimal loss. Yet none of these steps was a solution to the sugar plantation crisis, they were merely ways of prolonging plantation survival in spite of it.

The rising cost of labor was not the only problem the planters faced. Between 1820 and 1840, commercial sucrose extraction from the sugar beet, supported by government subsidies, was perfected in continental Europe. From the 1840s onward, combined German and French beet sugar production competed with the production of the Caribbean cane sugar industries. The price of sugar fell and, during the 1850s, the European market for Creole products slowly closed— especially for those goods coming from Spain's remaining New World colonies, Cuba and Puerto Rico. The market in the United States, however, remained open for sugar exports; as a result, Cuban producers became totally dependent upon a single overseas market.[11]

The Cuban planters believed they had a solution to the crisis when they adapted European refining techniques to their own sugar production; but these changes increased the productive capacity of the refining sector of their mills and left the planters in a production bottleneck. To make profitable use of greater refining capacity, both the cane field areas and the size of the field labor force had to be increased, and at a time when the cost of slaves and of transport was rising. Hence, the planters found themselves confronting a problem in the distribution of capital within units of production which were divided into two sectors: the completely unmechanized agricultural sector, in which production costs continued to rise, and the manufacturing sector, which ground the cane and processed the sugar—both operations dependent upon costly techniques of mass production. The planters had to cope with the outer economic limits of slave-based production. They wanted to industrialize the production of sugar, but because increased production could only come about with increases in the production of the primary materials, it would require employing a greater number of slaves to work in the field and also training other slaves to handle modern machinery. An ideological and political condition of slavery ran counter to this possibility.

Slave society had given rise to the image of the black slave: lazy, stupid, docile, and incapable of learning elaborate, nonroutine techniques. The planters themselves were never fooled by this image, knowing that the slaves mastered artisanal tasks requiring concentration and intelligence. They had learned from experience that the alleged ineptitude of the slaves was usually no more than a form of resistance to exhausting labor and subhuman living conditions. Nonetheless, they feared that slaves would reject the new techniques. Under these conditions, to speed up cane cultivation and to fully mechanize sugar manufacturing struck the planters as impractical. Industrialization and slavery appeared to exclude each other, so it would be necessary to fall back upon free labor to transform the plantations and to respond successfully to European competition. But the free workers of Cuba, whether white or of color, distrusted any system that would put them side by side with slaves, even though the salaries of agricultural workers in Cuba reached very high levels—almost double those of industrial workers in Europe and America.

The Retention of Slavery

The planters gave two reasons for not freeing their slave laborers. One was the experience of Jamaica. There, many of the freed people had deserted the scenes of their humiliation to relocate themselves on free land, where they could establish themselves as peasants. For the planters, the abolition of slavery could prove advantageous only if the density of population were sufficient to oblige every free person to become a wage worker on their plantations. Such was not the case in Cuba during the years 1840–50. The Cubans recognized that Spain was too weak to confront its abolitionist enemies, such as Great Britain, and observed that Jamaica, a British colony, was too disorganized economically to pay for the labor of its freed slaves. They calculated the value of their slaves at some 700 million francs, and wanted Madrid to compensate them if they were to turn Cuba into a plantation colony based on free labor. But Madrid was neither able nor willing to pay that amount.

Yet another question upset the Creole planters and led them to refuse to consider emancipation: they feared the creation of a black peasantry, which could turn the Creole social order upside down. In Cuba many of the peasants were whites who worked to provision both the plantations and the island population at large. Hence, they were the planters' principal potential allies in any eventual fight against either free people of color or slaves. The planters wanted no laws of the kind that had once been enacted in Puerto Rico, forcing the white peasantry onto the plantations; in Cuba, the political equilibrium was too uncertain for such measures.

This issue turned on percentages. From 1840 to 1860, Cuba's slave population was as large as its white population, raising concerns that were less urgent in Puerto Rico, where the ratio was only one slave to four whites. The memory of the Cuban slave revolts of the 1840s when dozens of whites had been killed and immense expanses of sugar cane burned, was fresh in the minds of the planters. Any political reform that might call into question the coercive relationship between white and black was considered an incitement to the slaves, and hence dangerous. Those educated by the abolitionists, it was believed, would take advantage of any reform to reproduce in Cuba the scenes remembered from French Saint-Domingue (now Haiti) at the beginning of the century. The political argument could be summed up in a single phrase: the planters would far rather see Cuba remain a slave territory subject to Spain than see it transformed into a black republic. Because no metropolis was able to resist this sort of argument, Spain procrastinated on the question of abolition, in spite of the persistent pressure of its European enemies.

Mechanization, the Colonato, *and Work under Contract*

If slavery was not to be abolished, what solutions could be offered which might preserve the international competitiveness of the Creole sugar plantations? The planters did not have enough capital to underwrite both the mechanization of their sugar mills and increases in the slave labor force. If the two different sectors of the sugar plantations could not be profitably connected, they would have to be separated. So it was that during the 1860s a new sort of cane producer, called the *colono*, appeared. In effect, some small-scale planters, whose funds were too limited to allow them to modernize their mills, gave up the production of sugar and became *colonos*. The *colonato* enabled large and medium-sized sugar estate proprietors to modernize without the risk of financial and political ruin. They maintained their own agricultural sector and purchased from the *colonos* the supplementary sugar cane necessary to make profitable and full use of their own mills. But the transfer of some praedial slave labor to a new category of producer did not resolve the question of finding a labor supply that could take on, and carry out, the cultivation of their own fields and the technical tasks required by the mechanized sugar mills.

The planters were forced to recognize that the monthly salary they would have to pay for each free worker they added would equal the wages paid to industrial workers in Europe. Even so, additional workers willing to accept such a salary could not be found on the island. From 1837 through 1853 many attempts were made to encourage immigration, but all of them were in vain. The few thousand European laborers brought from the Canary Islands, Catalonia, Spanish Galicia, and Ireland fled the plantations soon after they had arrived, and the Spanish authorities. fearing pressure from the countries of origin, were reluctant to subject them to conditions of coercive employment. The perplexed planters learned two lessons from this unfruitful experience: first, contracts should be hammered out to lock laborers into their jobs; second, that being the case, the use of white workers would be impossible. A new source of labor had to be found which would have the same characteristics as the slave labor force: no legal protection by a Western power; a large source of supply; and significant cultural differences, to attempt to insure that these working conditions would be accepted. The planters found potential laborers in Ethiopia, Egypt, and Polynesia; but the boats that might carry them never arrived in Cuba. Instead, peons and Yucatecan Indian prisoners were sold by Mexican *hacendados* to the Creole merchants. From 1848 through 1861, 1,047 Yucatecans reached Cuba. This traffic came to an end not only because of British pressure but also because of the difficulties of recruitment. Meanwhile, a new sort of traffic brought more promising rewards to the planters.

The Cantonese Coolies

In 1846 Pedro Zulueta, a Spanish merchant who fell into serious difficulties with English officials because of his involvement with the contraband trade in African slaves, proposed to bring 1,000 Chinese laborers to Cuba from a southern province of the Celestial Empire. His proposition was accepted by the Creole authorities, and Madrid agreed to the terms of the contract for this new labor force. According to the text of the contracts deposited in Cuban archives in Matanzas and

Havana, the Chinese laborers agreed to "work on the island of Cuba . . . at the orders of whatever person to whom the contract was transmitted." They agreed to fulfill all of the obligations specified under local law and to accept the salaries stipulated by the contracts, "although recognizing the higher level of salaries received by free workers in Cuba." Those who signed thereby acknowledged that "this difference in remuneration was compensated for by the advantages granted to them by their employers as indicated in the contracts." These advantages consisted of free transport to Cuba, the provision of lodging, medical assistance in the case of illness not lasting more than two weeks, the distribution of two and a half pounds of vegetables and eight ounces of salt meat each day, and the provision of two suits of clothing and one blanket each year. Thus, against the salary of four pesos paid monthly in silver or gold, and for the other advantages provided for in the contract, the Chinese immigrant should provide to his employer all of the services demanded, on a basis of a twelve-hour day over a period of eight years. He was also bound to accept the discipline of his employer, although no clause precisely specified the character of this discipline.

In 1852 new concessions for the importation of Chinese labor were agreed to by government officials in Madrid, and several obligations were imposed on the commercial companies involved. One-fifth of the contracts were to be filled by Chinese females, unless it was impossible to meet this condition because of opposition from the Chinese authorities. Parents were to bring their children, aged ten to eighteen years, who would be obliged to work for two pesos a month, and Chinese women would earn three pesos.[12]

The destitution of these immigrants explained the existence of such contracts. Unable to pay for their own transport, the migrants who signed up had to agree upon leaving China to render certain services to those who were paying for their trip. This system of work under contract had existed from the first years of the colonization of the Americas. English indentured servants and French engagés worked under such arrangements in the Caribbean islands and in North America between 1630 and 1730. An inherent characteristic of this system was that the real costs of the immigration agency were wildly out of proportion to the value of the labor obtained. At the Cerro market of Havana, for example, contracts of Chinese immigrants were sold for about 500 pesos, depending on the physical condition of the laborer, whereas the cost of their recruitment and the voyage came to only about 200 pesos.

This system of work by contract fulfilled two economic stipulations of the planters: it guaranteed low salaries, and it clearly specified the place and kind of work. An Asian immigrant represented the outlay of about 884 pesos, of which 500 pesos was the price of the contract as sold by the immigration agency, and 384 pesos the value of eight years' salary. A slave whose life expectancy was estimated at ten years was worth from 700 to 1,000 pesos from 1840 to 1850; hence, when the trade in African slaves was suppressed in 1865, Chinese laborers clearly constituted the cheapest labor source in Cuba.

The solution to the problem of costly free labor in a sparsely populated colonial territory had been rediscovered. The recruitment of Cantonese workers could proceed without foreseeable difficulty, except perhaps the great distance between China and the Antilles. The problems of Kwangtung (Guangdong) and particularly the Pearl Delta, near the city of Canton (Guangzhou), seemed propitious, from the planters' point of view.[13] The Delta was overpopulated and the available labor supply seemed almost as inexhaustible as that of the coast of the Gulf of Guinea, from 1760 through 1840. The native Chinese were ignorant of Creole customs and of the Spanish language, and they knew nothing of the existence of slavery. Moreover, the planters believed them to be docile, as the following quotation suggests: "We have need of men who will work side by side with the slaves; for this, only the native sons of a country governed by the whip will do. This requisite is fulfilled by the Chinese."[14]

THE RESERVOIR: CANTONESE LABOR

The Penetration of the Western Powers

During the years 1830 to 1840, England sought the opening of Chinese ports to introduce the commodities it was producing in India. One such commodity, opium, had been the cause of the first Sino-English War, which ended in January of 1841 with the cession of Hong Kong to England and the opening of the port of Canton to British commerce. Because both governments were dissatisfied with the agreement, however, the war was resumed. The English fleet occupied Ningpo (Ningbo), and then Shanghai in June 1842; some warships actually reached the Blue River (Jiangzi); and threatened Nanking (Nanjing). China capitulated, and a treaty of peace was signed at Nanking on August 29, 1842. The terms were severe: five ports on the South China coast had to be opened to English merchants, and the free movement of English merchandise on Chinese soil was henceforth to be guaranteed. Moreover, the recruitment of workers from South China, although not officially authorized by the imperial authorities, was begun as a result of pressure from English merchants.

The other Western nations observed uneasily this new and uncontested British imperial influence in China. With the outbreak of the Taiping Rebellion, they demanded commercial concessions, including the regulation of Cantonese immigration. But the Chinese imperial court resisted. France and the United States then joined Great Britain in a new war against the southern Chinese provinces; Canton, one of the cities of the south, was sacked during an expedition in December 1857. In 1858, the Chinese government indicated that it was ready to sign a treaty authorizing free Western commerce in all of China's territory. One stipulation concerned official authorization by the emperor for the immigration of his Chinese subjects. The imperial decree of 1718, which punished any Chinese attempting to leave China without the authorization of the authorities, became a dead letter. Between 1861 and 1871 other European nations signed similar accords, and Chinese emigration to Spain and its possessions was authorized by Peking in 1864.

The first Chinese arrived in Cuba thanks to Philippine intermediaries, who had been in contact with two English companies in Amoy (Xiamen), Tait and Company and Syme and Company. These companies organized the emigration of Chinese workers from the province of Fukien (Fujian) to Cuba; the Creole planters, however, were not satisfied with the services of these companies. After 1852, two other companies, Wardrop and Company and Pereda Machado and Company, obtained exclusive rights to import Chinese coolies into Cuba. The planters had recourse, however, to the forwarding agents of Tait and Company established in New York, Liverpool, and Boston, who carried out their business in South China—that is to say, in the two provinces of Kwangtung and Fukien.

In 1858, a movement against the shipment of Chinese workers to Cuba was initiated in Canton. Rumors raced through the city that the migrant workers were being carried off by force and then eaten by the Cubans. At the time, it was suggested that English Protestant missionaries were spreading these stories with the intention of discrediting their Catholic enemies. In any case, the consequences were dire. In 1858, the British seized a ship carrying six hundred emigrants recruited at Macao and forced the captain to release them in Canton. None of the six hundred was prepared to say he was emigrating voluntarily. Popular hostility toward the Spanish delegations grew, and in just one incident, eighteen Chinese recruiters were executed in Canton. The English sought to profit from this popular resistance, and from 1859 onward Chinese ports were closed to the companies and ships dealing with the Creole planters. England withdrew its ships from the traffic carrying Chinese emigrants to Cuba, and the United States followed suit after the election of Abraham Lincoln in 1861, leading authorities in Madrid to suspend its traffic.

These measures did not achieve their goal. The Creole planters in Cuba bent Madrid to their will, and the traffic was resumed by 1860. French and Russian fleets picked up where the English, American, and Dutch had left off. France was particularly active, supplying capital and ships to Creole companies, because Napoleon III had refused to accept the conditions that the English had exacted from the Chinese—conditions that amounted to a quasi-monopoly. In fact, the fight between these two sovereigns did not concern China so much as Africa, where France and Great Britain were disputing their domination of colonial territories. Nonetheless, the closing of Chinese ports compelled the Creole planters and their commercial partners to operate entirely out of Macao.

Macao, a colony founded in 1577, was the oldest European settlement in the Far East. The Portuguese had claimed this almost inaccessible port as theirs after paying a bribe to the viceroy of Canton. But the Chinese government treated the whole matter as a case of illegal land seizure and refused to acknowledge Portuguese claims. Macao itself was poverty-ridden, except for the Chinese quarter, where there was some commercial activity. But the colony was reawakened when it became the residence of the Spanish consul and the marshaling center for Chinese emigrés destined for the Spanish possessions. The alliance between the governments of Madrid and Lisbon prevented London from terminating the Spanish quest for Chinese labor. The British succeeded only in barring the provisioning with water and food of those ships carrying coolies from Macao, when they would drop anchor in Hong Kong, the deployment center for Chinese workers destined for the English colonies and for California.

Beginning in 1865, Great Britain utilized new means of applying pressure. By public declarations and in the press, it accused the Spanish and Portuguese of organizing a new system of forced labor in the guise of a program of free emigration. In 1871, when a liberal Portuguese administration gained power, policies changed in Great Britain's favor; the Portuguese liberals were sensitive to the British arguments, and the Creole planters found themselves in a precarious position. In April 1871, Spain had to order the end of the traffic, but again the Creole companies refused to agree. Once again in 1873, under both British and internal pressure, Lisbon passed a new law concerning emigration from Macao. The barracks where Chinese migrants awaited their embarkation from Macao were no longer to look like jails, and the armed guards who watched over them were to be eliminated. Moreover, the Chinese workers bound for Cuba were given Portuguese citizenship, and a new Portuguese consul, José Maria Eça de Queirós, was appointed to Havana. Eça de Queirós was a young socialist writer who soon found himself in the role of protector of the Cantonese laborers in Cuba. Finally, on December 27, 1873, Portugal put an official end to the shipment of indentured workers from its Macao colony.

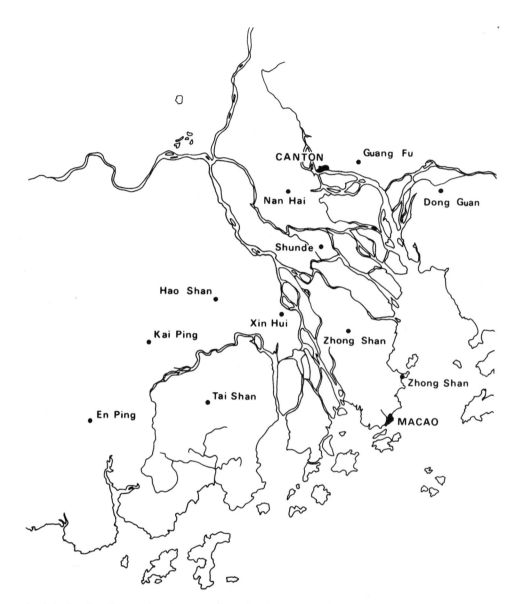

Areas of origin for the Chinese immigrants. From Denise Helly, *Ideologie et ethnicité: Les Chinois Macao à Cuba, 1847–1886* (Montreal: Les Presses de l'Université de Montréal, 1979). Reprinted by permission of the author.

Eighteen seventy-three was a fateful year for the Cuban planters and their coolie recruiters, witnesses to an incident that starkly revealed the behavior of the Creole company directors implicated in the coolie traffic. For years the imperial viceroy in Canton had used every available means to block the enforcement of the 1864 Sino-Spanish treaty, which had authorized the shipment of Chinese workers to Cuba. Since Macao was a scantily populated peninsula, coolies had to be recruited in the province of Kwangtung and brought to Macao. The viceroy actively hampered such recruitment. Therefore, in May 1873, two agents of Creole companies lodged their complaints before the emperor, claiming that the policies of the viceroy had occasioned serious financial losses to their companies and to the Cuban plantations. At the insistence of the Spanish chargé d'affaires, the Chinese government accepted the representations of the Russian, British, French, German, and American embassies in this matter. These governments, having no desire to support Creole interests, proposed an investigation to examine the fate of the Chinese emigrants.[15] The emperor accepted their proposal, and the text that follows this introduction is an outcome of this investigation.

The investigative body comprised one French and one American representative, who were to work under the authority of a highly placed Chinese functionary, Ch'en Lan Pin (Chin Lanpin), who was responsible for the educational and cultural welfare of overseas Chinese. Ch'en Lan Pin arrived in Havana from New Orleans on March 18, 1874, aboard the German ship *Strassburg*. Despite the planters' efforts to conceal the truth, the investigation caused an immediate scandal, whereupon the emperor decreed the end of shipments of Chinese coolies to Cuba. Then, in November 1877, after the publication of the *Report*, Spain signed a treaty with China officially ending coolie traffic. According to this treaty, the Chinese then under contract in Cuba were to have their contracts terminated, and Chinese consuls were named to towns on the island under the direction of the Chinese consulate general in Havana. Four consuls were named in 1879, with an eye toward the protection of Chinese subjects then residing in Cuba.

Another clause of the 1877 Treaty actually approved the voluntary emigration of Chinese citizens to Cuba. Very few free Chinese emigrants, however, would associate with the contract laborers. Spanish and Chinese financial interests were counterposed. A single Chinese company, China Merchant's Steam Navigation, retained the monopoly for transporting emigrants to the Antilles, and its directors proposed the emigration of 20,000 Chinese between 1882 and 1885. But permission for this project was not granted by the foreign minister in Madrid, who, repelled by the greed of its director, wanted to break the Chinese monopoly. In fact, it appears that highly ranked courtiers at the Peking court were sharing in the company profits. The Spanish foreign minister at the time wrote that "Chinese emigration to Cuba was left to private initiative, no official agreement being established for a continuous and controlled emigration."[16] England, the United States, and France remained the only countries to profit from the emigration of Cantonese peasants recruited as free workers for their plantations or mines.

The "Yellow Trade" to Cuba

PROFITS AND MECHANIZATION

Thanks to contract labor the crisis of slavery (which, in the view of the British, could have ruined the Creole planters in Cuba) was transformed into an era of prosperity. Between 1850 and 1868, sugar production tripled and the numbers of Cantonese contract laborers and the tonnages of exported sugars increased *pari passu* from 1847 to 1874. Between 1860 and 1870, Cuba could boast of thirty entirely mechanized sugar factories that, with the assistance of hundreds of slaves and Chinese laborers, swallowed up the harvest of thousands of hectares. During its investigations, the Ch'en Lan Pin Commission visited some of these plantations. Las Cañas, where they went first, ground the cane from 629 hectares of its own land in 1874, and the harvest from 134 hectares belonging to its *colonos* (cane suppliers). The plantation España was also visited by the commission; it had 938 hectares under cultivation, of which sixty-seven were in the hands of *colonos*.

Creole and metropolitan capitalists, as well as merchants, plantation owners, and big planters, were among the promoters of Asian labor importation—dubbed the "yellow trade" by Cuban historians. This highly speculative enterprise accorded to all parties significant rewards. It facilitated the mechanization of the sugar mills of the island's biggest planters, who in the past had often been the organizers and beneficiaries of slaving expeditions to the African coasts. The profits of the "yellow trade" reached U.S. $80 million and, depending on the year, yielded up to 150 percent or more on the capital invested. A witness from the years 1868–70 described a ship he had visited which was carrying 900 newly arrived contract laborers. This cargo represented a value of 450,000 pesos for the importers, whereas the original outlay had been 50,000 pesos, and the costs of the expedition less than 100,000 pesos. Thus, in this single shipment the firm cleared a profit of at least 300,000 pesos. What is more, in the period 1850–60, an expedition that had cost 150,000 pesos did not require more than a 30,000–50,000 peso cash investment, since the rest of the capital was advanced by the Junta de Fomento. From the outset this planter organization was supported financially both by the government and by the Creole and foreign banks.

Beginning in 1856, three firms protected by the Spanish Crown shared the right to carry Asians to Cuba. One of these, the Colonizadora, founded in 1854 by Rafael Torices with financing from the planters, controlled the traffic until 1860. This company exemplifies the vertical economic integration characteristic of those firms that controlled the lion's share of the emigration. The Colonizadora supplied the funds needed for its recruiting expeditions, assumed all other risks, had its own recruiting agent in China, owned its own barracks in Macao and Havana, had its own employees charged with the transfer of contracts, and even hired its own doctors for the medical supervision of the laborers. All the company lacked was its own shipping. It used English ships until 1859, then French ships, but later bought clippers and steamships sailing under Portuguese, Spanish, and Latin American flags. Small owners protested in vain to Madrid concerning this monopoly, which raised the costs of laborers' contracts.

Ultimately, an unauthorized importation of coolies by the Spanish court was begun, protected by the captain-general of Cuba, the highest ranking local authority, who made money from the illegal landings of coolies on the island. In 1863, import concessions were accorded to three new companies controlled by the big planters of Havana and Matanzas. Then, between 1869 and 1874, two other companies intimately connected to the big planters in the west of the island came to dominate the traffic until its end.

GRADUAL ABOLITION

The large sugar plantations, and the *colonos* that depended upon them, extended themselves through three provinces: Havana, Matanzas, and Las Villas, which together composed the western part of Cuba. The Ch'en Lan Pin mission did not reach the central and eastern provinces of Cuba, where peasants cultivated fruits and vegetables for island markets and tobacco (their cash crop) for export, and where cattlemen supplied meat to the island plantations and leather to the world market. In these regions there also lived a large free colored population that included merchants, artisans, and cane planters who, using outdated equipment, produced unrefined sugars for domestic consumption. In 1868, 276 owners were known to possess more than eighty slaves each in the western provinces; the average number of slaves per owner in the jurisdiction of Guantánamo—a coffee-producing zone in the east of the island—was only twenty six. The sugar planters of western Cuba controlled 90 percent of agricultural production, represented 77 percent of the colony's population, and owned 78 percent of its livestock. But in the central and eastern regions, the plantations were remote from the ports through which they shipped their sugar; they had limited productive capacity, their cane lands were never more than about 130 hectares per plantation, and their mills depended on animal power. For these modest enterprises, it was more viable for the planters to free their slaves and to rely upon wage labor instead.

The different groups of producers in the central and eastern provinces realized that Madrid had no interest in supporting them: Madrid refused to liberalize trade with the European countries and imposed taxes on both imports and exports. These producers provided the leadership for a reformist political movement and, beginning around 1840, made various demands on the government, which were supported by all of the whites on the island: free trade, reform of the customs duties, importation of white laborers, the end of the Spanish mercantile monopoly of the slave trade, representative government for local affairs, constitutional rights for Spanish citizens, the separation of military and civil power,[17] and representation in parliament in Madrid. But these demands were reduced to a lengthy list of frustrated hopes; no reforms were granted by Spain.

During the 1860s, sharpening competition with European sugar producers and British pressure for the abolition of both the slave trade and Cuban slavery deeply divided the Creole planters, east and west. The eastern sector, capital poor and excluded from the benefits of Asian immigration, felt threatened by the increasing competition of the European sugar industry and pressured for economic concessions from the metropolis. But in 1867, Madrid again rejected the demands for colonial administrative reform, indemnities for slave owners, and freedom of commerce, and instituted instead yet another tax—this one representing 10 percent of property values—while maintaining the customs system and asserting its hostility to any political change. Not surprisingly, perhaps, an insurrection broke out in the east of the island. This rebellion was supported by some planters of the central provinces, alarmed as they were by the ruin of the plantations in the east to which they had traditionally supplied fresh and dried meat. The insurgents' ranks also included many people of color in eastern Cuba.

In an attempt to resolve the crisis, an emancipation plan called the Moret Law was adopted by Spain in 1870. It freed slave children born after 1868 and slaves who were more than sixty years of age. Although plantation production was not hampered by these changes, the big planters from the west of the island were hostile to the plan, and arranged to expel from Cuba the governors who were responsible for its implementation. The planters wanted to slow the beginning of the abolition of slavery, which, in their view, would only bring other disagreeable measures in its wake. They assisted the Spanish army of Martínez Campos in its repressive activities against the nationalist insurgents in the east.

Faced with this coalition of Creole and Spanish interests, the rebels sought military and financial aid from the United States, to whom the annexation of the island had been proposed; but the Americans refused to enter the conflict. In the face of this rejection, and the opposition of the planters of western Cuba, the insurgent chiefs sought to make peace. Spain facilitated this in 1877, and a year later the nationalist leadership signed a pact to end the war. Only a group of men of color under the direction of General Antonio Maceo, a fighter for both the independence of the island and the abolition of slavery, carried on the struggle; but their futile resistance came to an end in 1879. A second insurgency in 1879–80 also ended in defeat. Some insurgents chose exile in the United States, where they organized a new movement in favor of the liberation of the Spanish colony.

In 1880, Spain adopted a program of progressive emancipation of slave labor, which was a response to the proposals from the big planters in the west. Spain instituted a patronage system in Cuba (the *patronato*), aimed at limiting the freedom of movement of slaves during the process of emancipation. The slaves, now "apprentices," were to receive modest "stipends," but they were obligated to remain for six years under the tutelage of their former masters, who would become their patrons. The system of patronage enabled planters to transform their slave labor force into a salaried labor force, while attempting to avoid the two dangers of sudden abolition: desertion by the newly freed, and increases in agricultural wages. Slavery was finally abolished in Cuba in 1886, with the release of the remaining apprentices from the *patronato*.

The political omnipotence of the planters who owned modern sugar mills was undergirded by the prosperity of the years 1840–80, which helped them to weaken European opposition. Thus, the planters were able to nullify the many attempts by Great Britain to sabotage their economy, compel the Spanish government to bend to their demands, and ensure the repression of their local political enemies.

The arrival of a hundred thousand Asian workers had facilitated the industrialization of sugar production and the maintenance of slavery by Cuba's powerful sugar interests. Great Britain, which had provoked the Creole sugar transformation of 1840–60 by attacking slavery and the Cuban recruitment initiatives in South China, had lost the decisive battle. The English never achieved their goal of ruining Cuba to the advantage of their own refining industry: the unrefined Creole sugar reached the American mills, and Cuba became a political and economic dependency of the United States.

The Pearl Delta

A brief look at Cantonese society makes it easier to understand to whom we are referring when we speak of Cuba's Chinese coolies.[18] In the middle of the nineteenth century, the vital center of Kwangtung province, the Pearl Delta, experienced an internal crisis aggravated by the aggression of the Western nations.

In this ostensibly agrarian province, male descendants of the same male ancestor were born into a particular clan, which had its own proper name. The unity of each clan was symbolized by its ancestral land holdings, which were the collective property of clan members; by a common cemetery; by an ancestral temple, which sheltered four generations of male ancestors; and by a common fund. This fund, managed by the senior males, made it possible to fulfill numerous obligations, including guaranteeing the cost of rituals owed to the ancestors, covering the needs of impoverished clan members, and paying for the studies of clansmen aspiring to posts within the imperial administration. These funds also served to purchase new common lands, which, when cultivated, enriched the clan. Hence, a man's membership in a clan established his identity and provided possible political influence through access to public affairs, material aid in case of need, and protection in the instance of conflict with another clan. But for certain men, this membership meant, above all, the acquisition of wealth.

Clan organization was animated by a distinctive dynamic. A clan was divided into households composed of two or three generations of males, their wives and children, and sometimes collateral relatives and impoverished allies. These patrilines had their own lands and an altar for the ancestors, who could usually be traced back at least four generations. The status of the different patrilines within the same clan was in no sense equal, and their relation to one another was marked by rivalry as much as by solidarity, each trying to consolidate its wealth in land and to promote its members to the imperial administration. In fact, the richest lines enjoyed a supremacy at the heart of the whole clan and utilized common funds with the aim of increasing their own means and influence. The less wealthy lines, unable to contribute in an equal fashion to the common fund, were relegated to positions of inferiority and dependence. Over time, the rich lines accumulated more and more advantages, such as decisive administrative positions, rents from both their own and their ancestral lands, and income from profitable activities bestowed upon them by the emperor, such as internal and external trade, controlled by the imperial authorities, who delegated the practice of trade to particular individuals.

The commercial exchanges that China maintained with foreign countries were carried out largely in the south, and from the eighteenth century onward this situation facilitated the accumulation of wealth and land in those lines that were closest to the imperial bureaucracy. The dynamic of internal clan organization revealed itself to be highly inequitable; for example, access to land was restricted to men of a line who had obtained through inheritance an equal part of the land from their father. A parceling of holdings followed, slowed only by the purchase of new land, which in turn raised the price of arable land.

Socio-economic cleavages at the heart of the clans were drastically accentuated during the years 1820–70, when natural catastrophes were added to already powerful demographic pressures and an agricultural system in disarray, following the suppression of numerous rebellions in the Blue River Valley.[19] Imperial policy was not modified to stem the effects of this demographic pressure; no land reform was adopted, no measures to increase productive capacity were instituted, few irrigation canals were dug, few reservoirs or grain warehouses were built, and no programs for the clearing of new land were instituted. The demographic growth in Kwangtung had important consequences for the clans, resulting in a diminution of land holdings for the less privileged patrilines, a reduction in their standard of living, and an increase in their indebtedness to the richer lines, who imposed usurious terms on their tenants. In 1833, the average Cantonese peasant had access to only one-tenth of a hectare,[20] while the successful patrilines were able to accumulate vast holdings. Since a village was frequently composed of members of a single clan, sharecroppers, renters, small peasants, and large land owners might belong to the same grand clan, but its internal solidarity would be seriously compromised.[21]

Confronted with growing misery, the members of the poorest lines—usually peasants themselves—sought to cultivate the most productive and commercially promising kinds of crops, such as cotton, tea, and silkworm mulberry. This alternative, however, was available only to peasants whose land was suited to such production; who had adequate family labor for cultivation and were relatively near a port or manufacturing center for sales and distribution. Many people lost their land and had either to engage in craft manufacture, become agricultural laborers, or move to urban areas. Finding wage labor in the cities was fraught with difficulty, due to the large number of shops in the villages and towns of Kwangtung. In effect, the presence of Western powers seeking to penetrate markets in South China gave rise to an increasing importation of manufactured products and a reduction in manufacturing activity in the region itself; Kwangtung had too little industrial activity to absorb an important fraction of its own ruined peasant population.

Other forces played a part in the deterioration of the Cantonese social system. Secret societies, which had developed an egalitarian ideology and were challenging the imperial order, were strongly established in Kwangtung. Because of the province's social crisis, these societies were able to augment their control in the peasant world, limiting and hindering any action by the imperial functionaries. The strongest patrilines responded by creating their own armed units, and the Peking government did nothing to intervene. The political instability that ensued aggravated social and economic difficulties in the southern districts of Kwangtung, which gave rise to the chaos of the 1840s and culminated in the Taiping Rebellion of 1848. For seventeen years, until 1865, the province of Kwangtung, among others, was the scene of clashes between imperial troops and the rebels. The cost of this conflict further impoverished the masses, already the victims of landowners' greed and of the armed bands that pillaged the harvests and imposed their own taxes. To escape the poverty and brutality, many villagers sought asylum in the provincial metropolis of Canton.

Peasants, artisans, ruined petty merchants, discharged soldiers, and beggars formed a parallel world in the south of the province, infiltrated by the secret societies and wracked by misery and instability. These people worked at all sorts of poorly paid and insecure jobs, which afforded them only bare survival, while the English, French, Spanish, and American merchants profited by recruiting the destitute workers for cheap migrant labor. Southeast Asia, the Americas, and Australia became the promised lands for poor Cantonese; the emigration of a member of these impoverished families became a means of assuring the subsistence of those who stayed behind.

As with other populations who emigrated in the nineteenth and twentieth centuries, the Cantonese left China under the pressure of material poverty; but as for other Europeans and Asians, the emigration was far more than a response to impoverishment.

For the Cantonese, emigration symbolized loss of identity and humiliation—exclusion from their society. By leaving Kwangtung, however, they sought to remedy their situation, to carry out a plan that was linked to the core representation of Confucianism, upon which clan organization depended. According to Confucian belief, the spirit of a person, detached from the body at death, carries on an autonomous and human existence, inasmuch as the spirit must continue to be nourished and honored. Such is the meaning of the rituals celebrated on the tombs and at the clan altars of those patrilines, where wooden tablets, representing the dead ancestors, are kept. If these honors are not conferred upon the ancestors their spirits suffer an unfortunate fate and become malevolent. Therefore, according to the patrilineal principle that governs clan organization, every male descendant must render homage to them. He honors his ancestors with the aim of maintaining his place in the community of the dead, as well as of the living; it is the ancestors who define his social status and on whom his identity is based. This community is embodied in the vision of a chain through time, made up of as many as a dozen generations, which tie the earliest ancestors to their many descendants. The continuity of the chain is a measure of the prosperity and happiness of the line itself—for the descendants as well as for the dead. To be sure, the clans are fragmented into lines, and the closest ancestral spirits frequently take precedence over their predecessors, particularly in the poorer lines; in the absence of material means, the most distant ancestors cannot be honored. Moreover, as the spirits of this latter group are petitioned by the multitude of their descendants, their favor or protection becomes less important, and preference is accorded to the closer ancestors.

In accord with Confucian belief, each male member of the line feels obligated to ensure that his line flourishes; to break the continuity of a line is to risk total social ostracism. Each descendant's goal is to see deposited on the altar of his ancestors the wooden tablet that represents his existence within the line, for to remain part of the chain of the living and the dead defines him as a man. If he must leave the land of his ancestors, he hopes to return to it, to await the day of his death and to be installed in the soil of his ancestors and of his descendants. But if, in a land other than his own, he is able to create a line that honors his spirit and follows the cardinal Confucian virtues of filial piety and respect for the aged, he can then envisage the transportation of the ancestral tablets to a foreign land and can contemplate self-exile. It is only on this condition, being able to found a family and therefore maintain the chain of ancestors and descendants, that a Cantonese emigrant can accept the abandonment of Chinese soil.

The men who left Kwangtung in the nineteenth century were usually the first of their line to emigrate, and most of them left alone, unaccompanied by their wives and children, for whom they had provided before departure. When their fathers' lands were divided, they renounced their claims in favor of a brother or a male relative who remained in the village and ensured the care of the ancestral shrine and of their spouses, children and aging parents. If unmarried, they hoped to return some months after, with the aim of marrying and having children.

Subjected to a grave social crisis, Cantonese peasants, craftsmen, and day laborers left their homes. Their willingness to work hard and to live modestly, repeatedly described by contemporaries in the countries to which they were exiled, were simple signs of their readiness to transform their unhappy departures into honorable exploits. The emigrants wanted to send their savings to the families they had left behind, and to accumulate wealth to permit them to purchase land upon their return to China. Or, if they could bring their wives and children to the new land, they put aside their savings so the definitive reestablishment of the patriliny in a new land would be assured.

It is estimated that one million Cantonese left the two provinces of South China between 1840 and 1875, the majority coming from Kwangtung. The number of emigrants from other provinces in the empire, where labor traffic was not organized by the West, was much smaller. The majority departed as free workers for the mines of California, Canada, or Australian Queensland, and for the French, Dutch, and English plantations of Southeast Asia. Some Cantonese were recruited for Surinam and other Dutch possessions, and the English and French islands such as Mauritius and Réunion.[22] Of the total number of emigrants, roughly 100,000 persons signed contracts to work in Peru, and 142,000 went to Cuba.[23]

A History Endured

The disillusionment of the Cantonese who signed work contracts for Cuba was immediate and total. They had in no way imagined that they were renouncing their condition as free men when they agreed to work in some distant, unknown land. They had no idea that they were the labor resource of a Creole sugar oligarchy determined to accept the end of slavery only on its own terms. The document that follows this introduction is a dramatic illustration of the painful deception of these people who, most of them between twenty and thirty years of age, had willingly exiled themselves to improve their own fate, only to discover that they would live as slaves.

If they were not carried off by force in the first place, then from their arrival in the Macao barracks, the migrants soon discerned the false promises of good treatment they had been given by the recruiters. Guarded by armed men and secluded in jail-like barracks, they were made aware of the terrible punishment inflicted upon those who refused to sign contracts or to embark upon the ships bound for Cuba. Some of the migrants who resisted were tortured. Others executed; and all had to suffer humiliation—such as the cutting off of the pigtail that the Chinese commonly wore. Once on board the "devil-ships" (as the Chinese dubbed them) that carried them on the three- to four-month trip to Cuba from Macao, every illusion was lost. Rebellions, assassinations of crews, reprisals against captains, suicides, and death by thirst cost the lives of some 16,000 of the 142,000 Cantonese who left for Cuba. The ships followed a long route that took them past the Straits of Sunda, with a stop at Batavia, and on to the Cape of Good Hope. They made a short stop at St. Helena for fresh water before heading for Ascension, Cayenne, the Barbadian coast, Trinidad, and finally Cuba. The steamships followed the same route, in spite of the opening of the Panama Canal; in 1865, Colombia, an independent nation opposed to slavery, prohibited even momentary landings by any ship carrying people against their will. The Suez Canal was not used, and by the time it was open to navigation, the coolie traffic was declining.

Most immigrants disembarked in Havana, where they were brutally examined by whites who paid large sums for their contracts, before being conducted, under guard, to their future places of work. Almost three-quarters of the Chinese were sent to the big sugar plantations of the western provinces.[24] A fraction of the remaining workers were sent to the tobacco and cattle-herding zones of the central and eastern provinces; some 20 percent were employed in crafts and artisanry such as cigar making and carpentry, 5 percent worked in laundering and domestic labor, and the rest were involved with the expansion of the sugar industry (stevedoring, railroad work, construction of municipal buildings, and railway maintenance).

Given the labor shortages on the island's largest plantations, the majority of the migrants ended up cultivating and cutting cane, and the rest were assigned to technical tasks in the sugar mills. In accordance with their original objective, the plantation owners employed Chinese laborers to manage the machines in the mechanized sugar mills. In this regard one enthusiast for Chinese labor observed that

> the Asian worker, intelligent, able, active, not inclined to routine and open to innovations, was able to help those well-trained planters who foresaw the application of their ideas, executing with an admirable precision the newly-adopted agricultural techniques and the

process of sugar manufacture realized by means of new machines. One must see them work in order to understand the intelligent adaptation of the Chinese to the regularity of industrial tasks, subject to the rhythm of the piston, to steam power, and to the demands of the thermometer.[25]

The adaptation of the Cantonese to industrial labor was so rapid that not a single informant to the 1874 investigation mentioned the technical difficulty in carrying out the tasks in the sugar mills.

Depending on the size of the plantation, the Chinese found themselves in groups of 20 to 200, living and often working side by side with 300 to 600 slaves. Their working conditions were no different from those of the enslaved men and women who made up the majority of the agricultural labor force. Like them, the Chinese were beaten, chained, deprived of food, and forced to work from fifteen to twenty hours a day. Moreover, they often went unpaid for their labor, or, if paid, they often received but a percentage of their due; and at the end of their eight-year term, many were coerced to sign new contracts.

The planters' intention was to squeeze maximum profit from coolie labor, in complete disregard for the so-called contracts they had signed. (For an example of a labor contract, see Appendix.) Moreover, to treat these nonwhite people differently than the slaves were treated would have meant deviating from the racist code of slavery and thereby inciting the slaves to revolt. According to the testimony of travelers, the fate of the coolies employed in establishments containing fewer slaves was no more enviable. All the legal rights that were written in their contracts (hours of work and rest, food rations, quantity and mode of payment of salary, judicial recourse) were denied them. As the logic of maximum profit led the Creoles to ignore the clauses requiring a contractual agreement between employer and worker, slave-based racist logic led them to apply to the Chinese the same corporal punishments visited upon the slaves. In this regard the Cantonese were doubly maltreated: on one hand as wage laborers, on the other as nonwhite workers.

Nonetheless, the relationship between the Chinese and the slaves was at times not only hostile but murderous. The Chinese refused to be assimilated to the category of nonwhite/slaves and they developed no concord with the black foremen who directed the field labor. To be sure, to avoid clashes between the two types of laborers, some planters provided coolie workers with coolie foremen, and allowed them quarters set apart from the slaves. But because they received salaries at all, and because some sought to establish relations with black women, the Chinese became potential objects of jealousy for some male slaves. (The emigration of coolies did not include women because it was difficult to recruit them in China and the planters refused to admit them to Cuba.[26])

The violation of the contract clauses and the conditions of life of the Cantonese almost totally prevented them from saving their wages so that they might return to China. This situation, coupled with their self-perceived status as free men, made them rebellious—sometimes violently so—against the authority of their patrons. The Chinese rapidly became familiar with the text of their written contracts in Chinese and Spanish and did not accept the innumerable failures of their patrons to meet their obligations. Beginning in 1847, rebellions and flight became common, and the Creoles immediately tried—though unsuccessfully—to subdue the Chinese workers. Between 1849 and 1873 a pressure game developed among the employers of the coolies, the captains-general of Cuba, and the government in Madrid, which was responsive to world opinion of the hour.

In 1849, a regulation transmitted from Madrid to Cuba spelled out the mutual obligations of patrons and coolies. The Catholic faith was to be inculcated in the Chinese; authorization was also given for punishing disobedient workers with the whip, the irons, and, in cases involving repeat offenders, recourse to local police authorities. Some concessions were granted in the regulations: a white foreman should, if possible, be placed at the head of each team of ten Chinese workers; corporal punishment should not be administered in front of the slaves; Saturday and Sunday were free days, during which coolies were given the right to pursue their own occupations; and, in case of a failure by their patrons to fulfill the terms of the contract regulations, coolies were to be allowed to appeal to the captain and local judge.

Another regulation, passed in 1854, forbade corporal punishment, reaffirmed the right of the coolies to buy their contracts, and designated the captain-general of Cuba as their protector; but the apparent clemency of the Creole authorities had no effect. According to a decree in 1858, Chinese workers who had finished their contracts were forced to sign new ones or leave the island within two months at their own expense. Another decree from Madrid in 1860 confirmed this regulation, specifying that those coolies "having failed to sign a second contract" must remain in the service of their patrons; on the other hand, the conditions under which the coolies could free themselves from their contracts were specified. It was left to the employer to decide on the price for the termination of the contract, plus indemnities for any hours of work lost and compensation for the cost of replacement.[27] The right of the patrons to impose these penalties was also recognized, but not the right of recourse to corporal punishment. The same Spanish decree spelled out as well that the contract laborers needed the authorization of their employers to marry.

A royal decree in 1862 granted residence rights to the Chinese upon the termination of their contracts.[28] They could, if they wished, sign a second contract and, if not, a letter of domicile (*cédula*) would be supplied to them for half a peso. Nonetheless, the practice of forcing the Chinese to renew their contracts for one, six, or even nine years had become customary. Confronted with these conditions, the Chinese continued to flee the plantations before or at the termination of their contracts, to find work with small landholders, peasants, or artisans or to join the ranks of the rebels in eastern part of the island. Authorities in Madrid and Havana passed new decrees with the aim of disciplining the Cantonese. According to the text adopted in 1868, and renewed in 1871, 1872, and 1873, every Chinese arriving after February 8, 1861, who did not possess a letter of domicile had to sign a contract or, if he had worked off his first contract, to leave the island within two months at his own expense. The Chinese who fled or who refused to accept a new contract were to be turned over to the authorities, who would bring them to the nearest municipal center to work on various community projects. This practice persisted until 1874.

The internal struggle among the employers of coolies and the Spanish authorities was not intended simply to bring the Cantonese to heel; it was also concerned with the proposed date for the end of the traffic in contract labor. In 1870, the captain-general emphatically demanded from Madrid the cessation of the coolie traffic. He noted the difficulties caused by the Chinese, stressing the role they played in aiding the Creole rebels. Madrid, pressured on the other hand by Lisbon, prohibited the traffic in 1871, but the planters and their merchants, who profited from the "yellow trade," vehemently opposed any stoppage of the shipments. During 1872, 1873, and 1874, 15,743

Cantonese arrived in Cuba, but thereafter the order from Lisbon to end the shipments of Cantonese from Macao, promulgated in December 1873, finally took effect.

In accordance with guarantees set out by the earlier regulations, hundreds of coolies invoked the protection of the captain-general by appearing before his representatives in their respective regions. They tried to obtain reparations for the physical outrages and legal injustices to which they had been subject, but they discovered that the functionaries—police and municipal employees of the island—were the willing tools of corrupt planters. As a result of their failure to obtain reparations, the Chinese either fled, committed suicide, or rebelled, by burning the cane fields, refusing to work, or assassinating their foremen. Many of them were eventually imprisoned or forced back to work. Two years before the arrival of the Ch'en Lan Pin Commission in 1872, 20 percent of the Chinese under contract had fled their plantations, that is, 8,380 men, of whom 1,344 were captured and sent to prison in 1873. Between 1850 and 1872, there were approximately five hundred suicides annually among the 100,000 Chinese on the island; during the same years, the average suicide rate for the slaves was about thirty five per annum, but there were doubtless many attempts not reported by the planters.

According to the testimony of the planters, some 3,000 laborers found a way to escape their contracts. In 1870, the captain-general attested that from 1868 on, coolies entered the ranks of the nationalist insurgency in exchange for a promise of emancipation. The Ch'en Lan Pin Commission sought to minimize this movement, by presenting the testimony of coolies who refused to follow their insurgent masters; but the three commissioners acknowledged that they had not been able to examine people in the zones controlled by the rebels.[29]

As a result of the corporal punishment, the labor, and the suicides, the planters themselves estimated that the annual mortality rate among contracted laborers approached 10 percent. In 1866, a Spanish journal calculated—as did the Ch'en Lan Pin Commission almost twenty years later—a mortality rate of 50 percent among the Chinese workers during the first years of their contracts; an American journalist estimated it at 75 percent.[30] The resistance and the mortality rate of the coolies was such that, in spite of massive arrivals of Cantonese in Havana, the cost of contract labor rose on the island. The second contracts were often paid at the rate of seven pesos a month from 1860 onward, and from ten to fifteen pesos during the 1870s.

The Chinese were horrified by the inhumanity and greed of the Creoles, and would neither accept maltreatment nor renounce their freedom. In 1874, workers began appearing before Peking's envoys in groups of one hundred or more to present their grievances. Accustomed as they were to justice, however imperfect, as it had been provided by the imperial functionaries in each of their ancestral villages, they trusted in the force of law. Of the 2,841 men[31] narrating their Cuban odysseys, only ninety said that they had emigrated freely, only two attested to humane treatment by their employers,[32] and only two said that they had signed a second contract freely.[33] To be sure, there were 68,825 men in Cuba in 1874, of whom at least 14,000 had letters of residence, whereas some 54,000 or more found themselves under contract, 44,000 of whom were on plantations.[34] The testimonies covered in the *Report* corroborate the descriptions provided by numerous French, American, and English observers who described the condition of the coolies in Macao and in Cuba.

The plantations visited by the three commissioners were selected by the Creole government, with the exception of Las Cañas, one of the largest plantations in Cuba.[35] The commissioners went to the enterprises with the largest number of coolies, but they also visited the principal municipal depots and prisons of the island. There they interrogated men who, for the most part, had already fulfilled their contracts, and others who had worked for railroad companies, brick factories, farms, cigar factories, and mines. Their testimony did not differ significantly. Because the coolies in the depots and prisons rejected the conditions of their contracts, it could be argued that they were especially insubordinate men; but their stories of arbitrary arrests and the circumstances of their coercion left no room for doubt.

Every man possessing a letter of domicile could, at the end of five years, become a subject of the Spanish Crown and, after 1874, obtain a Portuguese passport. The right of residence was matched by the obligation to convert to Catholicism and to obtain the endorsement of two whites who would serve as sponsors or godparents. The Chinese made desperate attempts to secure the right of residence, which was assured by a letter of domicile. Among the witnesses of 1874 were an indeterminate number of men who either possessed residence permits or who had gotten them before they were illegally confiscated by the insular police. The laborers explained how, despite the law, they were obliged to buy these documents from local officials at inflated prices. Some of them had completed the terms of their first contracts without agreeing to another when such a practice was permitted, while others had been able to purchase their contracts from their less successful patrons. To obtain the money for this, the Chinese either used their personal savings, the profits from the sale of manufactured goods, or their winnings from gambling; more lenient masters allowed their laborers to work on their own account during their rest days. Most of the time they had to pay substantial sums to the public officials to get their letters of domicile. In 1874, the Chinese told the commissioners that they had paid amounts from eight to 300 pesos,[36] although the legal cost for the right of residence was supposed to be only half a peso.

Starting in 1858, several hundred Chinese workers won the official status of free laborer, and the figures grew to 8,485 in 1871 and to 14,064 in 1872; but even emancipated workers were subjected to annoyance, abuse and thievery—particularly by the police. Chinese forgers aided by greedy Creole subalterns reproduced, falsified, and sold letters of domicile to people in hiding, who lived in fear of an examination of the coolie inscription registers, although such verification was not always made.

For the free Chinese, there were several means of achieving some security. There were the laborers who paid the estimated 100 pesos (approximate fee for 1865) required to leave Cuba.[37] Between 1865 and 1874, only 2,000 Cantonese managed to return to China,[38] but after the commissioners visit, more were able to improve their situation and go home. There were 46,754 Chinese on the island in 1877, suggesting that some 22,000 had either died or had left Cuba during the three years following 1874. Leaving the island before 1874 was difficult because the Creole officials refused to provide passports for the Chinese. The few that they did grant were only secured through the payment of inordinately large sums of money—from 70 to 200 pesos—and, once paid, most former contract laborers had too little left to allow them to return to China honorably.

The majority of coolies freed from their contracts formed work groups (*cuadrillas*) that sold their labor to farmers, small plantation owners, construction teams, or employers working in the ports. These Chinese teams provided such good protection to others who had fled their contracts that the captain-general disbanded them in December 1871 and they did not reappear until after the abolition of slavery in 1886.[39] Other former contract laborers plied minor trades and crafts (sec-ondhand clothes retailers, bone collectors, junk dealers, gardeners), opened shops as tailors, con-fectioners, greengrocers, and rooming-house keepers, or were bakers, domestic workers, cigar-makers, cooks, and so on. From 1858 onward, they established themselves along six Havana streets,[40] laying the boundaries of the Chinese quarter, still recognizable in 1959. In the 1870s, this phenomenon was repeated in other Cuban cities, setting the stage for the arrival of Cantonese merchants who came to settle between 1870 and 1880. Supplied with capital, about a thousand such merchants came from the United States, Mexico, and even Spain to profit from the Creole taste for exotic Chinese products and to sell to their countrymen merchandise imported from China.

Despite the arrival of the merchants, the community of free Chinese living in Cuba remained relatively insignificant, partly as a result of the emigration of the free Chinese workers after 1874. By 1899, only 15,000 free Chinese remained; 8,033 laborers, 2,754 domestics, 1,923 retailers, 471 stevedores, 301 junk dealers, 287 charcoal sellers, 196 laundrymen, and, surprisingly enough, 42 plantation owners. The merchants who had come to Cuba in the 1870s, along with coolies who had banded together, had managed to buy some small estates from planters in financial trouble; the first such purchase was recorded in 1879.[41]

CONCLUSIONS

The task of the Commission was to examine the condition of the Chinese working in Cuba, not to investigate those responsible for the "yellow trade," which had been officially condemned by the great powers. But the Commission did comment on the situation in general.

As an official Chinese mission of inquiry, it could not explore the circumstances that had pushed thousands of men from Kwangtung into exile and into so dreadful an experience on a Carib-bean island. The *Report* makes no mention of the social crisis that gripped the province, nor the inability of Peking to compel Spain to respect the terms of the immigration treaty signed in 1866. This treaty was supposed to limit contracts to five years, forbid the sale or the deception of Chinese subjects, and enforce free repatriation for the worker at the termination of the contract. The Com-mission did not explain how Chinese subjects could have been kidnapped with impunity from the districts of Kwangtung close to Macao: It had no interest in exposing Peking's ineptitude, or its lack of concern with the social violence that prevailed in the region.

On the other hand, the Commission repeatedly specified the responsibilities of the Spanish government, illustrating how it had failed to observe the 1866 emigration treaty: issuing numerous decrees forcing the Chinese into new contracts, refusing them residence rights in Cuba, and of-ficially prohibiting fines and physical punishment for the migrants, but without enforcement.[42] Its conclusions were even more telling in regard to the Creoles; it made clear that theft was their basic means of access to Cantonese labor,[43] and it defined the treatment of the Asian workers as tanta-mount to slavery.[44] The Commission also laid the responsibility for the coolie traffic at the door of criminal elements, Chinese and white, who flouted imperial law and scandalously deceived the em-peror's subjects.[45]

At the same time, the Commission was no more gentle in regard to the Chinese themselves. The *Report* reads:

> Some Coolies are industrious men, who emigrate willingly to better themselves, and who work cheerfully and well; some Coolies emigrate willingly, but being bad characters, do so to escape the results of gambling and crime, and carry with them their bad habits; some Coolies were kidnapped, being stupid fellows, and never can work intelligently; some Coolies, clever fellows, are induced to embark under false pretences, and on finding themselves deceived and entrapped, become desperate, their desperation being regarded by the employer as defiance, mutiny, disobedience, etc.[46]

All but two of the coolie witnesses had been either kidnapped or deceived by their recruiters, but the Commission nonetheless blamed them either for their stupidity or their naivete. The commissioners were extremely critical, remarking that "industrious men who work willingly and well, can support themselves at home, and do not emigrate voluntarily."[47]

Believing that the Chinese should have been able to earn adequate livings in their native China, the commissioners reproached those who had been deceived by the Macao recruiters and tempted by the promise of foreign opportunities. Thus, in the aftermath of the investigation ordered by the emperor and demanded by the principal Western nations, it was not only the traffickers and recruiters in Macao, or the Cuban and Spanish authorities, who were charged with responsibility for a tragic chapter in labor history that involved more than 100,000 Chinese workers in Cuba. Ignoring the social realities of rural Cantonese life, the Commission's *Report* attributed the workers' emigration to naïveté, stupidity, or malevolence on their part as well.

NOTES

The author and translator wish to thank Robert F. Barsky for his valuable assistance in the translation of the Introduction and Prof. Evelyn Hu-DeHart for her substantive editorial advice.

1. I employ the terminology of the Organization of Cooperation and Economic Development. Organisation de Coopération et de Développement économiques, *Migrations, croissance et développement* (Paris: OCDE, 1978), 18.

2. Works dealing with these issues are numerous; notable among them are: Lucie Cheng and Edna Bonacich, *Labour Immigration under Capitalism. Asian Workers in the United States Before World War II* (Berkeley: University of California Press, 1984); Stephen Castles and Godula Kosack, *Immigrant Workers and Class Structure in Western Europe* (London: Oxford University Press, 1973); Georges Tapinos, *L'économie des migrations internationales* (Paris: Armand Colin and Presses de la Fondation nationale des sciences politiques, 1974); Yann Moulier-Boutang, Jean-Pierre Garson, and Roxane Silberman, *Économie politique des migrations clandestines de main d'oeuvre, comparaisons internationales et exemple français* (Paris: Éditions Publisud, 1986); and Raphaël-Emmanuel Verhaeren, *Partir? Une théorie économique des migrations internationales* (Grenoble: Presses Universitaires de Grenoble, 1990).

3. Verhaeren, *Partir?*, 164.

4. Government of Canada, Statistics Canada, Demography Division, October 1989.

5. U.S. Department of Commerce, Bureau of the Census, *Statistical Abstracts* (Washington, D.C., 1988).

6. L. Dollot, *Les migrations humaines* (Paris: Éditions PUF, 1976), 124.

7. Verhaeren, *Partir?*, 88.

8. *Population Bulletin* 32, no. 4, (September 1977): 22, and David S. North and Marion F. Houston, *The Characteristics and Role of Illegal Aliens in the U.S. Labor Market: An Exploratory Study* (Washington, D.C.: Linton, 1976), 27.

9. Unless otherwise indicated, the materials in this part of the Introduction are drawn from Denise Helly, *Idéologie et ethnicité: Les Chinois Macao à Cuba* (Montreal: Les Presses de l'Université de Montreal, 1979).

10. Arthur F. Corwin, *Spain and the Abolition of Slavery in Cuba, 1817–1886*, Latin America Monograph No. 9 (Austin: University of Texas Press, 1967), 278.

11. In 1859, Cuba exported 41.9 percent of its product to the United States, 25 percent to Great Britain, 12 percent to Spain, 8 percent to France, and 6 percent to Germany. In 1877, Cuba exported 82 percent of its product to the United States, 4.4 percent to Great Britain, 5.7 percent to Spain, and 1.6 percent to France. Raúl Cepero Bonilla, *Obras históricas* (Havana: Instituto de Historia, 1963), 102–3.

12. Archivo Nacional de Cuba, Junta de Fomento, Book 201, 19–21.

13. Chinese place names and proper names are normally cited in accord with the transcription method used in the Commission report. At the first mention of such names, equivalent Pinyin transcriptions are provided in parentheses.

14. According to Feijóo de Sotomayor. See Duvon Clough Corbitt, *The Chinese in Cuba, 1847–1947* (Wilmore, Ky.: Asbury College, 1971), 10.

15. Corbitt, *The Chinese in Cuba*, 22.

16. Archives of Foreign Affairs Ministry (Ministerio de Asuntos Exteriores), Madrid, Legajo II, documento A/2365, 1870–1890. Letter of the Spanish Foreign Affairs Minister to the Spanish Consul in Hong Kong, 1879.

17. Significantly, Cuba was under a military government from 1820 onward, because the Spaniards considered it a territory under British siege.

18. Portions of this part of the Introduction are taken from Denise Helly, *Les Chinois de Montréal, 1877–1951* (Québec: Institut Québécois de Recherche sur la Culture, 1987), ch. 2.

19. Moreover, demographic growth in China, sustained through the seventeenth and eighteenth centuries, began to accelerate rapidly in the nineteenth century; within two hundred years, between 1651 and 1850, the population of China increased from 60,000,000 to 430,000,000 persons. See G. W. Skinner, *Chinese Society in Thailand: An Analytical History* (New York: Cornell University Press, 1957), 30.

20. Franz Michael, *The Taiping Rebellion: History and Documents* (Seattle: University of Washington Press, 1966), 15.

21. R. H. Tawney, *Land and Labour in China*, 3rd ed. (London: George Allen and Unwin, 1964), 32, and Daniel Kulp, *Country Life in South China* (New York: Columbia University Press, 1925), 121.

22. J. Ankum-Houwink, "Chinese contract migrants in Surinam between 1853 and 1870," *Boletín de estudios latinoamericanos y del Caribe*, no. 17 (1974): 42; Hughette Ly-Tio-Fane Pineo, *La diaspora chinoise dans l'Océan indien occidental* (Aix-en-provence: Institut d'histoire des pays d'Outre-mer, 1981), 69 and 112; Denise Helly, "La Réunion vue de Taïwan: le *Hua qiao zhi, liu ni wang dao*," *Annuaire des pays de l'Océan indien* (1981): 247.

23. Humberto Rodríguez Pastor, *Hijos del celeste Imperio en el Peru: (1850–1900)* (Lima: Instituto de Apoyo Agrario, 1989), 25. About one thousand workers under contract arrived in Brazil, another thousand in Panama, and several hundred in Mexico and Costa Rica. See Arnold Joseph Meagher, "The Introduction of Chinese Laborers to Latin America: The "Coolie Trade," 1847–1874," Ph.D. diss., University of California at Davis, 1975, 291–306.

24. Seventy-four percent, according to the "Padrón general de colonos asiáticos, 1872," *Boletín de Colonización* (October 15, 1873). Reproduced here as *The Cuba Commission Report: A Hidden History of the Chinese in Cuba*, the report of the Ch'en Lan Pin Commission, suggests the figure of 90 percent (sec. VII, 48) which differs from the official figures for 1872.

25. Ramón de la Sagra, *Cuba en 1860 o sea el cuadro de sus adelantos en la población, la agricultura, el comercio y las rentas públicas, suplemento a la primera parte de la historia política y natural de la Isla de Cuba* (Paris: Hachette, 1863), 57.

26. There were 56 Chinese females in Cuba in 1862, 32 in 1872 , and 81 in 1877—of whom 23 were under contract—and 58 who were free of any obligation.

27. *Cuba Commission Report*, sec. XLVI, 114–15.

28. Joaquín Rodríguez San Pedro, *Legislación ultramarina, concordada y anotada*, Madrid, 16 vols., Imprenta de los Señores Viotá, Cubas y Vicente, 1865–69, 2:449.

29. *Cuba Commission Report*, sec. XXXIV, 93–94.

30. *El Reino*, 6 September 1866. *Cuba Commission Report*, sec. XXXVIII, 99. James J. O'Kelly, *The Mambi-Land, or Adventures of a Herald Correspondent in Cuba* (Philadelphia: Lippincott, 1874), 271–90.

31. *Cuba Commission Report*, 34.

32. *Ibid.* sec. I, 36–38; sec. XI, 56–58.

33. *Ibid.* sec. XXV, 78–80 and sec. XXVIII, 84–85.

34. Available figures on the Chinese population are drawn from the following:

1855: 11,825. Felix Erenchun, *Anales de la Isla de Cuba, año de 1855* (Havana: Imprenta del Tiempo, 1856), 783.

1861: 34,816. *Censo de la Isla de Cuba, año de 1861* (Havana: Imprenta del Gobierno, 1862).

1862: 34,750 under contract, of whom 56 were women; 29,055 working on the plantations. Toledo Armildez, *Censo de la Isla de Cuba, año 1862*. (Havana: Imprenta del Gobierno, 1864).

1872: 72,506 individuals: 58,410 under contract (of whom 47, 583 were under contract on the plantations), 14,064 freemen, not under contract, and 32 free women. *Padrón general de colonos asiáticos, 1872*. Archivo nacional de Cuba, Comisión general de colonización, Havana. Published in *Boletín de colonización*, June 30, 1873 and October 15, 1873.

1874: 68,825, of whom one in five were living freely, without contract, in Cuba. *Cuba Commission Report* sec. XLI, 110. One contract laborer speaks of 100,000 Chinese living in Cuba (sec. XVIII, 70), but this must be erroneous.

1877: 46,754 individuals, of whom 81 were women (58 free and 23 under contract). "Resumen del censo de población de la Isla de Cuba en 31 de diciembre de 1877," *Boletín oficial del Ministerio de Ultramar* (Madrid: Imprenta Nacional, 1879), 904–5.

1899: 15,000. Census of Cuba, 1899, in Corbitt, *The Chinese in Cuba*, 92–94.

35. *Cuba Commission Report*, sec. XLIX, 120.

36. *Ibid.*, sec. XXII, 75–76.

37. *Diario de la Marina*, (Havana) May 6, 1865.

38. *Cuba Commission Report*, sec. XXXVIII, 84–85.

39. Antonio Chuffat Latour, *Apunte histórico de los Chinos en Cuba* (Havana: Molina y Cia, 1927), 96–100.

40. *Ibid.* 17.

41. *Ibid.* 86–90.

42. *Cuba Commission Report*, sec. XIII, 59–60.

43. *Ibid.* sec. XVI, 64–66.

44. *Ibid.*, sec. XXX, 88–90, sec. XXXV, 94–96.

45. *Ibid.*, sec. XIX, 70–71.

46. *Ibid.*, sec. XVIII, 69–70.

47. *Ibid.*

PART ONE

Despatch to Yamên

Translation of Despatch of Commissioners CH'ÊN LANPIN, MACPHERSON *and* HUBER, *reporting to the Tsung-li Yamên the results of their enquiry into the condition of Chinese in Cuba.*

The Commissioner CH'ÊN, and the Commissioners of Customs MACPHERSON and HUBER, address this memorial in reply:—

On the 10th day of the 10th moon of the 12th year of T'UNGCHIH [29th November 1873] was received the communication of the Yamên to the effect that "for the enquiry in regard to "Chinese emigrants to the Spanish possession of Cuba, CH'ÊN LANPIN, the officer in charge of "the Educational Mission abroad, has been. selected, that Mr. MACPHERSON, Commissioner of "Customs at Hankow, and Mr. HUBER, Commissioner of Customs at Tientsin, are likewise "appointed and are to accompany him; that this arrangement has been sanctioned by an Edict "of the 30th day of the 7th moon [21st September], that the head of the Commission is to "await in the United States the arrival of his associates, and that they are thence to proceed "together to their destination, where they are to institute an honest and complete enquiry, of "the results of which a full report is to be supplied, as a guide for subsequent action."

On the 12th day of the 10th moon [1st December], the receipt of these instructions was in the first instance acknowledged.

On the 26th day of the 12 moon [12th February 1874], Mr. HUBER arrived in the United States, and on the 3rd day of the 1st moon of this year [19th February], the deputed officer CH'ÊN LANPIN with him departed for Cuba, Havana being reached on the 29th day of the same moon [17th March], where apartments were hired in the hotel in which Mr. MACPHERSON was already residing.

On the 2nd day of the 2nd moon [19 March], (being thus united) we visited the Captain General the Governor of Havana, the official members of the Commission of Colonization, and afterwards the Consular Representatives of Great Britain, France, Russia, the United States, Germany, Sweden and Norway and Denmark, Holland, Austria, Belgium, and Italy.

On the 3rd [20th] we commenced an enquiry at the barracoon of Mr. Ibañez.

On the 4th [21st] we commenced an enquiry in the dépôt.

On the 5th [22nd] we continued the enquiry in the barracoon.

From the 6th [23rd] until the 11th [28th] inclusive we continued the enquiry in the dépôt.

During the 13th, 14th and 15th [30th, 31st and 1st April] the enquiry was prosecuted in the jail.

During the 17th and 18th [3rd and 4th April] the plantation Las Cañas was visited.

On the 22nd [8th] we proceeded to Matanzas, where, during the following days, the enquiry was prosecuted in the dépôt, prison and in the plantations "San Cayetano," "Concepcion" and "Armonia."

On the 28th [14th] we proceeded to Cardenas, where, during the following days, we prosecuted enquiries in the dépôt, prison and the plantations "Esperanza," "Recreo" and "San Antonio." A visit was also paid to the adjacent town of Cimmarones.

On the 3rd day of the 3rd moon [18th], we proceeded to Colon, where, during the following days, we prosecuted enquiries in the dépôt, prison and in the plantations "España" and "Flor de Cuba."

On the 6th [21st] we proceeded to Sagua, where, during the following days, we prosecuted enquiries in the dépôt, prison and in the plantations "Santa Anna," "Santa Isabella" and "Capitolis."

On the 9th [24th] we proceeded to Cienfuegos, where, during the following days, we prosecuted enquiries in the dépôt, prison and in the plantations "Juniata" and "Candelaria."

On the 13th [28th] we proceeded to Guanajay, where, during the following days, we prosecuted enquiries in the dépôt and prison, returning to Havana *via* the town of San Antonio.

On the 17th [2nd May] we proceeded to Guanabacoa, and on the same day prosecuted enquires in the Regla and Santa Catalina sugar-warehouses.

During these investigations, the hours of visiting the dépôts and prisons were always fixed by the local officials, and plantations also were only visited after the assent of the latter had been obtained. Besides, however, in the places where we stayed, as well as on the road, independent enquiries were instituted.

All investigations of Chinese were conducted verbally and in person by ourselves. The depositions and petitions show that $\frac{8}{10}$ths of the entire number declared that they had been kidnapped or decoyed; that the mortality during the voyage from wounds caused by blows, suicide and sickness proves to have exceeded 10 per cent.; that on arrival at Havana they were sold into slavery,—a small proportion being disposed of to families and shops, whilst the large majority became the property of sugar planters; that the cruelty displayed even towards those of the former class is great, and that it assumes in the case of those of the latter, proportions that are unendurable. The labour, too, on the plantations is shown to be excessively severe, and the food to be insufficient; the hours of labour are too long, and the chastisements by rods, whips, chains, stocks, &c., &c., productive of suffering and injury. During the past years a large number have been killed by blows, have died from the effects of wounds and have hanged themselves, cut their throats, poisoned themselves with opium, and thrown themselves into wells and sugar caldrons. It was also possible to verify by personal inspection wounds inflicted upon others, the fractured and maimed limbs, blindness, the heads full of sores, the teeth struck out, the ears mutilated, and the skin and flesh lacerated, proofs of cruelty patent to the eyes f all.

On the termination of the contracts the employers, in most cases, withhold the certificates of completion, and insist on renewal of engagements, which may extend to even more than 10 years, and during which the same system of cruelty is adhered to; whilst if the Chinese refuse to assent, they are taken to the dépôts, whence in chains, and watched by guards, they are forced to repair roads, receiving no compensation for their labour, undergoing a treatment exactly similar to that of criminals in jail. Afterwards they are compelled to again enter the service of an employer, and sign a contract, on the completion of which they are once more taken to the dépôts; and as this process is constantly repeated, a return home, and an attempt to gain a livelihood independently, become impossible.

Moreover, since the 2nd moon of the 11th year of HIENFÊNG [March–April 1861] the issue of Letters of Domicile and Cedulas has ceased, rendering liability to arrest universal, whilst those possessing these papers are constantly, be it on the street or in their own houses, called upon to produce them for inspection, or are even exposed to their being taken away, or torn up, and to themselves being carried away to the endless misery of a dépôt.

Of all these facts the depositions and petitions furnish detailed evidence.

Our stay in Cuba, commencing on the 29th of the 1st moon [17th March], ended on the 23rd of the 3rd moon [8th May]. Almost every Chinese met during this period was, or had been, undergoing suffering, and suffering was the purport of almost every word heard; and these men were seen by us all, and these words were heard by us all.

1,176 depositions have been collected, and 85 petitions, supported by 1,665 signatures have been received, of which copies and (English) translations are appended.

Replies to the Memorandum of queries sent by the Yamên in the 12th moon, and translations of Tables of Chinese embarked for and arrived at Cuba, received from the British Consul and the Commission of Colonization, of the Regulations now applicable to the Chinese in Cuba, of the Instructions issued to Masters of vessels conveying Chinese to Cuba, of eight Forms of Contracts, and of certain Tables of Chinese population prepared by the Commission of Colonization, also accompany this Despatch.

T'UNGCHIH, 13th year, 9th month, 11th day [20th October, 1874].

True translation.

(Signed)   A. MACPHERSON,

(Signed)   A. HUBER,
Commissioners of Customs.

PART TWO
Replies to Queries

This part contains the English version of the Replies to the Queries supplied by the Tsung-li Yamên for the guidance of the Commission during its investigation in Cuba.

陳 蘭 彬	(Signed)	[Chinese Signature.]
馬 福 臣	(,,)	A. MACPHERSON.
吳 秉 文	(,,)	A. HUBER.

REPLIES to queries contained in Enclosure I. G. $\frac{\text{Cuba}}{\text{No. 1}}$ of 1873. "Memo. of queries to be answered $\frac{\text{Cuba and Coolies}}{\text{Chinese Commission}}$ Nov. 1873."

I.

FROM WHAT PLACES DOES CUBA DRAW COOLIES?

The majority of the Chinese Coolies in Cuba sailed from Macao, Amoy, Swatow and Canton. They were mainly decoyed abroad, not legitimately induced to emigrate.

The petition of the *hsiu-ts'ai* Hsien Tso-pang (洗佐邦) and 14 others states, that "the "foreigners of Macao sent out vicious Chinese in order to kidnap and decoy men and to place these "in barracoons and on board of ships from which they cannot escape, chastise them there without "restraint, and conveying them against their will to Havana, after removing their queues and "changing their clothing, offer them for sale in the men-market." The *hsiu-ts'ai* Ch'ên Shao-yen (陳少嚴) states in his petition: "I was decoyed here by wicked men." The petition of Shih Chih-'ho (施致和) and 28 others states, "we were decoyed from Macao to this Spanish island of "Cuba." Wu A-kuang (吳阿光) in his petition states, "I was induced by the Coolie decoyers "to embark on board the vessel." The petition of Ao Ping-nan (區炳南) and 22 others states, "we were conveyed on board by violence." The petition of the military official (游擊) Chang Luan (張鑾) and 30 others states, "Portuguese and Spaniards, acting in concert, and aided by "vicious Chinese, make a traffic of decoying and selling men." The petition of Lin Chin (林金) and 15 others states, "we were decoyed by the vicious of our countrymen suborned by foreigners." The petition of Yang Yün (楊允) and 132 others states, "vicious men decoyed us into hiring "out our services." The petition of 'Huang Yu (黃有) and 15 others states, "we were induced "by the Coolie decoyers to embark on board of the vessel." The petition of the *hsiu-ts'ai* Li Chao-ch'un (李肇春) and 165 others states, "we were at various times brought by force to, or "decoyed into the barracoons of Macao, by certain vicious men of our own nation suborned by "Portuguese." The petition of T'ang Chan-k'uei (唐占魁) and 8 others states, "we, exercising "no foresight, were decoyed by vicious men." The petition of Chien Shih-kuang (簡仕光) and 96 others states, "we were decoyed by vicious men." The petition of Ch'iu Pi-shan (邱碧山) and 34 others states, "the Coolie decoyers devise means for deceiving men. Whilst professing "to offer employment to labourers, they in reality convert them into victims of their snares." The native of Fukien, Wang Chün-shêng (王均盛), states in his petition, "I was decoyed and "sold." The petition of Tsêng Jui-t'o (曾瑞託) and 4 others states, "we were either decoyed or "kidnapped on board of the Coolie ship." Chêng-chiu (鄭九) states in his petition, "I was "decoyed to Cuba, and sold to a sugar plantation." The petition of the native of Chihli, Chao

K'un (趙 昆), and 97 others states, "Spanish vessels come to China, and suborning the vicious of "our countrymen, by their aid carry away full cargoes of men, of whom 8 or 9 of every 10 are "decoyed." The petition of Tiao Mu (刁 木) and 3 other states, "vicious men have, at various "times, decoyed here tens and hundreds of thousands of peasants." The petition of P'an T'ai (潘 泰) and 89 others states, "misled by fair words, or decoyed, we were brought here to be sold as slaves." The petition of Yeh Nien (葉 年) and 20 others states, "we were decoyed abroad by the Coolie "brokers for sale to sugar plantations." The petition of Tsai Jih-shêng (載 日 生) and 1 other states, "not exercising care, we were decoyed to these Spanish cities." The petition of T'ang Lien-shêng (唐 聯 陞) and 106 others states, "Portuguese suborned the vicious of our countrymen "to bring us by force to, or to decoy us to, Macao, whence we were conveyed to Cuba, to be sold "as slaves to sugar plantations and other localities." The petition of Ts'ai Hêng (蔡 恒) and 79 others states, "we were decoyed into foreign houses by vicious men, where we were entrapped by "fair promises into embarking on board of vessels which conveyed us abroad for sale." The petition of Hsieh Shuang-chiu (謝 雙 就) and 11 others states, "we were decoyed by vicious men "and compelled by force to embark." The petition of Wu A-fa (吳 阿 發) and 39 others states, "we were decoyed to Macao by vicious men." The petition of Yeh Chün-fu (葉 君 福) and 52 others states, "we were the victims of fraud." The petition of Huang Fêng-chi (黃 逢 吉) and 11 others states, "we were decoyed to Macao by the offers of employment made by three vicious men, "Wên A-chiao (溫 阿 嬌), Lai Chi-ch'ang (賴 記 長) and Chung Lu-yüan (鍾 祿 元), and at Macao, "by the aid of their wicked associates, we were placed by force on board ship." The petition of Lai Shêng (賴 勝) and 9 others states, "we were decoyed and sold as slaves by foreigners." The petition of Liu A-shou (劉 阿 壽) and 4 others states, "we were decoyed to the Macao barracoons, "and though not inspected by any Portuguese officials, were, after the evening meal,—our queues "having been tied together, and guarded by foreign soldiers armed with firearms,—forced to "embark, whilst no one heeded the cries for aid which we uttered on the way." The petition of Chang Ting-chia (張 定 加) and 127 others states, "we were decoyed to and sold at Havana, "by vicious men." The petition of Chêng A-mou (鄭 阿 茂) and 89 others states, "we were induced "to proceed to Macao by offers of employment abroad at high wages, and through being told that "the eight foreign years specified in the contracts were equivalent to only four Chinese, and that at "the termination of the latter period we would be free. We observed also on the signboards of the "foreign buildings the words 'agencies for the engagement of labourers,' and believed that they "truthfully described the nature of the establishments, little expecting that having once entered "the latter, exit would be denied us; and when on arrival at Havana, we were exposed for sale "and subjected to appraisement in a most ruthless manner, it became evident that we were not "to be engaged as labourers, but to be sold as slaves."

Again it is gathered from the 1,176 depositions which have been recorded that of those who sailed from Macao Wên Ch'ang-t'ai (文 長 泰) and 65 others were kidnapped, that Tsêng Erh-ch'i (曾 貳 齊) and 689 others were decoyed, that Liu A-jui (劉 阿 瑞) and 50 others were entrapped into signing contracts in the belief that they were merely doing so in the place of others temporarily absent, that 'Huang A-mu (黃 阿 木) and 93 others were the victims of various snares tendered to them after they had gambled and lost, and that Ch'ên A-chi (陳 阿 吉) and 65 others emigrated voluntarily; that of those who sailed from

Amoy, Su A-ʻhai (蘇 阿 海) and 11 others were kidnapped, that T̲ʻang-chien (唐 建) and 22 others were decoyed, that Lin Shêng (林 盛) and 10 others were the victims of various snares tendered to them after they had gambled and lost, and that ʻHuang Shui-tʻou (黄 水 頭) and 5 others emigrated voluntarily; that of those who sailed from Swatow, Chʻên A-kuei (陳 阿 桂) and 4 others were kidnapped, that Chang A-lin (張 阿 林) and 27 others were decoyed, and that Lo Fu-chʻung (羅 富 崇) and 11 others emigrated voluntarily; that of those who sailed from Canton and Whampoa Yang Shih-fêng (楊 石 鳳) and 16 others were decoyed, that Chʻên A-chʻiu (陳 阿 秋) and 7 others were the victims of snares tendered to them after they had gambled and lost, and that Liang A-shêng (梁 阿 盛) and 11 others emigrated voluntarily; that the 2 who sailed from Hongkong, Li San-mou (李 三 茂) and 1 other, were decoyed; that of the 5 who sailed from Manila one, Wei Lêng (魏 冷), was kidnapped, whilst Wang Wei (王 爲) and the remaining 3 were decoyed; and that the one man who sailed from Shanghai, Chang Kuei-tʻing (張 桂 廷), was decoyed. Furthermore Chang Jung-chi (章 榮 記) deposes that foreigners decoyed to Macao from Pʻingyang (平 陽) in the prefecture of Wênchow (温 州) in the province of Chêhkiang more than 10 men, and Yü A-chao (余 阿 照) also deposes that foreigners speaking Chinese decoyed him to Macao, and there entrapped him into signing a contract, as if it were merely on behalf of another, temporarily absent.

It thus appears that of the Chinese labourers who have proceeded to Cuba, 8 or 9 of every 10 have been conveyed there against their will. The entire number who sailed for that island from the 27th year of TAOKWANG to the 3rd moon of the 13th year of TʻUNGCHIH, is, according to the statement prepared by the British Consul General, Havana, 142,422, of whom 43,273 sailed from Amoy, Swatow, Hongkong, Canton, Whampoa, Annan and Manila, whilst from Macao between the 27th year of TAOKWANG and the end of the 5th year of TʻUNGCHIH were shipped 63,455, and between the latter date and the 3rd moon of the 13th year of TʻUNGCHIH 35,694. These latter shipments took place in violation of the provisions of the communication attached to the Emigration Convention of the 5th year of TʻUNGCHIH, by which Macao is excluded from the localities at which the engagement of labourers is permitted; whilst, as proved by the depositions and petitions, the circumstances that have attended the introduction into Cuba of the majority of the Chinese are a breach of the 10th clause of the Spanish Treaty of the 3rd year of TʻUNGCHIH, which is to the effect that Spain agrees not to afford shelter to Chinese criminals or to *decoy* or *sell* any subjects of China.

II.

DO THEY SIGN AGREEMENTS?

In the Emigration Convention of the 5th year of TʻUNGCHIH, it is provided that the Emigration Agencies at the ports are to be inspected at will by officers of the two nations interested, and that these functionaries are also to be present at the time of signing contracts and of embarkation. The 11th clause also provides that Chinese under 20 years of age are not to be permitted to emigrate unless they produce a written authorization from their parents sealed by the official of the place of residence of the latter, or—in the event of it being impossible to procure such a document,—an authorization from the local official alone. In the 10th clause of the Spanish Royal Decree of 1860 it is likewise stated, that minors cannot sign contracts without the sanction of their parents or guardians. Of the Chinese now in Cuba the great majority were brought there by fraud or violence in order to be sold, and whether of age or minors either received no contracts, or were entrapped into accepting them, or constrained by force to sign them, or induced to affix their names as if doing so merely on behalf of others; whilst the documents themselves were in some instances delivered in the barracoons and in others on board ship. None of the indicated officers were present when contracts were signed, and none of the specified authorizations were produced, so that provisions prescribed by both China and Spain were violated.

The petition of Chu Chi-hsün (朱箕訓) and 10 others states, "we were decoyed into "foreign houses at Macao, in which we were forced to sign contracts, after which we were placed "on board ship, and conveyed to Havana." 'Ho A-ying (何阿英) in his petition states, "I "was confined in an upstairs room until I consented to sign a contract." Lo A-pao (駱阿寶) in his petition states, "I was compelled to sign the contract." Ku Ch'iao-hsiu (古橋秀) in his petition states, "I was beaten with great severity, and the suffering being unendurable I "could not but accept the contract, and with suppressed grief proceed on board, where were 600 "others, all wronged in a like manner." The petition of Chêng A-mou (鄭阿茂) and 89 others states, "we signed no contract, and after the lapse of a month were compelled to go on board "ship." The petition of Yeh Fu-chün (葉福君) and 52 others states, "after entering, the "gates were closed by a foreigner, and as all exit was prevented we perceived how we had been "betrayed, but there was no remedy; in the same chambers were more than 100 others, most of "whom passed their days and nights in tears, whilst some were dripping with blood,—the result "of chastisements inflicted on account of a suspected intention of escape, or of a declaration of "their unwillingness, when interrogated by the Portuguese inspector. The barracoon was of "great depth, and, at the time of punishment, as an additional precaution to prevent the cries "being overheard, gongs were beaten, and fireworks discharged, so that death even might have "ensued without detection; and witnessing this violence, there was no course open to us but "assent, receiving at the moment of embarkation a document, which we were told was a contract "for eight years." Jên Shih-chên (任世貞) remarks in his petition, "by what right can our "bodies be disposed of, without the signed authorization of our parents?" The petition of Li Chao-ch'un (李肇春) and 165 others states, "though years,—in some instances more than ten,— "have elapsed since we were decoyed here, our families know not whether we are alive or dead "or where we are."

'Ho A-hsien (賀阿先) and 235 others in their depositions declare that they signed their contracts under compulsion; 'Huang Ch'ao-ping (黃潮炳) and 192 others declare that contracts were handed to them in the barracoons; Kuo Chan (郭占) and 116 others declare that the contracts were handed to them on board ship; Wên Chang-t'ai (文長泰) and 231 others declare that the contracts were given to them at the time of inspection, by a Portuguese official. Su A-'hai (蘇阿海) and 42 others declare that no contracts were received by them; Li A-wu (李阿五) and 1 other declare that they were induced by fraud to sign contracts. Hsien Ch'êng-ku (冼成古)

declares, "as I was unwilling, the contract was given to me by force, and I was not allowed to
" speak." 'Hu A-pao (胡 阿 保) declares, "at the time of inspection I declined to sign the contract;
" the Portuguese official then forcibly seized my hand and when it had marked the paper took
" the latter away." Li A-pao (李 阿 保) declares, "a mark was made with my hand on a contract,
" and I was then given 10 cash." Lo A-êrh (羅 阿 二) declares, "after I had been locked up
" during half a month the contract was given to me." Chu Chieh (朱 撻) and 2 others declare
that they signed contracts without having been inspected by any official. Yang A-wang (楊 阿 旺)
declares, "another man signed a contract on my behalf." Huang A-yu (黃 阿 友) declares, "when
" 16 years old, I was induced to sign a contract, being told that I was merely doing so for another
" man." Wang A-jung (王 阿 榮) and 1 other declare that they signed contracts when 18 years
old. Ch'ên 'Hua (陳 華) declares, "I was decoyed when 11 years old." Ch'ên A-wu (陳 阿 五)
declares, "I was decoyed when 12 years old." Ch'ên A-fu (陳 阿 福) declares, "when 11 years old
" I received a contract in a barracoon." Lin A-ch'iu (林 阿 秋) declares, "I signed a contract on
" board ship and was paid two strings of cash." Liu I-ling (劉 益 齡) declares, "on embarking
" I was placed in confinement, and was given by the interpreter a contract made out in the name
" of Wang A-man (王 阿 滿)." Chang 'Huo-hsiu (張 火 秀) declares, "in the barracoon I saw
" that those who refused to go abroad were beaten on the cheeks, and placed under privies, so that
" consent was the only course open to me." Wang T'ing-kuei (王 廷 貴) declares, "I was
" decoyed, and declined to embark; I then was placed under a privy, and was told that if I
" persisted in my refusal I would never be permitted to come out, and, thus, I was constrained
" to assent." Liang A-shêng (梁 阿 盛) declares, "I saw those who refused to go abroad confined
" inside privies." Ch'ên Lung (陳 龍) declares, "when inspected by the Portuguese official, I
" declared that I was unwilling to proceed abroad. The interpreter then told me that if I persisted
" in my refusal I would be confined under a privy for three years." Lin A-lien (林 阿 連) declares,
" as I was unwilling to proceed abroad, the head of the barracoon told me, that unless I consented
" I would certainly be placed under a privy." Chang Lin-an (張 林 安) declares, "I ran away
" from a barracoon, was captured, and placed under a privy." 'Hung A-i (洪 阿 異) declares,
" after having been confined in a barracoon three days, I was given a contract made out in the name
" of a native of Sanshui (三 水), 'Ho A-yu (何 阿 有)." Ch'ên Shao-yen (陳 少 嚴) declares, "on
" board I was given a contract made out in the name of Chêng Ts'ai (鄭 材)." Wu Lien-shêng
(吳 聯 勝) declares, "I was forced to accept a contract and to sign the name of Wu A-chung
" (吳 阿 忠)." Wu Yao (伍 耀) declares, "on board, a contract was given to me, made out in the
" name of Ch'ên A-ssŭ (陳 阿 四)." Mai A-kuei (麥 阿 貴) declares, "the contract was given to
" me on board ship. It was made out in the name of Ch'ên A-fu (陳 阿 福)." Liang A-chang
(梁 阿 掌) declares, "the name on my contract was Huang Fu (黃 福)." Ts'ui Lan-fang
(崔 蘭 芳) declares, "the contract given to me was made out in the name of Liu Ch'i (劉 七)."
Yeh Tung-'ho (葉 東 合) declares, "the contract was in the name of Yeh Tung (葉 東)." Hsiao
Mêng-hsing (蕭 孟 興) declares, "when inspected by the Portuguese official a contract made out
" in the name of Lin Fu (林 福) was given to me." Li Ts'an (李 燦) declares, "the name on
" my contract was 'Huang Hsing (黃 姓)." Yeh A-hsi (葉 阿 錫) declares, "after embarkation I
" was given a contract made out in the name of Ch'ên Ch'ing-yün (陳 慶 雲)." Li A-shêng
(黎 阿 勝) declares, "the name on my contract was Ch'ên A-hsing (陳 阿 興)." Liang A-shêng

(梁 阿 盛) declares, "the name on my contract was Li A-êrh (李 阿 二)." Chang Luan (張 鑾) declares, "the name on my contract was Ch'ên Kuei (陳 貴)." Lin Achung (林 阿 中) declares, "on board a contract made out in the name of Liang A-fu (梁 阿 福), a native of Yangch'un "(陽 春), was given to me." Li A-pei (李 阿 北) declares, "the name on my contract was Lin Jih "(林 日), a native of Yangkiang (陽 江)." Li A-tê (李 阿 德) declares, "the name on my "contract was Liu A-'hung (劉 阿 紅). 'Ho A-ting (何 阿 丁) declares, "on board a contract "made out in the name of Chêng A-ta (鄭 阿 大) was given to me." T'an Pêi (譚 培) declares, "on board a contract made out in the name of 'Huang A-san (黃 阿 三) was given to me." Ch'ên A-tê (陳 阿 德) declares, "on board a contract made out in the name of 'Hou A-ku "(侯 阿 古) was given to me." Li A-yeh (李 阿 葉) declares, "on board a contract made out in the "name of T'an A-'ho (譚 阿 合) was given to me." Ch'ên A-liu (陳 阿 六) declares, "the name on "my contract was Huang A-san (黃 阿 三)." 'Hu A-ch'iang (胡 阿 祥) declares, "the name on "my contract was Ch'ên A-wu (陳 阿 五)." Chang A-ch'êng (張 阿 成) declares, "the name on "my contract was Wu Yung-chên (伍 永 貞)." Têng A-yen (鄧 阿 言) declares, "the name "on my contract was P'an Ying-yüan (潘 英 元)." Liang A-wan (梁 阿 萬) declares, "the "name on my contract was Hsieh Wu (謝 吾)." T'an A-ch'in (譚 阿 勤) declares, "the name "on my contract was originally Lan A-'huo (藍 阿 火), but on arrival at Havana another contract "made out in the name of Li A-ssŭ (李 阿 四) was given to me."

III.

IS CARE TAKEN TO SEE THAT THE AGREEMENTS ARE UNDERSTOOD ?

The petition of Li Chao-ch'un (李 肇 春) and 165 others states, "when the contracts are "being translated much is passed over, only a few clauses are read out, and Annan or Singapore "is stated to be the destination, so that, as we are not deprived of all hope of return, it seems "better, to avoid immediate death, to affix our signatures, and to embark." 'Huang Ch'ao-ping (黃 潮 炳) and 192 others declare in their depositions, "we received contracts in the barracoons "and these documents were not read to us." Kuo Chan (郭 占) and 116 others declare, "the "contracts were given to us on board ship and were not read to us." Wên Ch'ang-t'ai (文 長 泰) and 219 others declare, "the contracts were given to us in the presence of the Portuguese "Inspecting Officer but were not read to us." Wang Hsiang (王 向) and 8 others declare, "the "contracts were given to us in the presence of the Portuguese inspecting officer and were read "to us." Li A-fu (李 阿 福) and 2 others declare, "the contracts were given to us in the "presence of the Portuguese Inspecting Officer and were explained to us." Ch'ên T'ung (陳 通) declares, "the contract was given to me in the barracoon and was read to me." Ch'ên A-kuei (陳 阿 貴) declares, "a foreigner told me to affix my name to a contract, which he held in his "hand, but which he did not read to me." Li Ming (李 明) declares, "when being inspected by "the Portuguese official I declared that, as my parents were living I did not wish to proceed "abroad, and was then assured by the latter functionary that, if on arrival in Cuba I was "dissatisfied, the cost of a passage back would be supplied to me." Hsü A-fa (許 阿 發)

declares, "I asked where Havana was, and was told that it was the name of a vessel. I, in
"consequence, thought I was being engaged for service on board ship and signed the contract."
Hsieh A-fa (謝 阿 發) declares, "at the time of signing the contract, I was told that one foreign
"year equalled six Chinese months." Fêng A-k'ai (馮 阿 開) and 6 others declare, "the contract
"was read to me but I did not comprehend what the nature of the document was; and besides I
"myself cannot read." Wu A-fang (吳 阿 芳) declares, "I did not understand the meaning of
"the contract." Pei A-pao (貝 阿 寶) declares, "the contract was read to me, but I did not
"understand its purport." T'ang Yü (湯 玉) and 6 others declare, "the contracts were read to
"us, but we did not know what they contained."

IV.

DO THE LAWS PROVIDE ADEQUATELY FOR THE WELL-BEING OF THE COOLIES
ON THE VOYAGE?

The vessels—whether steamers or sailing vessels—which convey Chinese labourers to Cuba
appertain to various nationalities, and in consequence are not subject to any uniform system of
regulations. The rules prepared by certain Spanish merchants for the guidance of the masters
of vessels engaged in the traffic in question, prove to be, to a very great extent, not observed,
whilst it is difficult to comprehend the object of the 35th clause prohibiting the shaving of the
head by Chinese, and of the 20th clause which prescribes that when repairs become necessary,
the ports of China, Great Britain and the U. S. of America, are on no account to be entered, "as
"such a course would lead to the entire failure of the enterprise."

Of the more than 140,000 Chinese who sailed for Cuba, more than 16,000 died during the
voyages, a fact which is sufficient evidence of the absence of effective regulations.

The petition of Li Chao-ch'un (李 肇 春) and 165 others states, "when, quitting Macao,
"we proceeded to sea, we were confined in the hold below; some were even shut up in bamboo
"cages, or chained to iron posts, and a few were indiscriminately selected and flogged as a means
"of intimidating all others; whilst we cannot estimate the deaths that, in all, took place, from
"sickness, blows, hunger, thirst, or from suicide by leaping into the sea." The petition of Ch'iu
Pi-shan (邱 碧 山) and 35 others states, "If the master be a good man the sufferings are only
"those produced by grave maladies, but if his disposition be cruel there is no limit to the ill-
"usage, and there have been cases when more than half the number on board have died. Ten
"thousand hardships have to be endured during the voyage of several months." The petition of
Tiao Mu (刁 木) and 30 others states, "many die from sickness, and many jump into the sea to
"be devoured by the fish." The petition of Yeh Fu-chün (葉 福 君) and 52 others states, "the
"winds and waves on the ocean were great, and three months had passed away, but we had not
"arrived; as there was no water issued it had to be bought, and for a single cup a dollar was
"paid. The hatchway only allowed one man at a time to come down or go up, and the stench
"below from the crowd of men was most offensive, and the deaths thence produced were without

"number." The petition of Liu A-shou (劉阿壽) and 4 others states, "we cannot estimate the "number of deaths from ill-usage; the bodies were thrown into the sea."

Among the depositions there are found only the following instances of good usage received during the voyage. Ch'ên A-ch'iu (陳阿秋) and 1 other state that the masters treated those on board well. Fêng Chi (馮吉) declares, "the master treated me passably." P'an Ming (潘明) and 2 others state that they were well used, and received sufficient food on board. Yao A-ya (姚阿押) declares, "I was well used on board and the rations of food and fresh water "were sufficient." Yü A-kou (余阿狗) and 1 other state that they were well treated on board and received both water and rice.

On the other hand the depositions of Wang Shui-t'ou (王水頭) and 4 others, state that the water and rice on board were insufficient. Ch'ên A-chi (陳阿吉) deposes, "two of "those on board threw themselves into the sea because they had been flogged for taking water "when suffering from extreme thirst, and for refusing to allow their queues to be cut off." Liang A-chao (梁阿照) deposes, "I had money with me when decoyed on board, but the master "would not even permit me to redeem myself." Ho Hsi (何錫) deposes, "the fresh water on "board was insufficient." Ts'ai A-lu (蔡阿魯) deposes, "the water was insufficient and many "died from thirst; and besides, three men threw themselves into the sea." The deposition of Ch'ên Ch'ih (陳池) states, "that rice and fresh water were not sufficient and that those who asked for "water received blows." Yü Ming-hsing (余名興) deposes, "we were badly treated on board, "and sometimes a dollar was paid for two cups of water." Li A-pao (李阿保) deposes, "more "than 50 died from thirst and I heard that one Chinese was struck dead by the master for "stealing a cup of water." Liang En (梁恩) deposes, "both water and rice were insufficient, "and we were not allowed to go on deck." The depositions of Huang K'ai (黃開) and 2 others state that one dollar would buy only a single cup of water. The depositions of Lin Ch'üan (林泉) and 2 others state that the food was insufficient, that there was no fresh water and that they were constantly beaten. Kao A-tai (高阿代) deposes, "the treatment on board was bad "and the water was stinking. The surgeon was a bad man, and the sick at the moment of death "were thrown into the sea." Liu A-san (劉阿三) deposes, "20 men cast themselves over- "board." Chên A-shêng (陳阿勝) deposes, "on board 300 died from thirst." Chou Ch'êng (周成) deposes "all of us who seemed strong were placed in irons." The deposition of Li A-tê (李阿德) and 1 other states that the space for sleep allowed to each man measured only 1 ch'ih 2 ts'un. Fêng A-k'ai (馮阿開) deposes, "the surgeon struck all who complained "of sickness, and even tied them up and flogged them, and three sick men were killed by him." Li Chin-ch'üan (李錦泉) deposes, "the master was a very bad man; 12 sick men died through "his treatment." Liang Yu-tê (梁有德) deposes, "water and rice were both insufficient. I also "saw that three or four men, who by their physical powers caused apprehension to the master, "were severely flogged, and were placed in irons, from which they were only released on arrival at "Havana." Wu Yüeh (吳越) deposes, "the treatment on board was bad and 20 men being afraid "of the sea voyage committed suicide." Chou Jun-shêng (周潤勝) deposes, "one man who "complained to the mate of the rottenness of the fish was almost beaten to death by the sailors, "by the order of the master." Wu A-'hou (吳阿侯) deposes, "suffering from sea-sickness I was "unable to work, and was in consequence beaten by the mate." The depositions of Li Yu (李有)

and 23 others testify to their each having witnessed one case of suicide by jumping overboard. The depositions of 'Huang A-pei (黃阿北) and 4 others again testify to their severally witnessing one case of suicide. The depositions of Lung A-ch'uan (龍阿川) and 29 others testify to their each having witnessed two cases of suicide by jumping overboard. The depositions of Wang Chêng-fu (王正福) and 6 others testify to their each having witnessed three cases of suicide by jumping overboard. The depositions of 'Huang A-ch'ang (黃阿昌) and 4 others testify to the water and rice having been insufficient and to their each having witnessed four cases of suicide by jumping overboard. The depositions of Liu A-ssŭ (劉阿四) and 2 others testify to the cruelties each experienced, and to each having witnessed five cases of suicide by jumping overboard. Ts'ui An (崔安) deposes, "I saw eight men tied and flogged with great severity, two of whom were also "kept in irons until arrival at Havana." Li Hui (李惠) deposes, "I saw one man, a native of "Tungkwan (東莞), tied up and shot, and other five tied up and cast into the sea." Li Yü (李禹) deposes, "the treatment on board was bad; two men were beaten to death." Ts'ui Têng-lin (崔登林) deposes, "two men threw themselves overboard and two hanged themselves." Lo A-fa (羅阿發) deposes, "one man was beaten to death." Chao A-ling (趙阿凌) deposes, "the fresh water was "insufficient; three men also were shot." Li Wên-ts'ai (李文財) deposes, "the master intending to "arrest five men who had been decoyed, and were discontented, in error seized and chained five "others; upon this, the men whom he had desired to punish threw themselves into the sea." Li A-chieh (李阿皆) deposes, "five men who rose at night to relieve nature were shot by the "sailors." Shih A-kou (石阿狗) deposes, "the drinking of salt water caused much sickness, "which was incurable." Wang A-fu (王阿福) deposes, "eight men jumped overboard. They "did so because they had been decoyed and were dissatisfied." Hsieh Kuan-chieh (謝官姐) deposes, "one man jumped overboard because he was constantly beaten by the master and inter-"preter; moreover those who asked for water were beaten and many died of thirst." Tsêng A-tai (曾阿帶) deposes, "the interpreter was a Portuguese, and constantly kicked us." Ni A-'huan (倪阿煥) deposes, "the mate constantly struck us with a thick rope." Hsieh Fa (謝發) deposes, "I was chained to the bottom of the hold." The depositions of Kao Pao (高寶) and 1 other state that they were not allowed on deck even for air. Ch'ên A-shun (陳阿順) deposes, "two men committed suicide. On board a sailor wounded me with a knife and the scar is still "visible. The master with a firearm wounded two men." Li Shun (黎順) deposes, "water and "rice were both insufficient. Two men were shot, and two jumped overboard." Li Hsin (黎信) deposes, "two men who in want of rice created an outcry, were shot with a pistol." Hsieh A-kêng (謝阿庚) deposes, "the master was a bad man; food was insufficient and there was no water. "There were suicides by jumping overboard and hanging; and deaths from sickness." Ch'ên A-wei (周阿未) deposes, "Many leaped overboard, on account of being forced to cut their queues; "if we asked for water we were struck with an iron chain." Ch'ên I (陳翼) deposes, "the men "who had been decoyed were unwilling to go abroad, and entertained mutinous intentions. The "sailors discharged firearms from the hatchway into the hold, killed 20 and wounded 40 or 50. "The remainder were all placed in irons, and daily 30 were led on deck and there flogged." Li Pi-'ho (李璧和) deposes, "five men were lashed to the mast and shot. I myself was thrice "flogged on my naked person." Ch'ên Ch'in (陳琴) deposes, "many died of thirst; those who "took water were beaten." Lin A-yung (林阿用) deposes, "I was beaten because I was sea-sick.

" The food also was insufficient." Lu Chung (盧鍾) deposes, "as the food and water were both
" insufficient, we all created an uproar. The master shot the two leaders, and we were all severely
" flogged." Li A-ʻhui (李阿會) deposes, " I was hungry and asked for food; four sailors then forced
" me into a prostrate position, and flogged me, the scars resulting from the wounds being still
" visible." Wang Wei (王爲) deposes, " one man being unable to eat the beef, asked that salt
" should be allowed him (in its place). He was refused and threw himself into the sea." Huang
Tso (黃坐) deposes, " five men were killed on account of disturbances on board." Hsieh A-tso
(謝阿作) deposes, " we were not allowed on deck to obtain a little fresh air, and many died
" from the effects of the close confinement." ʻHuang A-fang (黃阿芳) deposes, " 11 men
" committed suicide. The day after I embarked we were all ordered on deck, and foot irons were
" attached to 173 physically strong men, besides 160 men were stripped and flogged on their
" naked persons with rattan rods." Wang Tʻing-kuei (王廷貴) deposes, " 24 men leaped
" overboard and two poisoned themselves with opium. They committed suicide because they
" had been decoyed and were unwilling to go abroad." Lai A-shih (賴阿時) deposes, " we
" all were being taken away against our will, and created an uproar. The master upon this
" directed the sailors to strike us with chains and 80 men were killed." Chu Tsʻun-fang
(朱村房) deposes, " one day suffering from extreme thirst I took a little water; and for
" doing so was struck by the master 25 blows on each hand." Wu Lien-shêng (吳聯勝)
deposes, " I myself saw a native of the Hwa (花) district kicked to death by the master for
" asking for medicine when sick : 36, of whom I was one, were tied up, beaten, and placed
" in irons from which we were only released on the vessel arriving at a British colony."
" Chʻên A-chʻing (陳阿慶) deposes, " two sick men went on deck to relieve nature, and were
" kicked to death by the sailors." Pʻang A-tung (龐阿東) deposes, " if through not under-
" standing the language the work was not well performed, we were beaten, and one of our
" number threw himself overboard." Liao A-ping (廖阿炳) deposes, " for drinking a small
" cup of water I was dragged on deck and flogged." Lo ʻHuai-chʻang (羅懷昌) deposes, " one
" man was beaten so severely by the master, that, the suffering being unendurable, he threw
" himself overboard." Lo Hsien-fa (羅先發) deposes, " one man was beaten to death on board ;
" five men committed suicide ; and two were shot because, having nothing to eat and suffering
" from hunger, they asked for food." Chang Chêng-kao (張正高) deposes, " the master was
" very cruel ; some died from thirst, others from flogging, others on the point of death but not
" dead were thrown overboard, and others, their sufferings being unendurable, cast themselves
" into the sea." Hsiao To (蕭多) deposes, " the food and water were insufficient ; flogging was
" constant, and two men committed suicide, whilst two others were so severely kicked by the sailors
" on account of smoking, that they died from the injuries thus caused." Li Pao (李報) declares,
" two men suspected by the master of mutinous intentions were hanged." Chʻên ʻHua (陳華)
deposes, " the master beat to death four men." Chʻên Chʻi-kuang (陳其光) deposes, " a native of
" Kiaying (嘉應) who created an outcry because he objected to his queue being cut off, was shot
" by the master, whilst others were flogged until their flesh was lacerated." Chên A-lin (甄阿林)
deposes, " the master was cruel. When thirst forced us all to go on deck in search of water, he
" regarding us as mutinous, discharged firearms and killed 40 men." Yü Kuan (徐觀) deposes,
" the mate displayed excessive cruelty ; suspecting that I and 15 others entertained mutinous

" intentions he confined, chained and constantly flogged us." The depositions of Ch'ên Hsio-chou (陳學周) and 1 other state that more than 30 men were shot during the voyage. Chang A-chin (張阿金) deposes, "the surgeon was a foreigner, and many died through his treatment; many "died from confinement in the hold, and others, decoyed unwilling to go abroad, killed them- "selves." Li A-ch'iang (李阿祥) deposes, "two men were suspected by the master of mutinous "intentions, and were hanged by his orders." Liang A-yu (梁阿有) deposes, "two insane "men were struck to death by the carpenter." Lin Chin (林金) deposes, "30 men committed "suicide." Ts'ui Lan-fang (崔蘭芳) deposes, "three men made an outcry, declaring that they "would not go abroad; of these two were killed by firearms, and one was hanged." Tsêng A-shêng (曾阿勝) deposes, "the men who were decoyed did not wish to go abroad, and in "consequence 60 were either shot by the master or committed suicide." Kuan A-hsiao (關阿曉) deposes, "on account of smoking four men were flogged until they spat blood, and died." Mo Shuang (莫雙) deposes, "four men committed suicide and the master shot three others." Liang A-chien (梁阿見) deposes, "I am the only child of my parents and was in great grief; yet no one "regarded me. During the voyage one man killed himself." 'Huang Ch'iu-t'ai (黃秋泰) deposes, "two committed suicide and two were beaten to death." Liang Piao (梁標) deposes, "water "and food were both insufficient; yet if any complaints were made, our clothing was removed, "and perhaps one hundred, perhaps several tens of blows were inflicted with a rod of four rattans "tied together." 'Ho A-fa (何阿發) deposes, "the master beat to death three men." Lin A-san (林阿三) deposes, "on the plea of there having been disturbances on board several men were "beaten to death; one man also jumped overboard." Ch'ên Lung (陳龍) deposes, "the master "was a bad man. Many being unwilling to go abroad threw themselves overboard. When being "prohibited from going on deck and being deprived of water we created an outcry, we were "regarded as mutinous by the master, and over ten were killed. They were killed by the sailors' "blows from bludgeons and knives. Near Malacca the vessels received injuries, but though the "water was entering the hold, the hatchways were not opened; and it was only when the water "reached our necks and when more than ten were already drowned that they were raised." Liu A-lin (劉阿林) deposes, "one man was beaten to death on board." Su A-wu (蘇阿五) deposes, "eight men were stripped of their clothing, severely flogged and then confined in "chains, which were only removed on arrival at Havana." Liu A-hsi (劉阿喜) deposes, "on "board four men were so severely flogged that they died on the following day." 'Huang A-ch'êng (黃阿成) deposes, "in consequence of my talking with some others, the master suspected me "of mutinous intentions and directed the sailors to tie up, strip, flog and chain me and 31 "others." Tsêng A-yang (曾阿養) deposes, "on board we were not allowed to speak." Wu Chên-ming (吳振名) deposes, "six men committed suicide." Liang A-ping (梁阿炳) deposes, "the master was apprehensive of a mutiny and tied up and flogged with great severity 30 "men." Fang A-ts'ai (方阿才) deposes, "200 men who were considered dangerous on "account of their physical strength were confined in chains." Wên Ssŭ (溫四) deposes, "one man on board committed suicide, and 50 men who were suspected of mutiny were "placed in irons." Lo A-fa (羅阿發) deposes, "on board two men committed suicide and two "men were beaten to death." Pêng A-shêng (彭阿生) deposes, "one man committed suicide "by swallowing opium." 'Huang A-tou (黃阿斗) deposes, "before the vessel sailed five men

"who attempting to escape jumped overboard, were shot, and after departure 24 men were tied
"up, severely flogged, and kept in chains in the forepart of the vessel, of whom two committed
"suicide by jumping overboard."

V.

IF ILL-TREATED ON THE VOYAGE, DO THE LAWS PROVIDE A MEANS OF OBTAINING REDRESS?

The 16th article of the Spanish Royal Decree of 1860 provides, that if on arrival of a
vessel it is ascertained from examination of the papers that the mortality during the voyage has
exceeded 6%, an enquiry into its cause shall be made, and that, if necessary, criminal proceedings
shall be instituted; and the 30th article also prescribes that in the cases in which the fines
indicated have been enforced by the Captain General, the Attorney General may in addition take,
in the name of the Chinese, legal action.

But not only on board of the vessel to which they have been decoyed are the lives of the
latter dependent on the will of the master and his officers without any means of appeal against
whatever injustice these may see fit to commit; but also on arrival at Havana they are at once
confined in barracoons, from which they can only go forth to labour under guard, being unable
to move a single step with freedom; whilst in any case their ignorance of the Spanish language
would render it impossible for them to put forward a statement of wrongs. Thus the right of
preferring charges is a purely nominal, practically useless privilege.

It is gathered also from the petitions that Ch'ên Ming-yüan (陳名願) and Yao Wên-
hsien (姚文先), both engaged as physicians, and Chang T'ai-lung (張泰隆), engaged at
Batavia as linguist, with the distinct understanding that the cost of return passages to China
should be furnished to them, were on arrival at Havana fraudulently sold, a wrong for which
despite the number of years that have elapsed, they have had no means of obtaining redress.
How much less then is any such redress possible for the general body of common labourers?

VI

ON ARRIVAL WHAT HAPPENS TO THE COOLIE?

By the 13th article of the Spanish Royal Decree of 1860, it is provided that vessels
conveying Chinese labourers to Cuba must—save in cases of sudden exigency—land them at
Havana. Thence the common practice has been to pass to that port, after undergoing quarantine
at Mariello in the neighbourhood of Guanajay.

The petition of Hsieh Shuang-chiu (謝雙就) and 11 others states, "on landing, four
"or five foreigners on horseback, armed with whips, led us like a herd of cattle to the barracoon
"to be sold." The petition of Ch'iu Pi-shan (邱碧山) and 34 others states, "Chinese (in the
"Havana barracoons) are treated like pigs and dogs, all their movements, even their meals, being
"watched, until, after the lapse of a few days, they are sold away." The petition of Li Chao-ch'un

(李肇春) and 165 others states, "at Havana, after a detention at the quarantine station our
" queues were cut, and we awaited in the men-market the inspection of a buyer, and the settle-
" ment of the price." The petition of Yeh Fu-chün (葉福君) and 52 others states, "when
" offered for sale in the men-market we were divided into three classes—1st, 2nd and 3rd, and were
" forced to remove all our clothes, so that our persons might be examined and the price fixed.
" This covered us with shame." The petition of Chang Ting-chia (張定加) and 127 others
states, " on landing at Havana we were exposed for sale, our persons being examined by
" intending purchasers, in a manner shameless and before unheard of by us."

Lin A-pang (林阿榜) and 1 other declare in their depositions, that, in the men-market
in which they were placed on landing at Havana, intending purchasers insisted on removing
their clothes, and on examining their persons in order to ascertain whether they possessed
strength, just as if an ox or a horse was being bought; and that in this manner Chinese are
subjected not only to hardships but also to shame. Kao A-san (高阿三) and 1 other depose,
that after arrival at Havana, before they were purchased, their clothes were removed, and their
persons were thoroughly examined, in the manner practised when oxen or horses are being
bought. Yen A-ʻhuan (嚴阿煥) and 1 other likewise depose, that when being sold their
clothes were removed, and their persons examined in order to ascertain whether they possessed
strength, in the manner practised when oxen or horses are being bought. Chang A-hsi (章阿錫)
and 1 other depose, that when being sold their clothes were removed and their persons were felt
and examined, just as is done in country districts when an ox is being bought. Chiang San
(江三) deposes, "in the Havana barracoon, for refusing to permit the removal of my queue, I
" was beaten almost to death." Li A-ling (李阿靈) deposes, " it is the custom when coolies are
" being sold to remove their clothing to enable the buyer to effect a thorough examination of
" the person."

VII.

DURING THE AGREEMENT TERM, WHAT IS HIS POSITION?

The petition of Li Chao-chʻun (李肇春) and 165 others states, " 90 per cent. are disposed
" of to the sugar plantations. There the owners rely upon the administrator for the production
" of a large crop of sugar, and the administrator looks to the overseers for the exaction of the
" greatest possible amount of labour. They all think only of the profit to be gained and are
" indifferent as to our lives. It matters not whether the workmen are miserable or contented,
" whether they starve or have enough to eat, whether they live or die. The administrator who
" gives only four unripe bananas as a meal, is considered an able servant, and if he gives only
" three he is regarded as still more efficient. The administrator who forces the Chinese to work
" 20 hours out of the 24 is a man of capacity, if he extorts 21 hours his qualities are of a still
" higher order, but he may strike, or flog, or chain us, as his fancy suggests to him. If we
" complain of sickness we are beaten and starved; if we work slowly dogs are urged after us to
" bite us. Those of us who are employed on farms or coffee estates, in sugar warehouses and

"brick-kilns, on railways and in baker, cigar, shoe, hat and other snops, are in each of these
"places of service, ill treated, flogged, confined in stocks and in jail, and tortured in every way
"as on the plantations." The petition of Hsien Tso-pang (洗佐邦) and 13 others states, "we
"are fed worse than dogs, and are called upon to perform labour for which an ox or a horse
"would not possess sufficient strength. Everywhere cells exist, and whips and rods are in
"constant use, and maimed and lacerated limbs are daily to be seen. Almost daily, also, we hear
"of suicides of our countrymen who have hanged themselves, jumped into wells, cut their throats
"or swallowed opium." The petition of Lin Chin (林金) and 15 others states, "the overseer,
"bludgeon in hand, drives us to labour night and day." The petition of Ch'ên Ku (陳古) and
2 others states, "the administrator and overseers are as wolves or tigers. In their hand is
"the knife and on their shoulders the musket, and when they detect only a little slowness in
"work they chastise us until the blood drips to the ground." The petition of Chang Luan
(張鑾) and 30 others states, "in Cuba, within its length of not 2,000 *li* are to be found
"thousands of prisons, tens of thousands of fetters, and a number which cannot be counted of
"human beings, ever crying out under wrong and in their pain with torn and lacerated
"bodies, and seeking death by hanging, drowning, or poison, or the knife." The petition of
Shih Chih-'ho (施致和) and 28 others states, "the flogging and chaining produce fatal
"effects, which the stronger may with an effort withstand, but under which the old and weak
"soon die." The petition of Chien Shih-kuang (簡仕光) and 96 others states, "the instruments
"of punishment are in constant use, not one of us can ever feel sure of passing uninjured a
"single day, nor is there ever sufficient repose." The petition of Ch'ên Yü-shu (陳玉樹) and
4 others states, "whether we are disposed of as domestic slaves, or sold to sugar warehouses, or
"shops, we are dealt with as dogs, horses or oxen, badly fed, and deprived of rest, so that a single
"day becomes a year." The petition of Kao Lao-hsiu (高老秀) and 16 others states, "Chinese
"in Cuba have to labour night and day, and do not enjoy one instant's tranquillity; we are in
"addition constantly beaten and treated in every way like oxen, horses, sheep or dogs." The
petition of Chao K'un (趙昆) and 95 others states, "we suffer from insufficient nourishment,
"excessive labour enforced night and day, flogging and chaining in the day, and imprisonment
"and confinement in the stocks at night, so that many have died directly of their sufferings, or
"have tried to escape and met death outside." The petition of Tiao Mu (刁木) and 3 others
states, "we work night and day, allowed only a very brief repose, scantily fed, constantly beaten
"and chained, considered no more than bad grass and treated like horses and oxen." The
petition of P'an T'ai (潘泰) and 89 others states, "in Havana the workmen are oppressed and
"beaten with whips and rods, at night they cannot shut their eyes in peace, they have not
"enough food, they are given no clothes, and it is impossible to reckon all those who have died
"from ill treatment." The petition of Chang A-yüan (張阿元) and 4 others states, "there
"is always a foreign overseer watching us, stick in hand, and throughout the year we receive
"floggings which draw out every drop of our blood, and cause some to die within two or three
"days." The petition of Chêng Hsing (鄭惺) and 5 others states, "sleep and food are insufficient,
"and great are the sufferings from confinement and the lash." The petition of Ts'ai Hêng
(蔡恒) and 79 others states, "we have suffered from the overseers, who, grasping whips, or knives
"or firearms, with their voices menacing as thunder and with their tiger's claws, were ever by

" our sides,—relying on their masters' power they treated us like horses or oxen, and on their
" favour our lives depended." The petition of Hsieh Shuang-chiu (謝 雙 就) and 11 others states,
" the overseers are more cruel than tigers or wolves. They have no pity in their hearts. They
" are as terrible as the thunder and beat us constantly with their whips or rods, or throw bricks
" at us, or kick us, always inflicting an injury from which sometimes death ensues." The petition
of Liu A-shou (劉 阿 壽) and 4 others states, "the overseers are cruel as tigers and wolves. If
" we work a little slowly, we are flogged on our backs with whips, or dogs are incited to tear us
" to pieces." The petition of Chang Ting-chia (張 定 加) and 127 others states, "the overseers
" rode about with cowhide whips and pistols, striking all, good and bad indifferently, inflicting
" blows on those at a distance with whips, and striking with sticks those within reach. Ribs were
" broken and spitting of blood was produced in this manner; other injuries, too, were inflicted on
" the head and the feet, but as they were not directly visible labour was still enforced." The
petition of Chêng A-mou (鄭 阿 茂) and 89 others states, "we commenced labour in the middle
" of the night; the savage overseers drew blood by their blows, and suicide was of constant occur-
" rence. At the end of the eight years half of our number had died." The petition of Ch'ên Ming-
yüan (陳 名 願) states, "but the sufferings of the general body of Chinese labourers are even
" greater. They have to endure hunger and chains, hardships and wrongs of every class, and are
" driven to suicide to the extent that no count can be made of the number of those who have
" thrown themselves into wells, cut their throats, hanged themselves, and swallowed opium."
The petition of Chu Chi-hsün (朱 箕 訓) and of 10 others states, "all in actual service, whether
" in the hills or on plantations, or in families, or on railroads, or on board ship, or whether doing
" forced labour in the prisons, are,—besides being exposed to various wrongs at the hands of the
' evil-minded,—subjected to the flogging of their overseers. These use whips the lashes of which
" are made of the muscles of oxen dried in the sun, and are three or four feet long, and the blows
" inflicted by which are intensely painful. Sucides are thus of constant occurrence; their number
" indeed is countless." The petition of Yang Yün (楊 允) and 131 others states, "suicides by
" hanging on trees, by drowning, by swallowing opium, and by leaping into the sugar caldrons
" are the results of wrongs and sufferings which cannot be described."

    Wu A-ch'iang (伍 阿 祥) deposes also, "I myself have seen men flogged until they
" vomited blood, and death ensued a few days afterwards." Li A-wu (李 阿 伍) deposes, "if
" on the sugar plantations the task assigned is executed at all slowly, the overseers at once inflict
" several tens of blows, drawing blood, lacerating the skin, and causing inflamed swellings."
Ch'ên Tê-chêng (陳 得 正) deposes, "if the work is not performed to the satisfaction of the
" administrator, imprisonment and working in chains are resorted to; or 20, 25, 50 or an indefinite
" number of blows are inflicted, causing the blood and flesh to trickle down." Chu Chia-hsien
(朱 甲 先) deposes, "the overseer said it did not matter if we died, as others could be bought
" to take our places." Ch'ên Pao (陳 保) deposes, "I saw the legs of a Chinese broken by a
" flogging." Ho A-tê (何 阿 德) deposes, "on the sugar plantation I was flogged until my flesh
" was lacerated, and the wounds were afterwards washed in alcoholic spirits causing intense pain."
Chêng A-chi (鄭 阿 吉) deposes, "I have been flogged with very great severity, and the scars
" on my person are still visible. I was flogged with a cowhide whip, and it constantly occurred
" that blood was drawn from the wounds and that my clothes were torn by the blows—yet I

"had committed no offence." Lin A-kou (林阿狗) deposes, "the administrator, when "intoxicated, would strike me on the head." Chou Liu (周六) deposes, "as the adminis- "trator acted with great cruelty, I ran away; I was pursued by hounds and on being "captured two of my fingers were cut off." Ts'ui An (崔安) deposes, "I saw a man "killed for simply striking an overseer." Ch'ên A-shun (陳阿順) deposes, "the adminis- "trator constantly inflicted floggings and incited the hounds to bite." Wang Ching (王敬) deposes, "I found the chaining and flogging so unendurable, during the first six months "of my service, that I attempted suicide by cutting my throat, and a month elapsed before "the wound was healed." Lu Shêng-pao (盧盛保) deposes, "monthly, the $4 were not "issued, and for a service of one year and a half, only $51 were paid me." Wang A-jui (王阿瑞) deposes, "I was sold to a brick-kiln, and during eighteen months received no wages." 'Han Yen-p'ei (韓炎培) deposes, "my master did not furnish me with food. He issued to me "orders for edibles to be handed to the plantation shop. These orders were regarded as money, "and their amount being placed to my debit, my earnings for the entire eight years were thus "deducted." Ts'ui F'êng-lin (崔登林) deposes, "on one occasion I went out to make certain "purchases. On my return I was severely flogged, and was compelled to work in irons during "three months." Yang Ch'i-man (楊其滿) deposes, "on one occassion, I was beaten with great "severity and it was not until I was so gravely injured that I vomited blood, that the blows "ceased. I also saw a flogging inflicted on another man, of such severity that finding the pain "unendurable, he leaped into a well." Yeh A-yao (葉阿耀) deposes, "for refusing to eat maize "I was almost beaten to death. My entire person was lacerated; on it there was not a single "spot uninjured." Li A-ta (李阿達) deposes, "on one occasion I received 200 blows, and "though my body was a mass of wounds I was still forced to continue labour." Li San-mou (李三茂) deposes, "on two occasions my trowsers were removed, and I was beaten with a rattan "rod on my naked person." Wu A-san (吳阿三) deposes, "the Chinese in chains were beaten "severely if they did not imitate the cries of sheep and dogs."

VIII.

ARE THE AGREEMENT STIPULATIONS CARRIED OUT?

Eight contracts issued at various dates between the 3rd year of HIENFÊNG and the 12th year of T'UNGCHIH have been examined. Of these only one—that has never been employed,— is framed in accordance with the provisions of the Emigration Convention of the 5th year of T'UNGCHIH.

The stipulations of the remainder are in most respects alike. Among these is a clause to the effect that labour cannot be enforced during more than 12 hours of the 24, whilst enquiries have shown that as much as 21 hours are exacted; another to the effect that Sunday shall be a day of rest, whilst it is ascertained that in the great majority of cases, no cessation of labour takes place on that day; a third prescribes that the daily rations shall consist of 8 taels' weight of salt meat and 2½ ℔s. of miscellaneous articles of food, all to be of good quality, whilst it appears, that the rations of meat supplied have been as small as a little more than 1 tael, and that the other articles furnished have been only potatoes, bananas or maize; and a fourth providing that in all cases of sickness, it matters not how long its duration, the labourers shall be sent to hospital by their masters to be properly cared for until cured, and that no deduction from wages is on this account to be made,—whilst investigation has proved, that in the larger number of instances, a Chinese complaining of sickness is punished by chains and blows, chastisements that have continually resulted in death, and that it has been but rarely that the wages have not been withheld; $ 8 are also specified as the sum to be advanced to the labourer before his departure, and the method of refund indicated is a subsequent monthly deduction by his employer in Cuba of $ 1, until the sum in question has been recovered; but though many have not received even a single *cash*, the almost universal practice has been to withhold not $ 8 but $ 12 during the first year of service. Again, a clause is found to the effect that at the close of the eight years, the labourer may without restraint seek employment, and that his original master cannot, on the plea of debt or of an agreement, retard his liberty or exact from him the performance of new tasks; but in despite of this provision it is proved that, in most instances, chaining and chastisement and other means are devised, in order to obtain an additional forced labour of even several years. It is likewise provided, that on the expiration of the contract term a period of 60 days shall be accorded in order to enable the labourer to arrange at the proper port for his return to his country, and that if he does not desire to go back he shall be at liberty to take such steps for improving his position as are permitted to the general labouring class in the island; yet it is ascertained that the labourers who refuse to be constrained into renewing their contracts are delivered to dépôts to work without wages, that they never enjoy the specified term for preparing for their return home, and that, the functionaries of the dépôts into which they are thrust becoming their masters, they are altogether precluded from independently seeking employment.

In these respects then the actual practice in Cuba is directly at variance with the various provisions to be found in the contracts inspected, as is testified by the recorded depositions and petitions.

IX.

IF THE EMPLOYERS VIOLATE THE STIPULATIONS, WHAT REDRESS HAS THE COOLIE BY LAW?

The 44th article of the Spanish Royal Decree of 1860 provides, that when Chinese labourers are wronged by their employers or are subjected to any breach of the conditions of the contract, they shall proceed to the official designated as their Protector, who shall duly investigate the matter. But though the Chinese in cases of violation of contract thus possess the right of bringing a charge before the authorities, their imperfect acquaintance with the people and the locality, and the restraint and the confinement to which they are subjected by their unscrupulous employers render it difficult for them to avail themselves of the privilege; whilst even when they succeed in preferring a complaint, redress would appear to be nearly impossible.

The petition of Ts'ai 'Hêng (蔡 恒) and 79 others states, "the paper without which we " could not move a single step was refused, but we had no means of complaint or protest in regard " to this injustice." The petition of Lin Chin (林 金) and 15 others states, "on the plantations " and farms we seek refuge in death by every form of suicide. It is impossible to enumerate all " the outrages to which we are subjected. The authorities when such cases reach their ears, " accept the master's bribes and give no heed to the crime. The instances of this class are innu- " merable." The petition of Huang Fêng-chi (黃 逢 吉) and 11 others states, "we had to endure " every kind of suffering. When our terms of service were drawing towards their close we thought " that we could rely upon our contracts, and that we would be able to go out and reap advantage, " but these documents were held as invalid, and our freedom was withheld." The petition of Lai Chih-chih (賴 質 直) and 3 others states, "foreigners are so untrustworthy as to disregard " altogether the stipulation of the contract that we are engaged for only eight years. After these are " expired they desire us to work again for a similar term." The petition of Ch'iu Pi-shan (邱 碧 山) and 34 others states, "after eight years of these sufferings, and the completion of the term of service, " a new contract for six years must be entered into." The petition of Yang Yün (楊 允) and 130 others states, "the contracts signed at Macao were for a term of eight years, but here we find there is " no limit to our labours." Chêng Shêng (鄭 盛) declares in his petition, "I and 24 others sold " with me, had each a contract stating that at the expiration of eight years we would be free, but " our employer, devoid of conscience, refused to accord to me my liberty, and coerced me into " working six more years. I could not avoid yielding, and now that I have finished the second " engagement, he again declines to permit me to go away, and has sent us all to the foreign " authorities." Ku Ch'iao-hsiu (古 橋 秀) declares in his petition, "I know of more than one " hundred who were with me, who on the completion of their contracts were forced either to " accept fresh engagements or to enter prison." The petition of Wu A-fa (吳 阿 發) and 39 others states, "foreigners in no way consider themselves bound by the provisions of the contracts. After " the eight years are completed they refuse us the cedulas and we are forced to remain slaves in " perpetuity."

Again, Yeh Yu (葉 由) deposes, "on the plantation we were constantly beaten. If we " complained to the officials, our employers presented them with money, and we were sent back, " and after our clothes were removed again flogged." Li T'ung (李 通) deposes, "I complained to " the officials because no rice was supplied; I, in consequence, was kept in chains during one " month." Wu Yüeh (吳 越) deposes, "on account of the unendurable sufferings on the " plantation many committed suicide. Complaints were made to the officials, but they gave no " heed." Ch'ên A-shun (陳 阿 順) deposes, "on the plantation was a prison, in which men were " constantly confined and chained. If we went only a few steps beyond the limits of the estate, " we were seized, flogged and chained, so that there were no means of preferring complaints." 'Ho A-pa (何 阿 八) deposes, "if we went outside only a few steps, we were regarded as " attempting to escape, and were seized, chained and beaten. Thus no one dared to prefer " complaints." Yu A-shih (游 阿 式) deposes, "according to the contract I was entitled to " clothes, which were not supplied to me; I therefore declined to work and was in consequence " chained and beaten." 'Huang Hsing (黃 輿) deposes, "on the plantation we are constantly " chained and beaten, but dare not complain to the officials through fear of being subjected "to even greater cruelties. I myself made an attempt to cut my throat." Huang A-shui (黃 阿 水) deposes, "whilst employed on the plantation, a native of P'anyü (番 禹), "by name A Kuei (阿 桂), was struck dead by the administrator. On the following day "we started in order to lay a complaint before the authorities, but we had proceeded only "half the distance when we were overtaken by the administrator at the head of a party of "armed men, and were carried back and chained." Kao A-lun (高 阿 倫) deposes, "we, nine "in all, proceeded to the officials but were sent back to the plantation, tied up and flogged by an "overseer—a white man—until his hand was fatigued." Lai Ch'uan-shou (賴 川 受) deposes, "the black overseers constantly beat us. I myself have already on four occasions been flogged, "and afterwards placed in foot-irons. On my endeavouring to offer an explanation when an "overseer abused me, he became angry and struck and chained me. Thus remonstrance is "denied to us." Lin A-t'ai (林 阿 泰) deposes, "my employer owes me $ 128. I came to Havana "to complain, but the official not only gave no heed, but also confined me in the dépôt, where I "have now been working without wages during two years." Lin A-cho (林 阿 著) deposes, "my "master owed me $108, and when I complained to the official I was brought back and again forced "to labour for five months, still receiving no money. As he stated that, as a punishment for my "bringing a charge against him, he would sell me to a sugar plantation, I and two others proceeded "to Havana in order to renew the complaint, and were there placed in confinement in the dépôt, "where I have now worked without wages during seven or eight years. My master has never "been called upon to reply to my accusation." Ch'ên A-yin (陳 阿 音) deposes, "a foreigner who "hired me for work on board ship owes me $ 100. I have preferred a complaint before the "officials, but no heed has been given to it." Hsieh A-fa (謝 阿 發) deposes, "I was "beaten if I worked a little slowly, and during the hours of labour was not permitted even to "relieve nature. On one occasion, having been flogged with great severity, I laid a complaint "before the officials, but my master by an outlay of money was enabled to bring me back, "and then compelled me to labour in irons." Liu A-wên (劉 阿 文) deposes, "some years since, "on account of the barbarous cruelty of the administrator, I complained to the officials. My "complaint was not accepted, and after returning, I and 39 others were forced to work in irons "for three months. Our wages for the same period were withheld." Ch'ên A-mu (陳 阿 睦) deposes, "on the plantation I was treated with great cruelty, being constantly beaten. Last "year, after a flogging of even unusual severity, I proceeded to the officials, and preferred a "complaint. My master having presented them with money was enabled to bring me back, and "chained my feet during several months and subjected me to an ill-usage greater than that "which I had to endure before." Tsêng Ch'ing-jung (曾 慶 榮) deposes, "of those with me, one "committed suicide by swallowing opium, and another by name A-fu (阿 福) was beaten to "death. The bodies were at once buried and no enquiry was made." Têng Kuan (鄧 寬) deposes, "during the two years which I passed on the plantation I was constantly beaten with "great severity. I made a complaint to the officials, but through my imperfect acquaintance "with Spanish, the result was that I was sent to the dépôt, where, with chained feet, I had to "work without wages on the roads and breaking stones." Lin A-chung (林 阿 中) deposes, "I and A-shêng (阿 生) and A-fu (阿 福) requested the administrator to issue to us our wages "in silver. The latter became angry and sent us to the dépôt where we had to work without "wages." Fêng Chi (馮吉) deposes, "after the expiration of the contract term I had to work "for seven years, during five of which I received as wages $17. My employer then wished to "substitute the paper currency, and as I declined to accept it I was within two or three days "removed to a dépôt by Government officials." Li Chia (李嘉) deposes, "at the end of the "eight years, my master denied that the contract term was completed. I therefore laid a "complaint before the officials, who retained me to perform, without wages, Government work on "the roads." Lo A-êrh (羅阿二) deposes, "on the expiration of the contract, I was sent to a "dépôt, where I passed four months. I was then removed by my master, who forced me to "labour in chains during three months. He daily beats me, and yesterday flogged me with great "severity. Five months have now elapsed, during which no wages have been issued to me. On "account of this and the other ill usage, I requested a fellow workman to, on my behalf, lay a "complaint before the officials. He has done so on three occasions and in each instance it has been "rejected, and I have thus to go on labouring; whilst if I ask for wages the threat of chaining "is made. I in all earnestness now meditate suicide."

X.

IF THE COOLIE BREAKS HIS CONTRACT, WHAT REDRESS HAS THE EMPLOYER BY LAW?

By the 77th article of the Spanish Royal Decree of 1860, it is provided that, in the event of repeated offences on the part of the labourer, the employer shall report the occurrence to the official designated as protector of Chinese, who shall, if the laws afford the necessary means, prescribe a punishment in accordance with their provisions, or if the contrary be the case, an augmentation of the disciplinary penalties. This clause thus enables the employers to without limit increase penalties which in a former clause were limited, and to impose punishments never contemplated by the laws, whilst in addition, in practice, they resort to whatever cruelties their fancy may suggest.

The statements collected show that on all the plantations the owners have established prisons, to which stocks and various implements of punishment are attached, and that the administrator and overseers constantly at will make use of hounds, knives, bludgeons and whips, so that the Chinese are in constant terror of death; and it is likewise testified that in cases too frequent to be enumerated, they are flogged when no offence has been committed or provocation offered, and that even after the contracts have expired they are chained and beaten. It is not likely, therefore, that they would voluntarily provoke such sufferings by any deliberate breaches of their agreements, and in consequence such instances are of the extremest rarity.

Thus, not only do the Regulations though prescribing reference to the protecting official confer on the employers the right of imposing and augmenting penalties; but, in reality, the latter inflict at will cruel chastisements of every class, without any authorization from the representatives of the Government.

XI.

DO EMPLOYERS TREAT COOLIES KINDLY:

Although a kind treatment of the labourers would be the right course it, in Cuba, is in the great majority of instances, that which is not followed. The petition of Chang Ting-chia (張定加) and 127 others states, "the daily food consisted of only maize and bananas. Our "monthly wages, in the meantime, are only $4 in paper, not equal to $2 in China, and insuffi- "cient to procure us even the additional necessary supplies of food and clothing. It is thus "impossible to save money." The petition of Yang Wan-shêng (楊萬勝) states, "I had to "labour night and day, suffered much from cold and hunger, was flogged when seriously ill, and "was chained and imprisoned even for resting a few moments." The petition of Wang Hua (王華) and 16 others states, "we are allowed three meals a day, composed of sweet potatoes, "maize, plantains and a piece of rotten salt beef, weighing 2 taels." The petition of Li Ying-sung (李英松) states, "I had to work night and day, was fed on only potatoes and plantains, and "was limited to a few instants of sleep." Liang Yu-shêng (梁有勝) declares in his petition, "I am beaten night and day, and my sufferings are unendurable." The petition of Li Chao-ch'un (李肇春) and 166 others states, "on the sugar plantations we are paid $4 (paper) worth "only a little more than $1 in silver, and not sufficient even for the additional food and clothes, "that are indispensable. On each estate there is a shop belonging to the administrator and "others; the things are of bad quality and very highly priced, but if we attempt to make a "purchase outside it is said that we are running away, and we are compelled to work with chained "feet. How is it possible, after the term of service, to have saved enough to pay for our passage "home?" P'an To-li (潘多利) declares in his petition, "if we make purchases at a shop "outside the plantation our wages suffer deduction during some months and we are forced to "work with chained feet for a similar period." The petition of Wu A-fa (吳阿發) and 39 others states, "the monthly wages of $4 are issued in currency, $2 of which are not equal to "$1 in silver." The petition of Lin A-ch'ing (林阿慶) and 1 other states, "we have not even "three meals a day, and the rations consist of only maize and rice. Our wages of $4 (paper) "do not even represent $2 in silver, and for the slightest cause a deduction is made." The petition of Yeh Nien (葉年) and of 20 others states, "out of our wages of $4 we are forced to "provide clothing and other necessaries, and whilst starvation is the compensation of our toil, "blows are accorded to us instead of repose."

Wang A-chi (王阿紀) also deposes, "at the commencement of my service, I was allowed "daily three meals; during the second year they were reduced to two and I was severely flogged." Yang Chin (楊錦) deposes, "the food issued consisted of rotten beef. If I did not eat, my feet "were chained." Chang Ch'ang-kuei (張長貴) deposes, "I was employed in a brick-kiln eight "years, during six of which no wages were issued." 'Ho A-jui (何阿瑞) deposes, "for making "cigars in a clumsy manner I was kept in irons during two months." Liang A-hsiu (梁阿秀) deposes, "I and 23 others, driven by hunger and by a consequent weakness which disabled us for "labour, begged our employer's son to increase the allowance of food, and for so doing we were "all chained and beaten. On the plantation also there were no habitations for us, and we were "told to provide them ourselves. Our monthly wages were but $ 3, and as even a grass hut for "two would cost $ 10, it was not in our power to obey. We explained this to our employer's son, "who became very wrathful, struck us indiscriminately, and together with certain negroes, seizing "knives killed one of our number, a native of Hiangshan (香 山), and wounded the remainder." Liang A-chao (梁 阿 照) deposes, "on the plantation is a shop owned by the master, at which "all our purchases have to be effected. The prices too are very high." The depositions of Chu Chia-hsien (朱 甲 先) and 76 others, also declare that all purchases have to be effected at the shops on the plantations. Liu A-wên (劉 阿 文) deposes, "all edibles have to be bought from "the steward." Liu A-yao (劉 阿 耀) deposes, "all articles have to be bought from the clerk." Fêng Erh (馮 二) deposes, "on this plantation, at present, two men are in prison chained and in "the stocks on account of making purchases outside." T'ang Ming-kwei (湯 明 奎) deposes, "monthly, as wages, we receive four tickets, which can only be employed in payment of purchases "at the plantation shop. Elsewhere they cannot be used, nor is it possible to change them for "bank notes." Tsêng Fu-min (曾 富 民) deposes, "as wages the master issues an order which "can be used in payment of articles bought at his shop, but cannot be converted into money, so "that no purchases can be made elsewhere." Ch'ên A-fu (陳 阿 福) deposes, "as I was young "I was directed to watch the horses which were grazing. Constantly my trowsers were removed, "and whilst held down by four men, I was flogged with a rattan rod." Ts'ai A-fang (蔡 阿 方) "deposes, "owing to sickness I worked less than the others, and in consequence chains were "attached to my hands and feet, and I was flogged on my naked person with a cowhide whip." Chang Shui (張 水) deposes, "when sick I was still compelled to labour, and as I performed less "than the others I was chained and beaten." Lo A-pao (駱 阿 寶) deposes, "the proprietor of "the sugar warehouse is excessively cruel. I have constantly suffered injury from his blows. "He wounds both skin and bone, and draws blood. He is most hurtful and venomous." Ch'ên A-lien (陳 阿 連) deposes, "I myself witnessed the death of an old man, whom the administrator "had directed to move a heavy implement. He was unable to do so and was at once struck dead." P'ang A-tung (龐 阿 東) deposes, "the overseers all carry cowhide whips for the purpose of "chastising the Chinese." Liu A-lin (劉 阿 林) deposes, "The administrator is of exceptional "cruelty. The owner has told him to flog without restraint, that it matters not if one is beaten "to death as ten others can be bought in his place." Hsieh A-ssŭ (謝 阿 四) deposes, "the owner "has urged the administrator and the overseers to flog us. He has said that it matters not if one "is beaten to death as he is rich enough to buy ten others." Liu A-jui (劉 阿 瑞) deposes, "the owner continually urges upon the overseers that a large crop of sugar is the only matter of "importance, and that no consideration should be shown to the labourers, as if one be beaten "to death ten others can be purchased."

On the other hand, among the depositions it is found that Chang A-wên (張 阿 文) declares that when working on a farm, belonging to a Frenchman, he was well used; and that T'ang Shêng (唐 生) declares that his master treated him passably, that he was sufficiently fed, and that when sick his wages were not deducted,—instances of what must be regarded as kind treatment, but unfortunately too few in number.

Again, Wang Chiu (王 九) alleges, that the owner was kind but the administrator the reverse. Ts'ai P'ei (蔡 丕) also alleges that the owner was kind, but that the administrator constantly flogged; Wang A-shêng (王 阿 盛) likewise declares that the owner was just but the administrator cruel, and 'Ho Hsi (何 錫) states that the owner was good, but the administrator exceedingly cruel. In these cases although the cruelties were not committed by the owners in person, yet, as the administrators are their servants, they are responsible for the acts of the latter, and consequently cannot be admitted to have accorded the considerate usage referred to in the query.

XII.

Do Coolies serve Employers faithfully?

Chinese after having been at the will of their importers sold out of the men-market and transferred to their purchasers, cannot be otherwise than obedient, through the terror inspired by the administrator and overseers, by the chains at their side, and by the rods and whips which goad them to labour.

The petition of Chêng A-mou (鄭 阿 茂) and 89 others states, "though we had neither "food nor repose, though the rations consisted of only plantains and maize insufficient to satisfy "hunger, we commenced labour in the middle of the night."

Yang Fa-ch'iang (楊 發 祥) also deposes, "my master was in debt, and sent me to work "on his creditor's plantation as a method of payment." Lu Chung (盧 錘) deposes, "my wages "were all expended in the purchase of additional edibles in the plantation shop. My debt was "ever proportioned to my earnings, but I dared not raise any objection." Chung Shêng (鍾 聲) deposes, "at the completion of the contract term, though a cedula was withheld, and I was "against my will constrained to continue labour, I had open to me no course but obedience." Wu Tê-shêng (吳 德 盛) deposes, "at the end of the eight years my master constrained me to "remain for an additional term of two years, and I dared not do aught but obey." Ch'ên A-yüan (陳 阿 元) deposes, "when I had worked during seven years I gave my master $150 in gold, "in order to redeem myself. He nevertheless retained me for another year, at the close of which "he did not furnish me with a cedula, so that my outlay was wasted." Ou Yüan (歐 元) deposes, "on the expiration of the eight years I applied for a cedula, but my master put me off from 'year to year. When I had thus completed other four years I handed to him $500 for the cost "of my passage home; and though two years have since passed away, he neither furnishes me "with a cedula, nor permits me to embark." 'Ho A-ssŭ (何 阿 四) deposes, "at the end of the "eight years no cedula was supplied to me, and I was forced to work for another term of four "years. A few days ago I asked my master for a cedula, and was told by him that I had to "serve for other six years. If this be the case, suicide is the best course open to me."

XIII.

Does the Law authorise Employers to punish the employed—how and why?

The 69th clause of the Spanish Royal Decree of 1860 is to the following effect:

" Employers are empowered to exercise a disciplinary jurisdiction in virtue of which they " shall be able to inflict the following penalties—

" 1. Arrest from one to ten days.

" 2. Loss of wages during the same time.

" The first of these may be imposed without the second ; but the latter cannot be resorted " to unless the first has been enforced." The 74th clause thus specifies the offences for which these penalties may be inflicted :

1. Insubordination towards employer or any representative of the employer.

2. Refusal to work, or want of punctuality in the execution of the tasks assigned.

3. The commission of an assault producing injury not rendering necessary suspension of work by the person injured.

4. Flight.

5. Drunkenness.

6. Violation of the Rules established by the employer,—[*note by translator*—Such rules not being contrary to the conditions of the contract, or to any of the provisions of the Decree (Art. 64)].

7. Any offence against morality, so long as it is not one of those which requires the intervention of a prosecutor, or, as being of that class, the party injured refrains from complaint.

8. Any other act intentionally committed and causing injury or loss to another person, but not constituting a crime of which the law can take cognizance.

Thus the Spanish Government distinctly limited the penal powers conferred on employers, and never intended to sanction the arbitrary infliction of chastisements and fines. The action of the Cuban proprietors has been however totally at variance with the course thus prescribed.

The petition of Chang Ting-chia (張 定 加) and 127 others states, " the prison was full " of instruments of punishment, the chains weighed from 50 to 20 catties, and there was no limit " to the number which one man carried ; and with the ankles thus burdened, labour had still " to be performed." Lo A-pao (駱 阿 寶) declares in his petition, " I was sold to a sugar " warehouse, where I was constantly beaten, so that the blood came out from all parts of my " body." Chang Kuan (張 觀) declares in his petition, " we have to labour 21 hours out of the " 24, and if we work half an hour less we are beaten severely, so that our skin and flesh become " lacerated and sore." Ch'ên Tê-ming (陳 德 明) declares in his petition, " if we went outside " to make purchases, we were brought back, confined in irons for three months and fined three " months' wages." Li Ch'i (李 齊) deposes, " on one occasion four Chinese killed an overseer— " a negro—they were confined in the plantation prison six months, after which two men were " hanged, and the two others shot on the plantation, in the presence of all the other labourers." Li A-tê (李 阿 德) deposes. " for smoking whilst at work, I was seized and held down by four men,

" received 24 blows, so that skin and flesh were lacerated; yet this chastisement is to be regarded
" as a light one. Chains are attached to our feet and we are goaded on with whips. If the
" administrator is of a kind disposition these fetters may be removed in two months, if he is not,
" they have to be worn six months. The chain extends from the neck to the ankles and may
" weigh 40 catties. I have myself been thus chained on three occasions. My offence was telling
" the administrator that, fed only on potatoes, I did not possess strength for my work. During
" the entire year we are not permitted to wash our clothes. If, when at leisure, we do so, and are
" seen by the negroes, we are chained and beaten. A man, too, was in chains eight months for
" simply effecting a purchase at a small shop in the neighbourhood." 'Ho A-pa (何 阿 八)
deposes, " on one occasion my master who observed me making a cigarette, ordered four negroes
" to seize my hands and feet, and I was flogged with a rattan rod so severely that my flesh was
" lacerated and the bones became visible. I was besides placed in the stocks and was again
" beaten with a whip by the administrator." T'an Fa (譚 發) deposes, " for buying rice, the
" administrator on one occasion confined me in irons during two weeks, and fined me one month's
" wages." Liu A-ping (劉 阿 丙) deposes " I was beaten for the slightest slowness, even for
" relieving nature." Pu A-hou (卜 阿 厚) deposes, " if thought to be absent too long when
" relieving nature the administrator and the white overseers would incite four large dogs, and men's
" feet have thus been bitten so severely that they were unable to walk." Chiang A-ch'i
(江 阿 起) deposes, " we were constantly struck and hounds were also incited to bite us." Liu
Hsin-fa (劉 新 發) deposes, " on one occasion I was flogged with such severity that my shoulder
" was broken, and that the blood drawn out of my back dripped over my entire body." Chung
A-tai (鍾 阿 代) deposes, " the owner of the plantation himself broke my arm by a blow."
Ch'ên Hsiang (陳 香) deposes, " I was transferred to a sugar plantation, where during five years
" I suffered great hardships. As I was flogged daily, I asked my employer why, as my tasks were
" well performed, I was thus chastised; and he replied that he had bought me not to labour but
" to be beaten." Yüan A-ts'ung (阮 阿 聰) deposes, " my master was very cruel. He beat all
" without discriminating between those who worked well and the inefficient, and even when we
" by chance met him on the road he would deal us a few blows." Lo A-êrh (羅 阿 二) deposes,
" I wished to redeem myself by payment of the price originally paid for me, but my employer not
" only refused, but also kept me in chains during one month, and flogged me severely." Sung
Hai (宋 海) deposes, " at present there are here 40 Chinese who though recently arrived and
" ignorant of the language work in chains." Yang A-ch'ang (楊 阿 昌) deposes, " my master
" acts with great cruelty. For one day's sickness he deducts a dollar." 'Ho P'ei-ch'i (何 沛 麒)
deposes, " I was sick during six months and my wages during an entire year were deducted."

XIV

DOES THE LAW PROVIDE FOR AN APPEAL BY COOLIES FROM THE PUNISHMENT AUTHORISED TO BE USED BY EMPLOYERS?

It is provided in the 71st Article of the Spanish Royal Decree of 1860, that the Chinese
shall in every case " possess the right of making complaint to the Protector, regarding any wrong

" done to them by their employers, whether such wrong consists in the infliction of punishments
" without sufficient cause or the imposition of unauthorised penalties, or in the breach of any of
" the provisions regulating the treatment of them." Thus, in the event of employers abusing the
disciplinary powers conferred on them, the right of preferring charges is accorded to the sufferers,
but numerous as the latter are, the proportion that has been enabled to obtain redress or even
make complaint is very small.

Lin Kuei-hsing (林貴興) deposes, " on the plantation, though wrongs of every kind have
" to be endured, there are no means of preferring complaints, as all egress is prohibited." Liu
A-lien (劉阿連) deposes, " the overseer flogs with great whips until skin and flesh are lacerated;
" thus wounded we still are forced to labour and no one is able to go out to make an accusation."
Li Yü (李禹) deposes, " as when I was at work on account of not understanding the language
" I was beaten with a cowhide whip, and found the chastisement unendurable, and as I saw
" that another man poisoned himself through being unable to support the cruelties, I preferred
" a charge before the officials. They gave no heed to my accusation. I afterwards was
" chastised even more severely, and after the completion of my contract term I embodied in
" a petition addressd to the Captain General, a statement of the wrongs endured by Chinese in
" Cuba, but this also met with no notice." Chu Chia-hsien (朱甲先) deposes, " as I saw Liu
" A-k‘o (劉阿科) receive 150 lashes dealt with severity, I, in indignation, proceeded to Havana
" in order to prefer a charge against the overseer. The official gave no heed to me, but sent
" me back to the plantation, where an exactly similar chastisement was inflicted upon me.
" The flogging continued from 8 to 10 A.M., and an hour afterwards Liu A-k‘o (劉阿科) threw
" himself into a sugar caldron." Liang En (梁恩) deposes, " one Liang Yu-shêng (梁有勝)
" being beaten to death by the administrator, I and three others made a complaint to the officials,
" but as the owner's agent presented them with $ 100, and the administrator sent them four
" negroes, the charge was unheeded, and I was sent back to the plantation where I had to work
" with chained feet during an entire year. I was afterwards transferred to another plantation
" appertaining to the same proprietor, when, as I had finished my term of eight years, I applied
" for a certificate of completion. I waited a year labouring in the customary way, and at its close
" left, intending to seek redress from the authorities; but the clerk of the plantation presented
" money to the guards, and I was arrested on the plea that I was attempting to escape, and I was
" delivered back to the plantation, where during four months I had to labour in foot irons."
Lin A-san (林阿三) deposes, " I was flogged without any cause. It depended on my master's
" caprice, on his good or bad humour. I did not dare to complain to the authorities, because
" such a course only resulted in being chained and flogged with even greater severity." Wang
A-ts‘ai (王阿才) deposes, " I constantly received injuries from flogging, I resolved to prefer a
" charge before the officials. My intentions were detected, and I was forced to work in irons
" during nine months." Li Tai (李帶) deposes, " one of us, able to speak Spanish, told our
" employer that rice was the customary diet of Chinese, and that, whilst at Macao it had been
" distinctly understood that Sundays were to be days of rest, the existing practice was different.
" Our employer gave way to anger, regarding these words as too daring; and afterwards our
" companion fell sick and was sent to the hospital where in a few days he died." Chou Tê-‘hua
(周德華) deposes, " they broke my finger merely because I was unable to express myself in

"Spanish." Ch'ien A-shêng (錢 阿 生) deposes, "my master was not good. He constantly "inflicted floggings, and broke my left arm, so that now it is disabled for work."

The petition of Li Chao-ch'un (李 肇 春) and 165 others states, "our countrymen are "murdered, cut their throats, and drown themselves, and the occurrences are either not reported to "the authorities, or if reported there is a brief inspection, and all is over. On the same planta-"tion there may be a friend or relative of the victim, but though he has witnessed all, he dares "not come forward to testify. If he did so his days would soon come to an end."

XV.

DURING AGREEMENT-TERM, WHAT TIME HAS THE COOLIE AT HIS OWN DISPOSAL—HOW CAN HE USE IT—AND DOES THE LAW PORTECT HIM IN TURNING IT TO PORFITABLE ACCOUNT?

The 10th article of the Emigration Convention of 1866 provides that of every seven days one is to be a day of rest, and that in the 24 hours work during more than 9½ hours cannot be enforced, and that all compulsory additional labour is prohibited. The 5th clause of the contract used in the 10th year of HIENFÊNG states that besides the specified times of rest, Chinese shall not be compelled to work on Sundays or holidays, and that on these days they shall be permitted to work as they may see fit for their own profit; and the 4th clause of the contracts used in the 3rd, 4th, 10th and 12th years of T'UNGCHIH, prescribes that Sundays shall be days of rest. The article—the 52nd—of the Royal Decree of 1860, which refers to the same point, is however somewhat at variance with the above provisions, as it directs the execution of the ordinary daily tasks even on festival days, when, despite the celebration of the festival, work shall have been permitted by the ecclesiastical authorities.

The contracts for these four years of T'UNGCHIH also stipulate that only 12 hours out of the 24 shall be devoted to labour. The 53rd article of the Decree of 1860 provides that under no circumstances whatever shall employers exact on an average more than 12 hours' work; and the 54th article, that even when an employer is empowered to distribute in the manner most convenient for his interests, the number of hours agreed upon, it shall be understood that no more than 15 hours can be exacted in one day, and that the labourer shall enjoy at leat six consecutive hours of rest; and the 45th article authorises their engaging in amusement during their days or hours of leisure. These three clauses, though not altogether in accordance with the Emigration Convention, evince a care for the interests of the class to which they apply, and have been disregarded by the great majority of the Cuban proprietors.

The petition of Ch'iu Pi-shan (邱 碧 山) and 34 others states, "a plantation is a veritable "hell; the Chinese are beaten the entire day, and the cruelties of the owner, administrator and "overseers are very great. Their bodies are covered with sores, their feet have no rest, and out "of the 24 hours they are granted only four for repose." The petition of Wang A-ching (王 阿 敬) and 22 others states, "the work is very hard. We get up at 3 A.M., and labour until noon; at 1 P.M., "we resume work until 7 P.M., when we rest half an hour and are allowed a ration of maize, after

"which work is continued up to midnight. We are struck and flogged, and out of our party of
"more than 200 men, only over 80 remain." The petition of Wang Hua (王 華) and of 16
others states, " we have to labour at night nearly until 1 A.M., and we have to recommence work
" at 4 A.M., and our bodies and our bones cause us so much pain that we cannot work with great
" activity." Ch'ên Tê-ming (陳 德 明) declares in his petition, " I was sold to a sugar plantation
" where I endured every hardship. I and the others got up at 4 A.M. and worked until 1 A.M."
The petition of Lin A-ch'ing (林 阿 慶) and 1 other states, " we are in the service of a railway
" company and have to work night and day. The overseer is very cruel, but whatever he alleges
" to the superintendent is believed by the latter. Those who have completed their eight years
" are not allowed to go away. We are constantly flogged by the superintendent at the instiga-
" tion of the overseer. We get up at 4 A.M., and cease work only at 1 A.M. On Sundays we do
" not rest." The petition of Yeh Fu-chün (葉 福 君) and 52 others states, " when sold to sugar
" plantations, we had to work night and day, having only three hours' sleep." The petition of
Ch'ên Ku (陳 古) and 2 others states, " on the sugar plantation we toil daily from 3 A.M. until
" midnight." The petition of P'an To-li (潘 多 利) and 2 others states, " we have to labour 19 or
" 20 hours out of the 24."

The depositions of T'ang Chien (唐 建) and 170 others testify that they have laboured on
the sugar plantations from 3 A.M. until midnight, and that on Sundays similar hours were
enforced. The depositions of Chang Chao (張 照) and 121 others testify that they have laboured
on sugar plantations from 4 A.M. until midnight, and that on Sundays similar hours were
enforced. The depositions of Wên A-chao (温 阿 照) and 20 others testify that they have
laboured on sugar plantations from 2 A.M. to midnight. The depositions of Ch'ên Wan-shêng
(陳 萬 生) and 47 others testify, that they have laboured on the sugar plantations from 3 A.M.
until 11 P.M. The depositions of Ch'ên Ch'ih (陳 池) and 27 others testify that they have
laboured on the sugar plantations from 4 A.M. till 11 P.M. The depositions of Ch'ên Ting-hsien
(陳 鼎 賢) and 6 others testify that they have laboured on the sugar plantations from 3 A.M.
until 9 P.M. The depositions of Tsêng Erh-ch'i (曾 貳 齊) and 7 others testify that they have
laboured on the sugar plantations from 2 A.M. until 11 P.M. The depositions of Li Ho (李 合) and 8
others testify that they have laboured on the sugar plantations from 4 A.M. until 10 P.M. The
depositions of Chang K'ai (張 開) and 6 others testify that the they have laboured on the sugar
plantations from 5 A.M. until midnight, and that the same hours were enforced on Sundays. The
depositions of Su A-'hai (蘇 阿 海) and 1 other testify that they have laboured on the sugar
plantations from 4 A.M. until 9 P.M., that during the collection of the crop the same hours were
enforced on Sundays, but that at other times work ceased on that day at 9 A.M. Liu A-san
(劉 阿 三) deposes, " on the plantation I rested during half the day on Sunday." The
depositions of Ch'ên Lin (陳 林) and 3 others testify that on the sugar plantations on Sundays
they ceased labour at 9 A.M., but recommenced it from 4 P.M. to 6 P.M. The depositions of
Kuo Chan (郭 占) and 1 other testify that on certain sugar plantations, during the collection
of the crop, the ordinary hours were enforced on Sundays, but that at other times work ceased
at 8 A.M. Lin A-i (林 阿 亦) deposes, " on the plantation in the 24 hours I rested two hours
" and a half." Wu Ch'ieh (吳 且) deposes, " on the plantation I got up at 6 A.M., and ended
" work at midnight." Li Yu (李 游) deposes, " on the plantation I commenced work at

"midnight and continued until 7 o'clock of the following evening." 'Huang Chieh (黃捷) deposes, "on the plantation I worked from 4 A.M. till 12 P.M. On Sundays I was allowed to rest "during two hours, in order to wash my clothes." 'Huang A-hsien (黃阿軒) deposes, "on "account of my refusing to work on Sundays, I was kept in chains during one month." Li A-yao (李阿耀) deposes, "in the sugar warehouse there were no fixed limits to the working "hours." The depositions of Huang A-ts'ai (黃阿才) and 3 others state that in a sugar warehouse they worked from 4.30 A.M. until 6 P.M. Ch'ên A-chi (陳阿吉) deposes, "in the sugar "warehouse I worked from 4 A.M. until 5 P.M." The depositions of Li Shê-fu (黎社福) and 4 others testify that they work in sugar warehouses from 4 A.M. until 11 P.M. Liang A-ch'êng (梁阿成) deposes, "I am engaged in an establishment for the hiring of cargo-boats, and work "from 4 A.M. until midnight. My master had promised that on Sundays labour might cease at "noon, but when I wished to act in accordance with this assurance the overseer forbade my so "doing and struck and kicked me, and as I am ignorant of the language I could not complain." Li Yü (李禹) deposes, "when employed in laying roads, I worked from 2 A.M. until 7 P.M." 'Hu A-tê (胡阿德) deposes, "when employed as a baker I commenced work at midnight and "continued it until 3 A.M. I rested from 3 A.M. until 5 A.M. I then resumed work until 7 A.M "when I again rested for an hour, after which work is again continued until 2 P.M." Hsü A-fêr (許阿苏) deposes, "when employed in a baker's shop, I worked from 10 A.M. until 6 A.M. of the "following day." Ch'ên A-'huan (陳阿煥) deposes, "I am employed in a cigar shop, I work "from 5 A.M. till midnight." Yü A-ch'ang (余阿昌) deposes, "I serve as scavenger, and have "to work from 9 P.M. until 10 A.M." The depositions of Ch'ên Mêng-ming (陳孟明) and 5 others state that in the dépôt they work from 6 A.M. until 6 P.M. The depositions of Chêng A-fu (鄭阿富) and 5 others state that in the Havana barracoon they worked from 6 A.M. to 6 P.M.

XVI.

CONSIDERING THE EXPENSE INCURRED BY EMPLOYERS IN PROCURING COOLIES, THE RATE OF WAGES IN CHINA, THE HOURS AND CONDITIONS OF LABOUR IN CUBA, AND THE FACT THAT THE COOLIE, KNOWING THE STATE OF THINGS IN CHINA, SIGNS A CONTRACT TO WORK IN CUBA; DOES THE EMPLOYER ACT EQUITABLY, AS WELL AS LEGALLY, IN HOLDING THE COOLIE TO HIS CONTRACT?

The "procuring Coolies" signifying the engagement of voluntary labourers, is a very different act from the sale of men, and the compulsory exaction of their assent, and the term, in that sense, cannot therefore be applied to the Chinese in Cuba, who for the most part have been the victims of either fraud or violence.

The depositions of every class that have been collected state that, in the most cases, the labourer in the first instance was handed only a few dollars, and that some were even paid but 300 cash or 10 cash or received nothing. Thus the original outlay incurred is insignificant, and the entire expense on account of a Chinese landed at Havana, may be estimated,— as is observed in the *Westminster Review*,—at $ 190, so that the ultimate profits of the importer become very considerable. To this effect is the paragraph in the petition of Jên Shih-chên (任 世 貞), Tai Erh-chieh (載 二 揵) and Liang Hsing-chao (梁 與 照) which states, "each Chinese decoyed "or kidnapped for sale here is disposed of for a sum varying from $ 400 or $ 500 to $ 1,000, leaving "on the average a profit to the importer of $ 200 or $ 300, so that the gain on ten thousand of "us must amount to two or three millions. In all some 200,000 have reached Cuba, representing "a profit of several tens of millions, a sum which, as it accrued from the sale of our bodies, ought, "justly speaking, to be remitted to our families."

The second question raised in the query is of course not regarded as referring to the cases in which men of wealthy families or of position have been decoyed; and it is impossible to put forward with certainty any rate of wages as that applicable in China to the men composing the general body of labourers, as their earnings would have differed according to individual qualities, and must have varied from year to year. A man, too, whose life is in the hands of those who have seized him, and who is being sent out of his country by force, is not able to take into account the considerations suggested, to discuss the provisions of a contract, or to weigh and compare various rates of compensation; whilst those who went of their free will were misled by false assurances, believing the actual gain to be greater, and the term of service shorter, and imagining that they would be treated as in their own country, exempt from tyranny and cruelty, and free to go or stay; and under this delusion they embarked, contract in hand, only to realize on arrival the great contrast of the reality. "The $ 4 wages," is observed in the petition of P'an T'ai (潘 泰) and 89 others, "are insufficient for support, the cost of all being "so great." Chiang A-lin (姜 阿 麟) deposes, "although the wages are nominally larger than in "China, the paper currency is so much depreciated, and prices are so high, that $ 8 or $ 10 do not "represent more than $ 1 or $ 2 would there." Lo A-chi (羅 阿 巳) deposes, "in China I "found 100 *cash* daily sufficient for the support of a family, whilst here the cost of living is so "great that $ 1 a day will hardly maintain a single individual." These statements indicate a sufficiently grave condition of misery; and that condition is aggravated by the fact that whilst the benefits conferred by the contracts—the rest, medical attendance, food and clothing—are far from being invariably accorded, hardships of which these documents contain no mention—the stocks, the lash, the rod and the bite of the hounds,—are inflicted without restraint.

In the engagement of Chinese labourers in China it would be just that the provisions of the Emigration Convention of the 5th year of T'UNGCHIH should be adhered to; but not only is the term of service—eight years—a breach of that document, but even after its completion, they are either forced into renewal, or handed again and again to the dépôts to await successive new engagements, a fresh violation of the contract stipulations, which subjects them to endless misery. "On the completion of the eight years," remarks Chang Luan (張 鑾) and those who signed with him, "instead of giving the freedmen's papers prescribed by rule, the Chinese "is removed to the dépôt, where he has to labour in irons, in company with the murderer and "deserter. Legally free, he is made a prisoner, and is treated as a runaway, although he has not "attempted to escape. Where and at what time have similar acts of injustice been perpetrated?" It is thus needless to discuss whether employers "act equitably in holding the Coolie to his "contract," as repudiation of the terms of agreement (to the prejudice of the Chinese) is the habitual practice of the class in question.

<hr>

XVII.

SOME EMPLOYERS ARE CRUEL BY NATURE AND HARSH TO THE EMPLOYED: OTHERS ARE KINDLY
AND TREAT COOLIES WELL; WHAT REMARKABLE CASES ILLUSTRATE EACH SIDE, AND
WHAT IS THE GENERAL STATE OF THE RELATIONS BETWEEN EMPLOYERS AND EMPLOYED?

When a master treats a servant well and gives no cause for complaint or accusation, there is nothing in his action which can result in any record of instances of it being preserved. On the other hand the cruelty and harshness of an employer aided by his administrator and overseers, the maiming of limbs, and the infliction of fatal injuries, though they may not generally be noticed or punished by the officials, cannot be effectually suppressed, and force themselves prominently before the eyes of all.

Thus Lai A-ssŭ (賴 阿 四) deposes, "I recollect the year before last a Chinese was "murdered, and that his body was cast into the sea. It was found by the guards, and was "recognised as that of a workman in the sugar warehouse. This however was denied by our "employer, and no further action was taken by the officials. Last year also, in the 7th month, "a native of the Hoyüen (河 源) district, by name A Erh (阿 二), was killed. The "authorities on this occasion sent for us to give testimony. Our master denied his guilt, and "imputed the crime to an overseer, a negro, and the latter was in consequence imprisoned. At "the same time another native of Hoyüen (河 源), who had declared that he had witnessed "the commission of the act by the master himself, was sold away to the mountains. Our master "also continually urged the negroes to beat us; he used to say, 'If one were killed, two others "could be bought.'" Fan Ssŭ-'ho (范 四 和) deposes, "the black overseers ever strike us, "whenever they see us, whether we are working or not; and the administrator also beats us. I "saw Ch'ên A-ssŭ (陳 阿 四) struck dead simply for pushing with a bundle of cane against "an overseer. It was then alleged that he had hanged himself." Lü A-chên (呂 阿 珍) deposes, "the overseers were negroes, and though I committed no offence I was constantly flogged. "I have seen men beaten to death, the bodies being afterwards buried, and no report being made "to the authorities." Hsieh A-shêng (薛 阿 盛) deposes, "with me were a native of Sinning (新 甯), by name Ch'ên (陳), and a native of K'aip'ing (開 平), by name Liang (梁). The "administrator accused them of cutting grass slowly, and directing four men to hold them in a "prostrate position, inflicted, with a whip, a flogging which almost killed them. The first "afterwards hanged himself, and the second drowned himself. The local officials visited the "plantation but instituted no proper investigation, and I and my companions were prevented by "our ignorance of the language from laying before them a statement of these crimes." Lo A-êrh (羅 阿 二) deposes, "I and my uncle Lo Nan-shao (羅 南 紹) were both sold to a railway "company. An overseer with an iron bar wounded my uncle so severely that he died in half "a month. I preferred a charge before the officials, and the overseer was arrested, but he was "released after a month's confinement and no other punishment was imposed." ʻHu A-ʻhua (胡阿花) deposes, "I heard that when Lin A-têng (林阿等) was murdered his body was "placed in a chamber and examined by the officials, and that the overseer was imprisoned." Hsieh A-ʻhou (謝阿侯) deposes, "four men out of a gang of 30 newly arrived, died in the "hospital four hours after they had entered it, on account of alleged sickness. Upon this 20 "men laid before the authorities a charge of murder, and at the request of the administrator an "official of low rank visited the estate. I, acting as interpreter, translated the evidence of two "witnesses who declared that sickness had been the cause of death. On the following day other "officials continued the enquiry. All were present, and on a question being put as to the prior "existence of sickness, the general answer was that the men had not been ill. The officer of low "rank then declared that, on the previous occasion, I had interpreted incorrectly, and I was "placed in prison. I was subsequently released on my master's bail." Liang A-kuang (梁阿廣) deposes, "with me was a Cantonese, by name A-liu (阿六). A little more than a month after "arrival, being unable to endure the cruelties, he hanged himself. The official visited the estate "for the purpose of making an inquiry, but our employer was rich and no further action ensued. "In Cuba the officials are at the orders of the rich." Wang Mu-chiu (王慕九) deposes, "finding the labour too arduous, I made a complaint to the officials, and the latter recommended "my master to be less exacting, and to supply me with sufficient food. He assented, "but when he had brought me back he forced me to work with chained feet during "seven months." ʻHuang Shih-jung (黃石容) deposed, "I was a witness of the sufferings "of ʻHuang A-kuang (黃阿光). Driven by the hardships he had run away. He was "captured, placed in chains, and so severely flogged that the blood and flesh dripped "down from him. He then, still in irons, was forced to labour, and being deprived of food, "in hunger ate some sugar-cane. This was observed by the administrator, who again flogged "him, and on the same evening he hanged himself. Twenty of us preferred a complaint to the "officials, declaring that we were unwilling to return to the plantation, but the master arranged "that 12 should be brought back under guard, the remaining 8 being, on the advice of the "authorities, sold to other plantations." Lin Ho (林合) deposes, "a native of the Shuntêh "(順德) district, by name Li Tê (李德), had worked on the plantation nine years, and "possessed 72 ounces of gold, which he handed for safe custody to an overseer. The latter, aided "by a negro, murdered him when in the field. The body was buried, and no report was ever "made to the authorities." ʻHuang A-tê (黃阿德) deposes, "last year I saw the murder of a "native of Hiangshan (香山). An official visited the estate in order to examine the body, "but never arrested the offender. The latter was a negro, and of this fact our master was aware, "but he simply inflicted on him a slight chastisement, and the matter was then considered "terminated. Negroes indeed receive better usage than the Chinese." Hu A-ssŭ (胡阿四) deposes, "a native of Sinhwei (新會), by name A-fêng (阿豐), was murdered by negroes. The "body was buried and no report was made to the officials." Chang Luan (張鑾) deposes, "I saw "the administrator flog a native of Tungkwan (東莞), by name Mêng (孟), so severely that his "whole body was lacerated; chains also were attached to his feet. The latter hanged himself. "The officials visited the estate, and entered into conversation with the administrator, but no

"questions were addressed to us."   Yeh A-ling (葉阿靈) deposes, "in the 10th year of T'UNG-
"CHIH, a negro murdered a Chinese.   The negro was a great favourite of our master, and the dead
"body was removed and buried.   Certain Chinese having discovered the place of burial, our
"master induced the authorities to chastise them.   He also intimated that they had committed
"the crime, and they were in consequence tried and eight men were sentenced to imprisonment."
Ch'ên Lin-shan (陳林山) deposes, "as, after the completion of our contract term, the adminis-
"trator flogged us with great severity, we all, 30 in number, became much discontented.   On
"information being given to him of our having expressed indignation at his cruelty he placed
"more than 10 in irons, and having bribed the authorities, procured the presence of certain of
"the guards, who shot four.   One of the four was a native of the district of Kaoming (高明),
"by name Li A-ch'i (李阿起), one was a native of the Kaoyao (高要) district, by name
"A-chao (阿照), one was a native of the prefecture of Hweichow (惠州), by name Li Kêng-yu
"(李庚有), and the fourth was a native of the Sinhwei (新會) district, and was named
"A-hsing (阿奥)."

The following instances of injuries were verified by personal inspection.   Scars of old
wounds on the bodies of:—

Yüan A-ts'ung. . . .	(阮阿聰)	Liang A-lin	(梁阿林)
Tsêng Jung-ch'ing . .	(曾榮慶)	Lo A-chi	(羅阿紀)
Wên A-chao	(温阿照)	'Ho 'Hai	(何　海)
Li A-'hou	(黎阿侯)	Lin Chao-chin . . .	(林照金)
Liu A-chi	(劉阿記)	Chung Shêng . . .	(鐘　聲)
Ch'ên A-'hung . . .	(陳阿洪)	Kao A-lun	(高阿倫)
Li A-k'ai	(李阿開)	Han Ch'ing-to . . .	(韓慶鐸)
Liang A-'hung . . .	(梁阿洪)	T'an Lien-chin . . .	(譚連進)
Mo A-hsün	(莫阿訓)	Liu A-t'ing. . . .	(劉阿廷)
Ho A-hsien	(賀阿先)	Chang Shih-chên . .	(張式震)
Liang A-kuei . . .	(梁阿貴)	Hung A-i	(洪阿異)
Yen A-yu	(顔阿有)		

Scars on the heads of:—

Ch'ü A-ping . . .	(區阿炳)	Miu Yang-chiao . .	(繆陽嬌)
Shên T'ai-kao . . .	(沈泰高)	Ch'ên A-shên . . .	(陳阿深)

Scars on the head and face of:—

Chu Ts'ai-fang   . . (朱村房)

Scars on the head and arms of:—

'Ho A-fa . . . . . (何阿發)

Scars from wounds self-inflicted in the hope of death, on the throats of:—

Huang A-ping . .	(黃阿炳)	Lin Lun-mei . . .	(林翰美)
Ch'ü Tan-k'o	(屈但壳)		

Actual wounds on the bodies of:—

Wu A-ch'in . . .	(伍阿琴)	Lan A-mu	(藍阿穆)

Actual wounds on the heads of:—

Chang Shêng . . . （張　生）   Yu A-t'ien . . . . （余 阿 田）

Actual wounds on the face of:—

Wu A-fang . . . . （吳 阿 芳）

Actual wounds on the chest of:—

Ch'ên Chung-hsiu （陳 忠 秀）

Actual wounds on the legs and thighs of:—

Wang Ta-ch'êng . . （王 大 成）   Ch'ên I-yu . . . . （陳 乙 有）

Ts'ai A-lu . . . . （蔡 阿 魯）   Ch'ü Chieh-k'ang . . （區 祖 康）

Lin Tzŭ-yu . . . . （林 滋 有）   Li A-lü . . . . （李 阿 呂）

The loss of the left ear by Liang A-yu （梁 阿 有）, deliberately cut off by his master.

The loss of a portion of one ear by Huang A-shêng （黃 阿 盛）.

The loss of sight by Li A-ta （李 阿 達）, the disease of the eyes having commenced immediately after a flogging, during which 200 blows were administered.

The injury caused to one eye of Liang A-'hua （梁 阿 華）.

The loss of two teeth of Ch'ên P'ei-ch'ang （陳 佩 長）.

The fracture of the arm of the *hsiu-ts'ai* Ch'ên Shao-yen （陳 少 巖）, of Li A-'hui （李 阿 會）, Yüan Ai-shan （袁 藹 山） and Ch'ên A-'hai （陳 阿 海）.

The maiming of the right hand of Lo Kuan-hsiu （駱 觀 秀） by a blow from a knife between the thumb and forefinger.

The loss of four fingers by Liu A-lin （劉 阿 林）, deliberately cut off.

The fracture of the fingers and toes of Li 'Hung （李 洪） and Li 'Ho （李 何）.

The fracture of one leg of Lu Shêng-pao （盧 盛 保）.

The loss of the use of one ankle by Wu A-kuang （吳 阿 光）, the result of wearing fetters.

The maimed condition of the feet of Hsü A-fên （許 阿 芬）, from the same cause.

XVIII.

SOME COOLIES ARE INDUSTRIOUS MEN, WHO EMIGRATE WILLINGLY TO BETTER THEMSELVES, AND WHO WORK CHEERFULLY AND WELL; SOME COOLIES EMIGRATE WILLINGLY, BUT BEING BAD CHARACTERS, DO SO TO ESCAPE THE RESULTS OF GAMBLING AND CRIME, AND CARRY WITH THEM THEIR BAD HABITS; SOME COOLIES ARE "KIDNAPPED," BEING STUPID FELLOWS, AND NEVER CAN WORK INTELLIGENTLY; SOME COOLIES, CLEVER FELLOWS, ARE INDUCED TO EMBARK UNDER FALSE PRETENCES, AND ON FINDING THEMSELVES DECEIVED AND ENTRAPPED, BECOME DESPERATE—THEIR DESPERATION BEING REGARDED BY THE EMPLOYER AS DEFIANCE, MUTINY, DISOBEDIENCE, &C. ALLOWING THAT AMONG THE COOLIES THERE ARE REPRESENTATIVES OF ALL THESE CLASSES TO BE FOUND, WHAT ARE THEIR FATES DURING AGREEMENT-TERM RESPECTIVELY?

Industrious men who work willingly and well, can support themselves at home, and do not emigrate voluntarily: "Born in China and never in want of food or clothing, we, like our

" ancestors," remarks the petition of Chang Luan (張 鑾), "did not dream of seeking a livelihood
" across the ocean." .

The depositions, on the other hand, show that men have gone abroad to escape the results
of crime and gambling, but even these did so in complete ignorance of the suffering which was
before them, whilst, tempted by lotteries, &c., they adhere to their evil habits in their new place
of residence, and are unable to lay by a single *cash*.

From the moment of their falling into the snare, an existence of suffering is the only one
known to both the stupid who are kidnapped and the clever who are induced to embark under
false pretences. Before embarking they are tormented by those who entrapped them, on board
by the master and all his subordinates, on landing by the employés of the men-market, after sale
by their purchaser, his administrator and overseers, and after the completion of their contracts by
the dépôt and other functionaries; but though they realise how they have been deceived
there is open to them no means of escape, and cruelty at last drives them to despair, and to seek
a means of death. The depositions show that besides those killed on the spot and those who
died from the effects of wounds, a countless number destroyed themselves by cutting their
throats, by hanging, drowning, poison, and casting themselves under wheels or into sugar-
caldrons, and that they are even goaded into offering up their lives by murdering their overseers.
Constantly, too, when but one or two have committed the crime, ten or twenty longing for death
will accuse themselves of the act. " It is because they cannot help it," is observed in the
petition of Li Chao-ch'un (李肇春), "that Chinese murder their administrator, for who is not
" afraid of exposing himself to death?" And in the petition of Chang Luan (張 鑾) and others,
it is stated, " the young strive for the shelter of a prison, voluntarily breaking the law in order to
" reach it." The depositions also of Huang A-p'ei (黃阿沛) and 21 others, declare that the jail
is preferable to the plantation. The position of all classes is described in the petition of Ch'iu
Tê-i (邱得意): " We are now," he states, "more than 100,000 Chinese in this island, whose daily
existence is that of criminals confined in jail." Again, in the petition of Kao Lao-hsiu (高老秀)
and 16 others, it is observed, "though all these wrongs are inflicted, we can only fold our arms
" and submit;" and in that of Chêng Hsing (鄭惺) and 5 others, " for these daily wrongs there is
" no redress;" and in that of Wu A-fa (吳阿發) and 39 others, " our existence is so miserable
" that the hours seem as days, and the days as years."

XIX.

**TAKING A BROAD VIEW OF THE MATTER, IS THE CONDITION OF COOLIES DURING AGREEMENT-
TIME AS GOOD AS THEY HAVE A RIGHT TO EXPECT? OR, IF NOT, WHERE DOES IT
FAIL TO BE SO—WHERE, HOW AND WHY, AND ON WHOM DOES THE RESPONSIBILITY
OF THE FAILURE REST?**

In many instances the very act of accepting the agreement was the result of compulsion,
and consequently an instance of unjustifiable treatment; the deaths from thirst, blows and
suicide are an indication of the treatment during the voyage; the stripping and shameless

examination of the person show how the Chinese are used in the men-market after landing; and hunger, want of sleep, neglected maladies and wounds of which they dare not complain, are the characteristics of their existence in their places of service. "The contract and stipulations are "violated with indifference:" "the state of things in no way fulfils the promises of the contract:" "we are constantly beaten, and are not treated in accordance with our contracts," are statements to be found in the petitions of Huang Yu (黃有) and 15 others, of Chao K'un (趙昆) and 97 others, and Yeh Nien (葉年) and 20 others.

Their condition therefore is not so good as they have a right to expect, and this assertion is applicable to those who came voluntarily, cognizant of the condition of the contract, as well as to those who were kidnapped and decoyed, and to whom the purport of the agreement was never explained.

Justly speaking, the responsibility lies on the men who, under the cloak of engaging labourers in a legitimate manner, obtain possession of their fellow men by violence and deceit, and on the vicious Chinese leagued with them. As to the latter, the 5th article of the Emigration Convention of the 5th year of T'UNGCHIH provides that, "Chinese employed to collect "emigrants must obtain a permission sealed by the local officials. Such Chinese shall be held "responsible for all violations of the laws, whether voluntary or otherwise, and shall in such cases "be arrested and punished by the proper authorities."

The numerous fraudulent devices that are resorted to, as described in the depositions, show the character of the agents by whom the labourers now in Cuba were entrapped. These unscrupulous men of course held no certificate from any official, and the traffic is a constant violation of the law. But those who could prove their guilt are already inside the trap, and no one is at hand to heed their cries; soon they have crossed the ocean, their families being ignorant of their departure, and all means of communication being denied, and in Cuba the interests of the sellers and buyers of men being identical, every plan is devised to prevent an ultimate return to their country. Thus the preferring of a charge becomes impossible, and the Chinese officials are precluded from effecting the arrests and imposing the punishments prescribed in the clause which has been quoted.

XX.

THE AGREEMENT-TERM EXPIRED, WHAT BECOMES OF THE COOLIE?

The following extracts from depositions furnish a reply:—

'Hu Ju (胡如) deposes, "on the expiration of the contract time, a cedula was withheld, "and I worked for other two years, under contract, on the same plantation. On the termination "I was sent to the dépôt, from which I was hired out for three years. These ended I was sent "back to the dépôt, where I laboured for five years without wages. I then again, during nine 'years, was hired out under various engagements, returning to the dépôt at the close of each." The depositions of Ch'ên A-fu (陳阿福) and 63 others state that cedulas were withheld on the completion of their contracts, and that they were delivered to dépôts. The depositions of Li

Ta-ts'ai (李大財) and 2 others state that after the expiration of the eight years they worked for another period of twelve months and were then sent to dépôts. The depositions of Ni A-ʻhuan (倪阿煥) and 11 others state that after the expiration of the eight years, they laboured for another period of two years, and were then sent to dépôts. The depositions of Yeh A-yao (葉阿耀) and 1 other state that after the expiration of the eight years they laboured for one year and were then sent to dépôts. Chang Hui (張會) deposes, "I would have been beaten to death if on the " expiration of the eight years I had declined to enter into a fresh one for a period of six years." The depositions of Lin A-hsiu (林阿秀) and 3 others state that after the expiration of the eight years, they laboured for another period of six years and were then sent to dépôts. The depositions of Chang Chao (張照) and 12 others state that on the completion of the contract a cedula was withheld, and that they were handed over to dépôts by the officials. The depositions of Hsü Chien-fa (許建發) and 2 others state that on the expiration of the eight years they worked in brick-kilns for four and a half years, after which they were seized by the officials and handed over to dépôts. Huang A-mu (黃阿木) deposes, "on the expiration of the eight years, " I worked for another term of six years, after which, owing to my not possessing a cedula, I was " seized by the officials and handed over to a dépôt." Liang A-shêng (梁阿盛) deposes, "on " the expiration of the eight years, I worked for another period of three years. I then obtained " a cedula and laboured as a charcoal burner during one year, after which I was placed in a dépôt " where I worked four years without wages." Li ʻHo (李合) deposes, "after the expiration of " the eight years, I worked in various ways during four years. I then was sent to a dépôt." Lin A-i (林阿亦) deposes, "after the completion of the contract I worked for another period of " six months. I then was sent to a dépôt." Lin Yüeh (林月) deposes, "on the completion of the " eight years, I worked in various ways during seven years, after which I was sent to a dépôt." Ts'ai Hsia (蔡霞) deposes, "after the expiration of the eight years, as my legs were diseased, I " was sent to a dépôt." Huang shih (黃詩) deposes, "on the expiration of the eight years, I " worked for two other terms, the first of two years, the second of four years, after which I was sent " to a dépôt." Wang Fu (王福) deposes, "after the expiration of the eight years, I worked for " another period of five years, after which I was sent to a dépôt." Lu A-hsing (陸阿杏) deposes, " after the expiration of the eight years I received from my master a cedula; but at the end of " the 12 months I was not allowed to renew it, and was sent to a dépôt." Ch'ên A-ch'ing (陳阿慶) deposes, "on the expiration of the eight years, my master asked me to renew the " contract. As I declined my feet were chained for two nights, and I was sent to a dépôt." Ch'ên A-hung (陳阿洪) deposes, "after the expiration of the eight years, I worked for another term of " three months. My master still desired me to remain in his service, and on my refusing he " struck me on the back with a stick, and dealt me blows with bricks, and sent me to a dépôt." Lo A-yü (羅阿玉) deposes, "on the expiration of the eight years, I entered into another " contract for three years. I then was sent to a dépôt where I worked during 10 years." Ch'ên Wan-shêng (陳萬生) deposes, "after the completion of my contract, I worked for another " term of 11 years, I then was sent to a dépôt." Ch'ên Yu (陳有) deposes, "on the expiration " of the contract, my employers desired me to enter into a new engagement for six years, and " on my refusing, attached irons to my feet, and compelled me to labour." The depositions of Wu Yü-shêng (巫毓勝) and 2 others state that they were originally sold to a dépôt, and after the expiration of the eight years, they entered into new agreements. Ch'ên Kou (陳 苟) deposes, "men who had completed their contracts were not allowed to go away. If they "persisted in refusing to renew their engagements, they were sent to the dépôt." Lü A-wu (呂 阿 武) deposes, "after the expiration of the contract, on my applying to my master for a "cedula, he desired the police to conduct me to jail." Wu A-hou (吳 阿 侯) deposes, "after the "expiration of the eight years, I laboured on Government work, without wages, during five "years." The depositions of Ch'ên A-'hung (陳 阿 紅) and 3 others state that on the eve of the expiration of the contract they were chastised with increased severity and that, of the gang of 40, 34 were placed in irons and sent to the dépôt. The depositions of Ch'ên A-'hêng (陳 阿 恒) and 3 others state that a few days before the completion of their contracts they were placed in chains and severely flogged, and that they were told that if they consented to renew their engagements they would be released, and that they would be sent to the dépôt if they declined; they add that, when being escorted there, two were tied together, as is practised in the case of robbers, and that they were not permitted to remove their clothing from the plantation. Hu A-ssŭ (胡 阿 四) deposes, "at present in the prison in this plantation a man is confined whose "contract is on the eve of expiration. He is forced to labour with both feet chained."

XXI.

Can he choose between staying in and leaving Cuba?

The petition of Jên Shih-chên (任 世 貞) and 2 others states, "we were here sold to "plantations, where we suffered from hunger and cruelty during eight years. As we were forced "to purchase additional supplies of food and clothing at the plantation shop, we saved nothing, "and at the end of the contract term, when we thought that we would be able to procure other "and better remunerated employment, so as to be able in a few years to amass sufficient for a "passage home, our employer delivered us to the dépôt, whence on the following day we were "sent out to labour in chains, on the roads, receiving no wages, and in every way treated like "criminals of the jail. Afterwards we were forced to sign fresh contracts, and to enter the service "of planters, of the wages paid by whom out of $15 the official retained $10, whilst out of $30 "they handed to us only $6; and when these fresh engagements were terminated we again were "handed to the dépôts. In these we passed several months, after which contracts were again "imposed upon us, so that by means of these successive engagements, not one day of freedom "was accorded to us." The petition of Huang Erh (黃 二) and 5 others states, "last year in the "3rd moon our contracts expired, but still we have been kept at work up to this date. More "than a year has thus already elapsed and the superintendent (of the Guanabacoa Railway Co.) "declares that he desires us to enter into other contracts for four years." The petition of Liang A-tê (梁 阿 德) declares, "on the completion of my contract term I imagined that I could seek "employment elsewhere, but my master chained me and flogged me and forced me to engage "myself for six years." The petition of Yü A-hsia (余 阿 洽) declares, "I was sold to a railway "company with an engagement for eight years, but though that term expired seven years ago, no

" cedula has as yet been issued. I sometimes want to take a walk outside, but I cannot through dread " of my master knowing of it, and of his flogging, chaining and ill-treating me." The petition of Liu A-shou (劉阿壽) and 4 others declares, "after we had completed our eight years, our master " refused to issue cedulas, and desired us to work six more years. If we refused we were beaten " and chained. Those who have no money to hire a *padrino*, who wish to go to other places of " service, are exposed to be arrested by the guards, and sent to the dépôt." The petition of Chu Chi-hsün (朱箕訓) and 10 others declares, " to procure from the officials a Letter of Domicile " and a cedula an outlay of $50 or $60 and baptism and adoption by a foreigner were indis- " pensable, so that it was useless for a poor man to endeavour to obtain these documents." The petition of Li Ying-sung (李英松) declares, "on the termination of the agreement I was refused " the necessary papers, and my master was even wrathful at my applying for them. I was " delivered to the officials, who would not permit me to speak, and was confined in prison for six " years, labouring but receiving no wages, a helpless victim of cruelty." The petition of Yeh Fu-chün (葉福君) and 52 others declares, " when the completion of the eight years term was " approaching, every one was consoled at the prospect of speedy liberty, of saving money, and " going back to China, but our employer was so heartless as to insist on our binding ourselves for " other six years, sending those who refused to the dépôt, where they had to labour on the roads the " whole day, with chained feet, receiving no wages, and not having enough to eat, whilst the " severity of the toil was augmented by the burning sun." The petition of Ho A-ying (何阿英) declares, " I purchased my liberty in the 6th year of T'UNGCHIH, but in the 9th year I lost my " cedula, and up to this time I have been kept in jail working for the benefit of others. There " is no one to whom I can appeal." The petition of Chang Kuan (張觀) declares, " after we " have toiled for so many years we ought indeed to be set free, but instead we are sent to the " dépôt, where we are forced to work without wages." The petition of Chang Mêng (張孟) states, " having no papers I was seized by the guards and placed in the prison. I was employed " in it as a sweeper, receiving neither wages nor clothes, so that imprisonment like a criminal " is the termination of my seventeen years' service." The petition of Chang Shih-lien (張石連) declares, " I was sold to a market-gardener, under whom I worked during eight years. At their " close my master desired me to stay other four years, after which he sent me to the dépôt. " I have now been in it five years, employed on municipal work. I am an old man and should " like to procure a document permitting me to go out and beg. I cannot obtain one, and I pray " that you will aid me in the matter." The petition of Yüan Ai-shan (袁藹山) declares, " at " the close of the eight years I was forced to sign another engagement for two years. My contract " was detained by the overseer, and he never returned it. I subsequently was seized by foreign " guards, and I have now been over three years in the dépôt. We have to endure endless " hardships. I am now sixty-six years old, and I beg that you will procure me a mendicant's " pass, so that I may go out and beg for food. The change would revive me."

Again the 37th clause of the Regulations published in Cuba, and dated September 1872, prescribes that " all immigrants arrived after the 15th February 1861, who shall be found " employed, without being in due form contracted, on a plantation or in an industrial or commercial " establishment or private residence, shall be conducted to the chief town of the jurisdiction." These extracts are evidences of the extent to which a Chinese, whether he desires to go away or remain, is deprived of freedom of choice, for as is remarked in the petition of Lin Chin (林 金) and 16 others, "the foreign authorities consider the Chinese as a source of wealth for themselves. "To whom then can we apply for redress?"

XXII.

IF HE ELECTS TO STAY, WHAT FOLLOWS?

The 1st clause of the Regulations, dated September 1872, prescribes that, "every Chinese "immigrant arrived after the 15th February 1861, is compelled to leave the island on completion "of his contract, or should he desire to remain, to re-contract himself in the capacity of "immigrant labourer or workman, according to the provisions of Article VII. of the Royal Decree "of 1860, and of Articles 51 and 52 of the Instructions of 1868, and of the Decree of 18th "October 1871." As, however, the smallness of the wages, aggravated by the necessity of purchasing food and clothing in addition to those supplied on the place of service, renders it impossible to lay by sufficient for the cost of passage, and as the latter is not supplied by the employers, the rules now in force retain on the island under the control of the dépôts, all Chinese, and those who stay cannot be regarded as following a course suggested by free election. Thus the petition of Tsêng A-shih (曾 阿 石) remarks, "I pray you "to aid me in escaping from a life-time slavery, by procuring for me my freedman's papers, "a boon for which I shall ever be grateful." Liang A-tê (梁 阿 德) observes in his petition, "my hope is to be rescued by you, so as to find it in my power to obtain a situation "in another locality, where in two or three years I may save sufficient for the expenses of my "return." Again, the depositions of Ch'ên T'ung (陳 通) and 1 other state that they were forced to pay monthly $3 to foreigners who acted as their godfathers or padrinos, and that passports for a return home were refused to them by the officials. Hu A-ju (胡 阿 如) deposes, "though I held a certificate of completion of service, issued by my master, it was necessary to in "person hand to the officials three ounces ($51) when applying for a cedula." The depositions of Wên Ch'ang-t'ai (文 長 泰) and 6 others also declare that for their cedulas they each expended $51. The depositions of Wu Yüeh (吳 越) and 1 other declare that they each expended $8 in the purchase of cedulas. The depositions of Hsü Shu (許 數) and 1 other declare that they each expended $102 in the purchase of cedulas. Fêng A-hsiu (馮 阿 秀) deposes, "I purchased a cedula from the secretary of the officials for $59½." Chou Jun-fêng (周 潤 勝) deposes, "I paid $17 for my cedula; although on it was distinctly noted that it was issued "gratis." The depositions of Wang Chêng-fu (王 正 福) and 2 others declare, that they each purchased their cedulas for $100. The depositions of Ts'ui Têng-lin (崔 登 林) and 2 others declare that they each expended $68 in the purchase of a cedula. Kuan A-nêng (關 阿 能) deposes, "I, in the first instance, purchased my cedula for $100, "and besides annually for its renewal I have to pay $1 or $2 or $5 or $10." P'an Yo-hêng (潘 岳 衡) deposes, "I expended $90 in the purchase of a cedula." Li Shun

(李 順) deposes, "I expended $50 in the purchase of a cedula." Hsü A-fa (許 阿 發) deposes, "a cedula being refused on the completion of my contract term I had to expend $300 in order "to obtain its issue by the authorities." Ch'ên A-fa (陳 阿 發) deposes, "I expended $20 in "the purchase of a cedula." Wu A-ssŭ (伍 阿 四) deposes, "I expended $255 in purchasing "a cedula from the officials." Chiang A-ch'i (江 阿 起) deposes, "after the expiration of the "contract term, I worked for another period of five years. I then gave the officials $85, but did "not even by this outlay succeed in purchasing a cedula." Liu A-chi (劉 阿 記) deposes, "I "had to expend $36 for the renewal of my cedula although properly the fee is only $0.50." 'Huang Tê (黃 德) deposes, "on applying ɔ the officials for a cedula, I was seized and placed in "a dépôt." Liang A-ying (梁 阿 英) deposes, "I expended $51 in the purchase of a cedula "from the officials, but after having worked independently for two years, the officials of another "locality, after inspecting it, took it away on the plea that it had not been issued under their "jurisdiction." Wan Ch'ang-hsiu (萬 長 秀) deposes, "I expended $51 in the purchase of a "cedula, but it was torn up by the officials of another locality and I was sent to a dépôt." Wu Wên-fan (吳 文 番) and 5 others depose that they were deprived of their cedulas by the authorities and were placed in the dépôts. Wu A-fu (吳 阿 福) deposes, "my cedula was "burnt, and I was removed to a dépôt." Li A-tou (李 阿 斗) deposes, "I expended $51 in "purchasing a cedula, and after working independently during eight years, the authorities "declared that the document was fictitious, took it away and arrested me." Li A-'hung (李 阿 鴻) deposes, "I expended $135 in purchasing a cedula, but afterwards, on the plea that "it was fictitious, I was arrested and placed in a dépôt." Li Hsi-pao' (李 阿 寶) deposes, "after "the expiration of the contract term, I worked for another period of six years; at its close by an "outlay of $68 I bought a cedula. The functionary who sold it to me assured me that I could "make use of it in any locality, but the guards of the place where I went declared that it was "not in order, and sent me to a dépôt." Lin A-lung (林 阿 龍) deposes, "my cedula having "been stolen, I was arrested and taken to prison." T'an A-hsing (譚 阿 興) deposes, "as I lost "my cedula during certain disturbances caused by the insurgents, I was arrested and placed in a "dépôt." Ch'ên A-kuei (陳 阿 桂) deposes, "having lost my cedula I was placed in a dépôt." Wang Tzŭ (王 滋) deposes, "my cedula having been stolen I reported the fact at the dépôt and "was detained there." Kuo Chi-hsiu (郭 紀 秀) deposes, "one Sunday, I went out without "carrying my cedula on my person, and was arrested and placed in a dépôt." Liang Lien (梁 連) deposes, "certain guards whom I met tore up my cedula but did not arrest me."

XXIII.

IF HE ELECTS TO LEAVE, WHAT FOLLOWS?

The 2nd clause of the Regulations of September 1872 is to the following effect: "The "immigrant who, on completion of his contract, desires to leave the island shall be removed to "the dépôt of the chief town of the jurisdiction, so that his embarkation within two months "may be effected as laid down in Article VII. of the Royal Decree of 1860, and in Article 54 of "the Instructions of 1868, and if at the close of this term, he has not prepared the sum required "for the cost of passage, or if though possessing sufficient funds, he has not taken his departure, "he shall be liable to be re-contracted, so that the Municipalities may be spared the outlay "involved by a large assemblage in the dépôt of such immigrants, and so that other evils arising "from such assemblages, together with those resulting from the withdrawal from active labour "of a large number of Chinese, may be avoided." The whole purport of this rule certainly indicates a desire rather to enforce new contracts, than to facilitate departures. The 25th clause of the Regulations of May 1873 again is to this effect: "Chinese who have completed their "original and subsequent contracts, and who desire to quit the island, shall receive passes to "enable them to proceed to Havana in order to procure passports in the manner prescribed in "the Orders of the Colonial Goverment of the 13th July 1872, and shall deliver their original "contracts and the certificates of completion to the Central Commission. Those residing in "Havana shall be conducted by their employers before the Central Commission, to which at the "same time the above specified documents must be delivered. Failing their production or the "guarantee spoken of in the said order the passport shall be refused," and the order quoted prescribes that the guarantee must be satisfactory to the Central Commission. All these forma-lities—the inspection of contracts and certificates of completion, or procuring guarantees that are liable to rejection, and, the obtaining of passes and passports, are obstacles causing many difficulties to Chinese who may desire to leave. Thus the petition of Wu Chin-ch'êng (吳錦成) and 123 others declares, "it constantly happens that men who, having completed their time, "apply for a passport, not only lose the money which they have paid to the person to whom they "have confided the application, but also fail to recover the cedulas which had to be delivered "with it." Tsêng Lin (曾林) also deposes, "I had sufficient money for a passage home, and "wished to return, but my master would not furnish me with a certificate of completion, "and desired me to enter into a new engagement," and T'ang Chien (唐建) declares that a passport may cost from $ 70 to $ 200.

XXIV.

DO MEN ELECT TO LEAVE OR TO STAY, AS A RULE?

As the majority of the Chinese have been brought to Cuba against their will, and as the sufferings endured during the eight years of service result in the deaths of so large a proportion, it may be assumed that the survivors long to escape from a spot which has been to them so perilous; but the difficulties impeding their departure—the withholding of the certificates of completion by employers, the compulsory renewal of contract and the detention in dépôts—prove insuperable. Thus Lu A-hsing (陸阿杏) deposes, "since my contract term was completed I "have still been a victim of wrong. My discontent is great, and I desire to depart, it matters "not where. Any locality is better than this island. The injustice has become unendurable and "death is preferable." The depositions of Liang A-hsin (梁阿新) and 2 others declare, that their only desire is to be away from Cuba. Chou A-tung (周阿東) deposes, "I can only implore "that I may be rescued out of this island. I will pay with my life for such a boon." Yün Lin-shan (雲 林 山) deposes, "my only desire has been to leave, but the frauds to which I have been "subjected have prevented my laying by the passage money, whilst besides the fact of a passport "costing more than $100 is an obstacle rendering departure impossible." Hsieh A-jui (謝 阿 瑞) and 1 other depose, "even if my confinement in the dépôt ceased, and I were permitted to engage "in profitable employment, I would go away. I would not remain here." T'ang Yü (湯 玉) deposes, "even if I could acquire wealth here I would not remain."

XXV.

THE FIRST PERIOD ENDED, DO THOSE WHO ELECT TO STAY RECEIVE HIGHER PAY AND ENTER INTO NEW CONTRACTS ON MORE FAVOURABLE CONDITIONS?

In the Decree of the Colonial Government of December 1871 it is provided that all Chinese—other than those domiciled—not employed on estates, or in commercial establishments or in private residences, are immediately to be arrested and confined in the dépôts; that all Chinese so employed, but not formally re-contracted are to remain under the temporary guardian-ship of the individuals in whose service they may be, until the Government can ascertain whether they are deserters or whether they have been guilty only of the fault of neglect to re-contract themselves in a legal manner; that a contract is to be entered into between their guardians and such Chinese thus placed under them to the effect that monthly wages of $12 are to be paid, $4 of which are to be handed to the workmen and $8 to be deposited in the hands of the Government, and that Chinese who, whilst the census is being carried out, complete their first contracts, are to have the option of remaining under the guardianship of their masters or of entering the nearest dépôt; and that during the same period no papers of any class whatsoever are to be issued to Chinese, save passes for those serving under original contracts, whom their masters may desire to transfer from one locality to another. Again, the 14th article of the Regulations of May 1873 is to the following effect: "Chinese arrived after the "15th February 1861, who, having completed any contract, are either unwilling or unable "to procure its renewal, shall be delivered by their employers to the local authorities, and "the expired contracts and cedulas must be handed in at the same time." The expression "those who elect to stay" is thus hardly applicable to the class in question. The petition of Lin A-yu (林 阿 有) also states, "on the completion of the contract term not only was the "liberty to which I and the others—42 in number—were entitled withheld, but we were also "placed in irons and treated as criminals." The petition of Lai Shêng (賴 勝) and 9 others declares, "on the contracts we have signed in Chinese it is plainly stated that we are engaged "for eight years, and that after having completed our time, we shall be free either to work for "our own account, or to return to China, but now when our terms of service are finished, liberty "is withheld and we have no means of obtaining it." The petition of Tsêng A-shih (曾 阿 石) declares, "when my eight years were completed, my employer placed me in irons in order to "coerce me into continuing labour, and he still not only withholds my freedom, but also declines

" to augment my wages, and I am forced for the moment to consent to his demands in order to
" be released from my fetters." Shên A-ts'ai (沈 阿 才) deposes, " on the completion of the eight
" years my master forced me to remain in his service for other four years but did not increase my
" wages." Ch'ên Tê-lin (陳 德 林) deposes, " on the expiration of my eight years I made a fresh
" contract with my master for two years at monthly wages of $ 6, but he only paid me $ 4." Ch'ên
A-chi (陳 阿 吉) deposes, " after the expiration of the eight years I was forced to work for two
" additional months, and I was only released on payment of $ 17." Ch'ên I (陳 翼) deposes,
" when our contracts expired nine months' wages were due to us, and we applied to the new
" master for payment. Upon this, he directed us to continue our labour and to await the return
" of our former employer. We—16 in all—then inquired what wages would be issued to us,
" and were told that we should receive only the former rate of $ 4. We replied that after our
" original engagement had been completed a higher rate ought to be conceded, and that if it were
" not granted we should prefer to be delivered over to the authorities. The administrator then
" declared that our first contracts had not yet expired, and that it mattered not whether
" willingly or reluctantly we must work on the old conditions; and when we persisted in our
" refusal the overseer brought cords and chains, and stood round us, as if intending to place us in
" fetters. Upon this one of our number conversant with Spanish urged upon the administrator
" that our contracts had really expired, and that we refused to work on the former terms. An
" overseer then struck me with a whip-handle inflicting an open wound on my head. Two of
" my companions succeeded in escaping observation, and reporting the occurrence to the
" authorities. The latter then sent for us and the administrator and a consultation took place
" between the latter and the officials which ensued in ten being sent back to the plantation. I
" and five others who refused to return were sent to the Colon dépôt." Wên Ch'ang-t'ai (文 長 泰)
deposes, " when my contract expired I was locked up by my employer and compelled by him to
' enter into a fresh contract." P'ang A-tung (龐 阿 東) deposes, " after the expiration of the
" eight years, if I had refused to enter into a fresh contract I would have been flogged and
" chained." 'Huang Ch'üan-hsi (黃 全 喜) deposes, " though I had been a source of profit to my
" master,—he hiring me out for $ 25 per month, and paying me only $ 3 or $ 4,—on completion
" of the contract term he handed me to a Government official. The latter told me that if I
" could not pay $ 51 for a cedula, he would contract me to another employer, and that I must
" pay him $ 4 of my earnings." Lu Shêng-pao (盧 盛 保) deposes, " after the expiration of the
" eight years, my employer kept me in chains during six months, and then handed me to
" a dépôt, without delivering my original contracts. The officials alleged that I was a
" deserter, and I was beaten so severely that my ankle was broken. As the surgeon neglected
" me and I was starved in the hospital, the injury became incurable and I was forced
" to become a beggar, and now even my beggar's pass has been taken away by the guards,
" and I sleep in the street." Ch'ên A-shun (陳 阿 順) deposes, " after the expiration of
" the eight years, I worked for another term of seven years, and at their close my
" cedula was detained by my master who declined to deliver it unless paid $ 68." Ch'ên Hsiang
(陳 香) deposes, " my cedula was forcibly taken away by my second employer. I procured
" another, of which I was also deprived by certain officials, who exacted money, and as I was
" unable to satisfy this demand I was placed in a dépôt and forced to work without wages."

Ch'ên A-ho (陳 阿 和) deposes, "when on the expiration of the eight years a new contract is
" entered into and wages are increased to the extent of a few dollars, the fact of payment being
" made in the paper currency renders the augmentation altogether nominal."   Tsêng A-shih
(曾 阿 十) deposes, "I and 39 others whose contracts had expired were not sent to a dépôt, but
" our master forced us to work in chains, and inflicted on us daily a number of blows, equal to
" the number of dollars paid us monthly as wages."   Lo A-chi (羅 阿 已) deposes, "on the
" expiration of the eight years I was forced to enter into a contract for another term of four years,
" an increase of wages of $4 being accorded to me.   I afterwards worked for an additional period of
" three years."   Lin Ho-chuang (林 合 莊) deposes, "on the expiration of the eight years I was
" forced to enter into a new engagement for six years at monthly wages of $15.   At their close
" I was handed to a dépôt."   Ch'ên Man (陳 滿) deposes, "on the expiration of the eight years
" I was forced to enter into a new engagement for four years at monthly wages of $11.   At their
" close I was handed to a dépôt, where I had to work without wages."   Wang Shui-t'ou
(王 水 頭) deposes, "after the expiration of the eight years, I worked for another period of six
" years at monthly wages of $8.   I then was sent to a dépôt, where I laboured during six years
" without wages."   Ch'ên Ting-hsien (陳 鼎 賢) deposes, "on the expiration of the contract term
" I was handed by my employer to the officials.   They compelled me to enter into another
" engagement for two years at monthly wages of $6.   I subsequently obtained a cedula, but the
" year before last, having no money for its renewal, I was arrested and placed in a dépôt."

XXVI.

WHAT MEANS ARE PROVIDED FOR THE RE-PATRIATION, OR DEPARTURE, OF THOSE WHO DESIRE TO LEAVE CUBA?

By the 9th clause of the Emigration Convention of the 5th year of T'UNGCHIH, the term
for which engagements can be entered into is limited to five years, and on their completion the
employer is bound to furnish the sum specified in the contract for the cost of passage back to
China.   The clause also provides that in the event of the immigrant electing to remain and of
his being permitted to do so by the authorities, he shall, if he re-engages with the same employer,
receive only half the amount prescribed as cost of passage, the employer however to again bind
himself in the new contract to, at the close of the second term of five years, provide the entire
sum specified; on the other hand if the Chinese does not again enter the same service, the
employer has to at once deliver to him the amount in question.   On the immigrant is also
conferred the right of demanding the same concession, in the event of his being incapacitated by
sickness, before the close of the contract term, and of, if it be refused, seeking redress from the
authorities.   Among the forms of contract inspected only one is framed in accordance with
these provisions.   Its 2nd clause defines five years as the period of the contract; the 6th states
that if at their completion the immigrant desires to return, he shall receive $75 for the cost of
passage; the 7th, that if a second contract is entered into with the same employer, the immigrant
shall at the end of the first receive $35.50, and on the termination of the second, the entire

amount of $75; and the 8th, that even if on arrival the immigrant is incapacitated by sickness, the cost of a return passage shall be at once supplied to him. This form of contract is however blank, whilst the others which have been used contain clauses at variance with the Emigration Convention.

The 18th clause of the Spanish Royal Decree of 1860 is to the following effect: "Two "months after the termination of his engagement, the Chinese must either have renewed his "contract, or have quitted the island; this provision becomes successively applicable to him on "the completion of each engagement into which he enters, and in the event of his not fulfilling "it, he shall be employed on public works, until after deducting the cost of maintenance the sum "accumulated to his credit is sufficient to defray the cost of passage to the locality which he may "select, or which, if he fails to do so, the Captain General may designate for him." The 55th clause of the Instructions of 1868 provides that Chinese desirous of quitting the island but not possessing the necessary funds, shall, if after working one year for Government the sum to their credit is insufficient, be sent away at the cost of the dépôt; and the Royal Decree of 1871 *(note by the translator*—ordering the expulsion of all classes of Chinese not working under contract) directs, that the deportation of vagabonds and paupers is to be effected at the cost of Government. These various clauses evincing a certain consideration for the interests of the Chinese, are however but empty words. In practice, the Chinese, deprived of all free choice, is forced either by his master or the dépôt to sign a fresh contract, and receives no wages for the labour he performs during the interval which, in the latter case, he passes in that establishment. The actual gains, too, of those whose new engagements are effected by the dépôts, prove to be insignificant, whilst it is as little to be hoped that their functionaries will burden themselves with the expense of sending Chinese home, as it is that the latter can find it in their power to take counsel with the Captain General as to the destination most suitable for their interests.

Hsien Tso-pang (洗佐邦) and 13 others state in their petition, "formerly Coolies arrived "from Canton and Fukien with contracts for only five years, but of these they were deprived "here (Havana) in the barracoons, whilst those who have embarked at Macao have all been "contracted for eight years, a rule the origin of which is unknown to us. Passports of departure "must be bought, the prices exacted being in proportion to the supposed affluence of the "applicant, varying from tens to hundreds of dollars. How then can even a few hope for a return "home?" The petition of Lin Chin (林金) and 16 others declares, "when the time has expired "and the cedula is asked for, the master defers giving it day after day, and at last by an arrange-"ment with the officials, our countryman is seized and coerced to sell himself again for eight "years." Wu Shêng (吳勝) states in his petition, "on the completion of the eight years I was "delivered over to the officials. By them I was sent into the mountains to aid in the execution "of certain Government works, quarrying stones, &c., &c., and whilst thus engaged my arm was "broken. No compassion however is displayed towards me, and no steps are taken for my "relief, and I know not where I can apply even for food." The petition of Wu Chin-ch'êng (吳錦成) and of 124 others states, "we have heard that men who have been permitted to leave "have been starved to death during the passage, or are taken to other places and again sold." The petition of Kao Lao-hsiu (高老秀) and 16 others states, "some who have been able to think "of a return home, through their ignorance of the movements of vessels expend all their earnings

" whilst waiting and thus lose their opportunity, or, if known to possess a little money, they are
" murdered and robbed."

XXVII.

ARE THERE CHINESE IN HAVANA AND OTHER CUBAN CITIES? TO WHAT CLASSES DO THEY
BELONG? WHAT IS THEIR CONDITION AND HOW ARE THEY TREATED? WHAT ARE
THEIR VIEWS OF LIFE IN CUBA?

Chinese who on their arrival have been disposed of for service in Havana and other Cuban
cities, are employed in sugar warehouses, and in cigar, shoe, hat, iron, charcoal, bakers',
confectioners', stone-cutters' and carpenters' shops, and in bricklayers' and washing establishments, in railways and gas works, and as municipal scavengers, in brick-kilns or on board
cargo-boats, and as domestics and cooks. There are some, also, who having obtained Letters of
Domicile, have engaged in a trade of small proportions. Of all these the great majority are,
according to their own statements, subjected to wrong. Besides, enquiry has shown that, in the
various cities, those who have been delivered to the dépôts and who thus detained undergo
extremer hardships, form the most numerous class. These are constantly seen on the highways
working in gangs like convicts, digging, or carrying stones, and watched by guards who goad
them on with the whip and the rod.

The following extracts from depositions will indicate the treatment accorded in the various
cities. Li A-chiu (李 阿 九) deposes, "after holding a cedula during six years it was taken away
" by the officials, and I was forced to labour on Government works." Yao A-ya (姚 阿 押)
deposes, "my cedula was taken away by the officials, and I was placed in the Colon dépôt."
Wên Ch'ang-t'ai (文 長 泰) deposes, "seven years ago Chinese of every class, those who had
" completed their contracts and those who had not, were forced to labour in the construction of
" the church which stands in front of this hotel (at Sagua). A white man was in charge of every
" four Chinese, and the slightest slowness on the part of the latter was punished by blows. I
" myself saw within a very brief space of time, seven men commit suicide by jumping into wells,
" and besides, the voluntary deaths by hanging and the deaths from violence were exceedingly
" numerous." Ch'ên A-chên (陳 阿 振) deposes, "I was robbed of my cedula, and was in conse-
" quence placed in the dépôt." Ch'ên Shui (陳 水) deposes, "I have to pay yearly an ounce for
" the renewal." Ho A-êrh (何 阿 二) deposes, "I had held a cedula during seven years, when
" certain disturbances having taken place, I quitted the town to convey information to the
" Government officials, and subsequently falling sick lost my cedula, and was confined in a dépôt."
Li Cho (李 卓) deposes, "I was hired out to labour by the authorities of the place, and if my
" wages amount to $20, I have at least to hand to them the half." Lo A-ch'ang (羅 阿 昌)
deposes, "owing to the wages being small I left a shop in which I had been employed in free
" service. The owner, in revenge, induced the police to deprive me of my cedula, and to confine
" me and force me to labour in the dépôt." Ch'ên A-fu (陳 阿 福) deposes, "having been deprived
" of the use of one arm through an accident caused by machinery, I was expelled from the dépôt

" and have now been a beggar during more than ten years." Ts'ai A-lu (蔡阿魯) deposes, " whilst in the dépôt my legs became diseased. I was in consequence expelled from it and forced " to beg." Liang A-po (梁阿鉑) deposes, "in the Colon dépôt I have seen two men beaten for " breaking wind." Ch'ên A-shun (陳阿順) deposes, "the police on discovering a Chinese without " a cedula demand a bribe of $4. Sometimes, too, in order to extort money they seize the cedulas, " and if it is refused, tear them up and deliver the holder to the officials." Yang Chin (楊錦) deposes, "seeing some Chinese and negroes fighting, I endeavoured to put a stop to the quarrel. " The police arrested me as well as the others, took away my watch, money and cedula, and " confined me in the stocks. I now serve as cook in this dépôt." Pei A-pao (貝阿寶) deposes, " on my losing my cedula the local officials sent for me, and gave me certain work to execute, " promising wages at the rate of $17 monthly, but though I laboured for an entire year they paid " me nothing." Li Yen-ch'un (李衍春) deposes, "men arrested for not possessing cedulas can " procure release by a payment to the police, but the release is soon followed by a fresh seizure." Chang Erh (張二) deposes, " cedulas can always be bought here, the price varying from $50 to " $200. If the applicant is known to possess any money, the sum asked is invariably greater. " The functionaries of the dépôt detain any cedulas which Chinese may hold and after their " death, sell them." Chuang A-i (莊阿意) deposes, "after the completion of my contract I kept " during seven years a shop for the sale of meat. I afterwards opened one for the sale of " miscellaneous articles. Of my four assistants one was wounded by a blow from a knife and " died. Subsequently a white soldier entered my shop and endeavoured to remove a number " of articles without payment, and on my resisting, beat me with a stick, and when my " assistants endeavoured to interfere, stabbed one in the left ribs and another on the head. " The first has been sent to the hospital, but the wounds of the other may be examined. My " own arms, too, have been so injured that I cannot move them with any freedom. The people " here declare that the killing of a Chinese is no more than the killing of a dog. I have " complained to the officials in regard to the last assault, but though six days have elapsed, we " have not been sent for to give evidence." Yang A-t'ien (楊阿田) deposes, "I came to Cuba in " a ship from California, on board of which I was employed, and losses by gambling compelling " me to remain, I was seized and placed in the dépôt of this city (Colon). I have now been here " four months, receiving no wages and constantly beaten. Chinese are certainly treated as if " they were fowls or dogs." The petition of Wu Chin-ch'êng (吳錦成) and 123 others states, " when four or five Chinese converse together in the street, a policeman will accuse them of " conspiracy, and if they assemble four or five in a house, shutting the door, they will be charged " with gambling, and unless we at once offer money we are taken to jail. We may be left there " two or three years without being tried and we may petition four or five times without any reply " being vouchsafed. On each occasion of petitioning we must request a friend to engage an " advocate for our protection and after the payment to him of a certain sum of money our " statement is forwarded. But if we do not afterwards fulfil the wishes of the official addressed " (give the sum demanded) we are never released "

XXVIII.

ARE THERE CHINESE IN THE COUNTRY ?   TO WHAT CLASSES DO THEY BELONG ?   WHAT IS
THEIR CONDITION, AND WHAT DO THEY SAY ABOUT IT ?

Chinese are disposed of, but not in large numbers, to tobacco and coffee estates, to farms and market gardens.   The great majority however are employed on sugar plantations, and it is there that the greatest wrongs are inflicted upon them, wrongs far graver than those endured in the cities.

The following extracts will indicate the condition of those working in the country districts. Ch'ên T'ung (陳通) deposes, "on all plantations there are jails, in the smallest of which 12 "or 15 can be confined."   Ch'ü Tan-k'o (屈但壳) deposes, "in the day-time we work in irons, "and at night are confined in the stocks.   On the plantation there are three cells, one of iron "and two of wood.   In the former 30 individuals are constantly placed, and in the others several "tens are as often detained."   Ch'ên Chin (陳金) deposes, "for reporting myself sick, I "received 200 blows on the back, which became lacerated.   I was forced to work as usual on the "same day and at night the wounds were rubbed with salt and lime-juice."   Li Yün (李閏) deposes, "I have seen four men shot dead on the plantations."   Huang Ch'ao-ping (黃潮炳) deposes, "on a plantation I had to work in irons during three years, and I never knew why this "chastisement was inflicted."   Liang Tao-'han (梁道漢) deposes, "on the cane fields there "are ground fleas which penetrate and lay eggs under the skin, and eat and corrupt the flesh, "and no cure is possible; and as no shoes are furnished, we are constantly unable to move our "feet."   Ko Ch'i (柯溪) deposes, "on the expiration of the eight years, I worked for another "term of two years.   My savings out of my wages I had entrusted to my master, and as he joined "the insurgents, I lost all I had laid by."   Ch'ên Kou (陳苟) deposes, "I had saved by self- "denying economy $ 100.   These were stolen from me.   The thief was discovered, but he "divided with the administrator what he had taken."   Wu A-hsiang (伍阿祥) deposes, "I "was sold to a plantation belonging to one of the local officials, who for six months' service only "paid me two months' wages, and forced us to catch squirrels for food in order to save the cost "of dried beef."   Wên A-nêng (温阿能) deposes, "there were men confined in the jail of "the plantation, but they were removed in anticipation of the visit of the Commission."   Chang Hui (張惠) deposes, "on the plantation there is at present a man who was beaten two "days ago.   He is now locked up so that he may not be seen by the Commission, as it is feared "that he may be interrogated."   Ts'ai Hsi (蔡細) deposes, "Passing the gates of a plantation, "I was seized by white men, who robbed me of what I had with me, and of my cedula.   I "complained to the officials, and the result was that I was confined in the Cardenas dépôt." Ch'ên A-yu (陳阿有) deposes, "passing a plantation, I was seized by certain of the overseers, "who robbed me of my cedula."   Ch'ên A-'ho (陳阿和) deposes, "I gave my cedula to the "head of the gang for renewal, but he ran away and took it with him, and I was seized and "placed in a dépôt.   The *ti-pao* (capitan de partido) would sell me another cedula, but I do not "possess the necessary funds."   Ho A-kuan (何阿官) deposes, "I handed my cedula to my "master for safe custody, and going out without it, was arrested.   I was then forced to work in

" the repairs of drains, and in all, had to labour ten years without wages." The petition of T'ang
Lien-shêng (唐 聯 陞) and 106 others states, " last year, for the work of the Trocha, a locality
" most unhealthy and close to the insurgent districts, the Government dispatched $\frac{1}{10}$th negroes
" and $\frac{9}{10}$ths Chinese. Of the latter a third perished, and those who survived, instead of receiving
" on their return the freedmen's papers which had been promised to them, are now confined in
" the various dépôts. It is because officials, planters and other men of influence, think only of
" using us for their own ends to augment their wealth, that they are thus so devoid of scruples
" and so deficient in honour, and it is useless to protest against these violations of good faith."
Liu A-sung (劉 阿 枞) deposes, " at the Trocha a shop was opened by a small official whose
" opium and miscellaneous articles could be purchased. These were sold on credit, payment
" being secured by deduction from the wages." Chang A-wên (張 阿 文) deposes, " at the
" Trocha all eatables were extremely dear. A cup of good water cost half a dollar, so that it was
" impossible to save money. The climate was very bad, and the labour very hard." Liu A-lien
(劉 阿 連) and 3 others depose, " when being conducted to the Trocha we were tied together each
" in turn, and thus transported in the railway." Li A-yao (李 阿 耀) and 127 others depose that
they, when proceeding to the Trocha, were promised cedulas by the officials, and that not only
is this pledge disregarded, but they are sent to the Havana dépôt, and forced to perform unpaid
labour.

XXIX.

ARE THERE CHINESE IN THE PRISONS ? FOR WHAT CRIMES ? HOW PUNISHED ? HOW TREATED ?

The jails to be found in the Cuban cities are substantially constructed, lofty, clean, and
cool, contrasting most favourably with the low, damp and hot chambers of the dépôts, and the
filthy and close quarters allotted to Chinese on the plantations. The prisoners, too, excluding
those in the chain-gang who work on the roads, and who suffer like the similar class in the
dépôts, are burdened with no labour heavier than the making of cigarettes, and are but lightly
chastised ; so that the treatment accorded to the criminals may be regarded as considerate.

The following extracts from depositions supply information in regard to the points referred
to in the query. Wang A-fu (王 阿 福) deposes, " I left my master's service after working for
" him during fourteen years. He upon this accused me of deserting and I was arrested and
" sentenced to two years' imprisonment." Liang Kuei-chung (梁貴鍾) deposes, " on one occasion,
" I went out on horseback, neglecting to take with me my cedula, and was placed in prison by a
" guard whom I met, and who demanded the production of my papers." Li Hsiang (李香)
deposes, " I was arrested and imprisoned but I am ignorant of the cause." Wu A-chao (吳 阿 照)
deposes, " my master having joined the insurgents, I proceeded to the authorities in order to
" report the occurrence, and was imprisoned because I did not possess a cedula." Wu Ch'ieh (吳且)
deposes, " I was imprisoned on a false charge of theft, and though four months have since elapsed
" I have not been examined by any official." T'ang A-lung (唐 阿 隆) deposes, " after being
" confined for six months in a jail, in which I was placed by the official of another locality,

" I was removed to the Havana prison. I have committed no offence, and can only conjecture
" that a foreigner with whom I had difficulties when carrying on a trade with certain
" detachments of troops, calumniated me. I have now been imprisoned here (Havana) three
" years, and though I have addressed four petitions to the Captain General my case has not
" even been tried." The depositions of Yang A-ssŭ (楊 阿 四) and 6 others state that they
belonged to a gang which, during the previous year, was working on a plantation, their
cedulas having been inspected and accepted as in order by their employer ; that owing
to the latter being in their debt $ 1,300, to their refusal to perform night work, and
to a desire on the part of the authorities to extort money, the documents in question were
declared to be fictitious, that their remonstrances pointing out that the cedulas had already been
admitted to be genuine were disregarded; that they and four others were imprisoned, and that they
were even prohibited from removing their clothes from the plantation. Liang Yu-tê (梁 有 德)
deposes, " having entered into conversation with three Chinese whom I met on the street, I was
" arrested by the police on the charge of inciting them to run away. I was confined in the
" Guanajay jail. The food is not sufficient, but on bribing the jailer, an improvement takes
" place." 'Ho Hsi (何 錫) deposes, " I was the head of a gang, and was arrested on the false
" charge of employing deserters." Chang Ch'ang-kuei (張 長 貴) deposes, " as I had refused to
" lend the ti-pao (Capitan de partido) money and a saddle, he falsely accused me of stealing
" certain articles from another Chinese, and I was imprisoned. Another reason was that I was
" disliked on account of having married a white woman. At first on admission I was beaten by
" the jailer, but he ceased doing so after I had paid him $ 3." Lo A-fa (羅 阿 發) deposes, " I
" chanced to be passing four Chinese who were fighting and, though I had nothing to do with
" the dispute, the ti-pao (Capitan de partido) arrested and imprisoned myself and Hsü A-wu
" (徐 阿 五)." Ch'ên Ch'êng-ch'i (陳 成 琪) deposes, " having obtained a cedula, I opened a
" shop for the sale of sundry articles. A Spaniard falsely declared that his wife had entrusted
" to me $ 400, and I was in consequence arrested and imprisoned." Hsü A-hsing (徐 阿 興)
" deposes, a policeman whom I met having directed me to produce my cedula for inspection,
" declared that it was not properly mine, and a discussion having arisen, he incited his dog
" to bite me. I kicked his dog, and for so doing was arrested and imprisoned by the
" ti-pao (Capitan de partido)." Jung A-k'uan (容 阿 寬) deposes, " I was accused of stealing
" my cedula from another man, and was in consequence imprisoned. No trial, however,
" has even taken place." Sung Chin (宋 晉) deposes, " on a cedula being refused at the
" completion of the eight years of service I went away, and worked independently during six
" years. I was then seized, and placed in this (Matanzas) prison." Têng A-ssŭ (鄧 阿 四)
deposes, " holding a cedula, I procured for the owner of a plantation 20 labourers, all of whom
" possessed a similar document. Nevertheless the police accused me of hiring men whose terms
" of contract service had not been completed, seized me, deprived me of $ 70 in silver and of
" $ 200 in paper, demanded another sum of $ 200 as the price of my release, and, as I was unable
" to pay it, placed me in prison. No trial, however, has taken place." Liang A-yu (梁 阿 友)
deposes, " on the 3rd moon of this year, a Chinese sent out to collect accounts failed to return.
" Enquiries on every side being made (by his master) I reported that, a few nights previously,
" I had heard what resembled the noise of a horse. An investigation which followed this

" testimony resulted in the discovery of the corpse, and I was arrested and imprisoned. All
" know that I am suffering injustice, but, as I have not been tried, I cannot be released, and my
" confinement has already lasted one month." Lung A-ch'uan (龍 阿 川) deposes, "the year
" before last I bought a cedula for $ 68. During the first month of last year, at the time of
" renewal, the police declared that the document was fictitious, and placed me in a prison." Lin
Wa (林 瓦) deposes, "a white man, who owed me several tens of dollars, and to whom I had
" refused to lend certain articles which he wished to borrow, accused me of stealing cigars, &c.,
" of which a Chinese had been robbed, and though the Chinese himself declared that I was not
" the culprit, no heed was given to this exoneration, and I was placed in prison." Liang Hai
(梁 海) deposes, "I bought from a Cantonese named A Fa-tsai (阿 發 仔) a gold watch-chain.
" Certain persons came to inspect the chain, and accused me of having purchased stolen property;
" and I was removed to prison where I have been confined twenty months without trial." Li
Ta-ts'ai (李 大 財) deposes, "the assistant cook, a negress (whom I was censuring for delay
" in the preparation of my master's dinner), accused me of striking her with the small knife
" with which I cut paper, and the cook, a white woman, sent for the police who arrested
" me and placed me in prison." Ko Ch'i (柯 溪) deposes, "the officials demanded money
" from me, and as I was unable to comply they declared that my cedula was fictitious and placed
" me in prison." Ch'ên Hsing (陳 興) deposes, "I was arrested and placed in prison for having
" a pistol in my box." Wu A-yao (伍 阿 耀) deposes, "I went out to purchase certain cooking
" utensils, and met a white man who told me that he had some for sale. Before I had settled
" with him in regard to the price, police came up who declared that the articles in question had
" been stolen. The white man ran away and I was arrested and have already been in jail three
" months." Hsü A-hsiang (許 阿 湘) deposes, "when Li A-liu (李 阿 流) had been robbed
" and murdered by a negro the master bribed 'Ho Chang-yu (何 章 友) to testify that I was
" the criminal. All the Chinese were indignant at this, and 'Ho Chang-yu (何 章 友) himself
" admitted that he had been induced to give false evidence. I, however, am still in prison
" without a trial." Miao Chi-yu (繆 巳 有) deposes, "the negro cook of the establishment in
" which I was employed as domestic, one evening came home drunk, and seizing a knife ran
" after me. I went upstairs to inform my master, and the negro whilst following me, fell down
" and wounded himself. He then declared to the master that the injury had been inflicted by
" me, and I was sent to prison, tried, and sentenced to six years' imprisonment." Ch'ên A-lin
(陳 阿 林) deposes, "whilst purchasing vegetables, the money which I was carrying fell out
" of my hands on an adjoining stand of melons, and when I was picking it up, I was accused
" of committing a theft, was arrested, and imprisoned. Owing to my ignorance of the language,
" I was sentenced to one year's imprisonment; through an outlay of $ 10 I am exempted from
" all labour but that of watching the yard." 'Ho A-hsien (賀 阿 先) deposes, "the police who
" were in search of a deserter met me, and, declaring that I resembled him, and that I also had
" committed a robbery of $ 200, arrested me and placed me in prison. I have already been in
" jail six months, but have not been examined by any official." Liang A-yu (梁 阿 有) deposes,
" my master cut off my left ear for going out. An official who happened to pass, observing how I
" was maimed, inquired in what manner the injury had been inflicted. Both I and my master were
" arrested and placed in prison, but the latter, in three days, by an expenditure of $ 2,000, obtained

" his freedom. In the meantime my confinement continues, and my money and other property
" cannot even be removed from my master's premises." Lo Kuan-hsiu (駱觀秀) deposes, " the
" administrator dealt me a blow with a knife between the thumb and forefinger, and at the same
" time wounded the head of A Kuo (阿郭), a native of Yangkiang (陽江). Our employer
" reported the occurrence to the official, and we and the administrator were all placed in jail.
" The latter was released on the following day, but our imprisonment still continues." Wu Yeh-
ch'êng (吳葉成) deposes, "four negroes in league with certain recently arrived Chinese killed
" the new administrator. By an outlay of money on the part of our employer, the participation
" of the negroes was not mentioned, and the crime was imputed to us—ten in all—whose contracts
" were on the eve of expiration, and we were consequently imprisoned." Wu Shao (吳紹)
deposes, "an overseer owed me $100, and on my asking him for payment, struck me, and dashed
" me to the ground. I had a knife on my person, and stabbed him to death. I was arrested
" and imprisoned, but have not been sentenced." Liang A-hsiu (梁阿秀) deposes, "when our
" employer's son, aided by the negroes, seized knives and killed one of us—a native of Hiang-
" shan (香山), and wounded all others, we seized the weapons and killed him. We, 22 in all,
" were arrested and placed in prison; one died there, four were sold away to Havana, sixteen
" were sent back to the plantation, and there are still two in jail." Hsieh A-kou (謝阿狗)
deposes, " we stabbed to death the administrator, on account of his cruelty. We, 24 in all,
" proceeded to the jail and surrendered ourselves. Our master, by an outlay of $680, induced
" the officials to order 12 of our number to return to the plantation, and on our refusal, an officer
" of low rank discharged fire-arms, wounding nine and killing two. There are 22 still in jail, and
" we consider it preferable to the plantation." The deposition of Chang A-hsiu (張阿秀) and
4 others states, "four of our gang of 40 having been killed by the violence of an overseer, eleven
" of us murdered the latter. We find the jail preferable to the plantation." Wu Hua-ch'ang
(吳華長) deposes, " I prefer remaining in jail." Ch'ên A-ch'iu (陳阿秋) and 22 others depose
that the jails are preferable to the plantation. Huang Shih-pao (黃石寶) deposes, "the labour
" on the plantation is more severe than that enforced in jail." Wang A-ts'ai (王阿才) deposes,
" I bought a gold watch for 1½ ounces, which a foreigner accused me of having stolen, and I was
" in consequence placed in prison, where I have each week to manufacture 16,000 cigarettes, and
" if this number is not completed I receive 12 blows."

XXX.

THE CONTRACT COOLIE IS A MAN WHO HAS PLEDGED HIMSELF TO WORK ACCORDING TO CONTRACT
FOR A TERM OF YEARS: HE IS NOT A SLAVE. IS HE TREATED AS A MAN WHO HAS
CONSENTED TO BE BOUND BY A CONTRACT, OR AS A SLAVE? ARE THERE SLAVES IN
CUBA—OR WERE THERE, AND WHAT IS OR WAS THEIR TREATMENT?

The distinction between a hired labourer and the slave can only exist when the former
accepts, of his own free will, the conditions tendered, and performs in a like manner the work

assigned to him; but the lawless method in which the Chinese were—in the great majority of cases—introduced into Cuba, the contempt there evinced for them, the disregard of contracts, the indifference as to the tasks enforced, and the unrestrained infliction of wrong, constitute a treatment which is that of "a slave, not of a man who has consented to be bound by a contract." Men who are disposed of in Havana, who are afterwards constantly, like merchandise, transferred from one establishment to another, and who, on the completion of their first agreements, are compelled to enter into fresh ones, who are detained in dépôts and delivered over to new masters, whose successive periods of toil are endless, and to whom are open no means of escape, cannot be regarded as occupying a position different from that of the negroes whose servitude has so long existed in the island, and who are liable to be hired out or sold at the will of their owner. Thus 'Hu Ju (胡 如) deposes, "I have been here twenty-seven years. The inhabitants truly "desire to reduce the Chinese into slaves for life." Ch'ên A-shun (陳 阿 順) deposes, "the "officials and merchants of Cuba desire to convert the Chinese into slaves for a life-time." Liu A-t'ang (劉 阿 唐) deposes, "on the plantations, the Chinese are treated exactly like the "negro slaves." Lin A-lung (林 阿 龍) and 6 other depose that on the sugar plantations the Chinese are treated exactly like the negroes. Li Ch'êng-hsün (李 承 訓) deposes, "in Cuba we are "treated exactly like slaves." Liu A-jui (劉 阿 瑞) deposes, "I am treated exactly like a negro "slave." Lin A-t'ai (林 阿 泰) deposes, "on the plantation, the slaves and the Chinese are all "treated alike." Hsü Shao-lin (徐 紹 麟) deposes, "the inhabitants are accustomed to employ "the negro slaves, but their treatment of us is even worse than that of the latter." The petition of Hsien Tso-pang (沈 佐 邦) and 13 others states, "the subjects of other countries come and "depart without hindrance, and in their transactions endure no wrongs, and it is hard to "understand why Chinese should be subjected to such outrages, to a treatment worse than that "of the negroes." Ch'ên Tê-lin (陳 德 林) deposes, "at the close of three years I was disposed "of to another plantation, by which, after the lapse of a similar period, I was again sold." Lin Yüeh (林 月) and 7 others depose that they were resold by certain plantations, to another plantation. Li A-chieh (李 阿 晉) deposes, "I was resold by a farm to a "sugar plantation." Tsêng Erh-ch'i (曾 貳 齊) deposes, "my employer disposed of me "to a cooper." Ch'ên A-chi (陳 阿 吉) deposes, "I was resold by the local officials to "a sugar warehouse for $70." Li A-pao (李 阿 保) deposes, "I was originally sold "to a railway company for $238; at the close of three years I was disposed of to a "jeweller for $170; and afterwards I redeemed myself by an outlay of $306." Liang Piao (梁 標) and 1 other depose that they were resold by their employer to bakeries. Li A-tou (李 阿 斗) and 1 other depose, that they were sold to other employers by the plantation by which they had been originally bought. Liu A-tai (劉 阿 戴) deposes, "I was resold to the "plantation by a bricklayer." Yu A-shih (游 阿 式) deposes, "I was resold by the plantation to "a market garden." Lin A-yung (林 阿 用) deposes, "after I had worked for three years I was "resold to a second employer for $163." 'Hu A-pao (胡 阿 保) and 4 others depose that they in all were sold to six different employers. Ch'ên A-'hai (陳 阿 海) deposes, "when my right "arm was broken, I was resold to a cigarette manufactory." Wên A-hsien (溫 阿 先) deposes, "out of the 82 who were bought with me, 77 were resold." Liao San (廖 三) deposes, "three "months after arrival on the plantation, I was resold to another one." Liang A-shêng (梁 阿 盛)

deposes, "after I had worked for a year I was resold to a sugar plantation." Li Jun-chu (黎潤珠) deposes, "I was resold by the plantation to a railway company." Lin Erh (林二) deposes, "after working nine months in the service of the Railway Company I was resold to a "plantation." Lo A-erh (羅阿二) deposes, "after working two years for the Railway Company "I was resold, and employed as a domestic servant. I remained in this position three years "when, my master becoming impoverished, I was again disposed of to the Havana Municipality "for $ 102." Chung Shêng (鍾聲) deposes, "after working seven years at the gold mines, I was "conducted by my master to Havana and then sold for $ 85." Wang Ts'ung-shêng (王從盛) deposes, "originally I was employed in the gold mines. I afterwards was sold to charcoal-"burners." Ch'ên A-wu (陳阿五) deposes, "I was resold and became a domestic at Havana." Chang Jung-chi (章榮紀) deposes, "I was resold after a year's service." Lin A-p'ing (林阿平) deposes, "after three years' service I was resold." Ch'ü Jung (區榮) deposes, "I was resold to a "plantation, and by it again sold to a sugar warehouse." Kuan A-hsi (關阿喜) deposes, "I "have been sold twice to employers in Havana." Liang A-yu (梁阿有) deposes, "I was resold "for service in a shop." Ch'ên Shao-chi (陳紹基) deposes, "I was resold to a shoemaker in "Havana." Ts'ui Lan-fang (崔蘭芳) deposes, "I was resold to a shoemaker." Wang Kuei-chieh (王貴姐) deposes, "I was ill at the time of arrival, and was sold to an establishment at "Matanzas, which was in the habit of purchasing the sick, curing them, and then reselling them." Liao A-ping (廖阿炳) deposes, "I was disposed of by the Havana barracoon to a similar "establishment at Matanzas (for sale)." T'ang A-lung (唐阿隆) deposes, "three years ago, the "Governor of Havana brought back to Havana all Chinese, and resold them as slaves for six "years." The petition of Su Chin-shêng (蘇進生) and 11 others states, "again, on the 10th of "the 9th moon of the 11th year of TUNGCHIH, the authorities, in concert with the planters, "devised means to force us to recontract for six years. During the night all were arrested and "shut up in the fortress, in the dépôt, or in the jail, and it was not until a month had elapsed "that the Consuls who had taken pity on such sufferings succeeded in obtaining the release of "those who could furnish security. The remainder, over 160, were sold by the 2nd military "officer of Havana to the hills at $ 102 each." The petition of Wu Chin-ch'êng (吳錦成) and 123 others states, "we were decoyed to this island, where those of us who have not completed "their eight years are subjected to much ill treatment, and the others, whose contracts have "expired, are also the victims of wrongs. For example, when travelling by rail we are not "allowed on the better cars, and in the hotels and in the shops we are kept apart in the same "manner as the black slaves." The petition of Jên Shih-chên (任世貞) and 2 others states, "but though the officials, the merchants and the planters are all indebted to us, they, with "heartless cruelty, torment us daily and hourly, refuse to treat us as human beings, disposing of "us as slaves and acting towards us as if we were brute beasts. We learn that friendly relations "now exist between China and the greater powers of the West, and that it is by the efforts of the "latter that the traffic in negro slaves has been suppressed. Why do they not render to us a "similar service?"

XXXI.

HAS THE SPANISH GOVERNMENT LEGISLATED IN FAVOUR OF THE COOLIE? HAS IT MADE LAWS FOR HIS GENERAL WELFARE AND PROTECTION? ARE THE LAWS EFFECTIVE? IF NOT, TO WHAT EXTENT AND IN WHAT RESPECTS INEFFECTIVE, AND WHY?

The 31st clause of the Spanish Royal Decree of 1860, directs that the Captain General shall be the chief protector of Chinese, and that he shall exercise this function in the various jurisdictions, by means of his delegates, the Governors and Lieutenant Governors, who, in turn, shall be aided by the Captains of districts; the 10th clause provides that minors can only contract themselves with the consent of the persons under whose charge they are; the 12th clause provides that vessels carrying Chinese shall be supplied with a quantity of water and sound food, proportioned to the number of individuals who have to be conveyed and the distance to be traversed; the 21st clause provides that Chinese, the rights of the importer over whom have been forfeited (through certain violations of Regulation), shall be at liberty to contract themselves; and the 22nd that should they not desire to do so, the Captain General shall exact from the consignee a sum sufficient to defray the cost of the re-exportation of the entire number; the 32nd clause provides that in their relations with the tribunals of justice, immigrants shall be defended in the lower, by the Attorney of the Court of Justice of the Peace, and in the higher, by the Attorney General; the 33rd clause provides that under no circumstances whatever and notwithstanding any stipulations to the contrary, shall employers exact from Chinese, on an average, more than 12 hours' work; the 54th, that when a contract empowers the employer to distribute, in the manner most convenient to his interests, the number of hours agreed upon, it shall be understood that no more than 15 hours can be exacted in one day; and the 69th, that the duration of an imprisonment imposed by an employer cannot exceed 10 days.

These provisions, characterised by a care for the welfare and protection of the Chinese, have however never been observed, and are in practice null, whilst on the other hand, the restrictions resorted to by the dépôts in order to enforce renewal of contracts, and to render continuance of labour unavoidable, are daily becoming more oppressive. Thus the petition of Chien Shih-kuang (簡仕光) and 69 others complains of the baneful laws and evil deeds of Spain; and that of Li Chao-ch'un (李肇春) and 165 others alleges that, "within the last few years, the planters "have, in concert with the authorities and the Commission of Emigration, enforced very unjust "rules." These statements certainly indicate that the laws in favour of the Chinese have not been effective, and the following extracts will explain the cause of this failure.

The petition of Chang Luan (張鑾) and 30 others states, "again, officials here are "often merchants, others are completely under the influence of the planters, and all ignore the "outrages committed, and do not even make an inquiry into the cases of suicide or murder. "Of late years, too, the issue of cedulas has ceased, or they can only be obtained by a large "outlay. On the other hand, the dépôt is enlarged, and police make raids on every side, with "the view of forcing the Chinese to enter into fresh contracts, so that the wishes of planters may "be satisfied and officials enabled to share in the labourer's earnings. Towards such officials, "and the citizens of fortune who govern the dépôts, gain flows in a deep and rapid stream, as

" at their will they hire out to labour or recall from it, our countrymen, whom they have
" converted into serfs, not of an individual but of the entire island, serfs deprived of all hope
" of again seeing their homes." The petition of T'ang Lien-shêng (唐 聯 陞) and 106 others
declares, " we are coerced into entering into fresh contracts, of the wages specified in which the
" greater portion is retained by the officials. At the close of these new contracts the same course
" is followed, and is afterwards successively adhered to. Thus the Government works of the
" island are executed free of cost, and the relations between the planters and the officials are
" tightened by mutual gain, whilst our sufferings, in the meantime, become more and more
" oppressive."

XXXII.

CAN THE CAPTAIN GENERAL ORDAIN LAWS WITHOUT REFERENCE TO SPAIN? OR IS THE LAW
PROPOSED IN CUBA REQUIRED TO BE CONFIRMED BY SPAIN? HAS SPAIN REFUSED
TO CONFIRM ANY PROPOSED LAWS? OR, HAVE LAWS PROPOSED IN CUBA NOT GONE
INTO OPERATION?

By the 56th clause of the Spanish Royal Decree of March 1854, all previous legislation
on the subject of the introduction of labourers into Cuba was abrogated, and the Decree of 1854
was itself annulled by that of July 1860 which is still in force. The 31st clause of the latter,
by appointing the Captain General to be Protector of Chinese, renders the government of them
one of his normal functions, but the 81st clause reserves to the Spanish Government " the right
" of at any time suspending or prohibiting the introduction of Chinese labourers into Cuba."
" The resolution," it proceeds to declare, " it may arrive at on this question, shall be made
" public in the Madrid and Havana *Gazettes*, and the term on the expiration of which importa-
" tions must cease, shall begin from the date of publication in the latter. This term shall not
" be less than eight months, and all importations taking place after its termination shall be
" regarded as appertaining to the category of those specified (as subjecting the importer to
" forfeiture of his rights) in Article 20. It must be understood by importers, that the fact of
" their engaging in this traffic is a recognition by them that its suspension or prohibition confers
" upon them no right to any compensation."

Subsequently, in February 1868, the Captain General made public other Regulations
containing 83 clauses, the objects of which were stated to be, the extinction of abuses which had
arisen through a disregard of the Provisions of the 1860 Decree, and the establishment of perfect
order in all matters connected with Chinese immigration.

In July and August 1870 the Captain General urged the prompt cessation of this immigration, and in June 1871 was published a Royal order acceding to the request; but on the
18th October a Decree was issued by the Captain General, declaring that the permission thus
accorded would not be availed of.

Again, on the 14th September 1872, Regulations—containing 40 articles—for the recontracting of Chinese, framed by the Central Commission of Colonization, were made public by the Captain General, and though assent to them was subsequently refused by the Spanish Government, they are still in force. The Regulations, containing 65 articles, of the 7th May 1873, were also published on the authority of the Colonial Government, alone.

No answer can be supplied to the last paragraph in this query. No means existed for obtaining information as to "laws proposed but not gone into operation."

XXXIII.

WHAT PARTS OF CUBA ARE IN REBELLION?

The regions extending north-west of Santiago de Cuba, south-east of Sagua, and north-east of Cienfuegos are infested by migratory bands of insurgents.

XXXIV.

HAVE COOLIES AIDED REBELS, AND, IF SO, UNDER WHAT CIRCUMSTANCES—WHERE, HOW, AND WHEN?

The petition of Chang Luan (張鑾) and 30 others states, "The rebellion in Cuba is one of "Spanish subjects against the Spanish Government; many instances have occurred of planters, "when joining the rebels, endeavouring to induce the Chinese labourers to do likewise, and of "the latter, even at the risk of death, refusing, or of, if constrained to go, at once returning. The "number of those who have acted thus is not considerable, as is proved by enquiry. Again, "though plantations and the Trocha are close to the districts held by the insurgents, we "have heard of no instance of a Chinese flying to the latter. A Chinese labourer can "scarcely be expected to return good for evil, but born in a country where the principles "of right are respected, he is able to refuse to attach himself to disturbers of law and "order. The people of Cuba, however, instead of recognising and being grateful for the "display of such feelings deny their existence, and use this denial as an excuse for fresh "prohibitions and restrictions." Ho A-hsien (賀阿先) deposes, "when my master joined "the insurgents I ran away to Havana." Wang A-jui (王阿瑞) and 1 other-depose, "when my "master joined the insurgents, I went away to another plantation." Tsêng Li-chieh (曾李姐) deposes, "my master joined the insurgents, but I attached myself to a gang of labourers and "worked under its head." Mo A-mu (莫阿穆) deposes, "my employer joined the insurgents, "but I remained, and worked for the new owner." Chang Jung-chi (章榮紀) deposes, "my "master joined the insurgents, but I went away and performed work for the officials." Yin Shou-k'un (殷守昆) deposes, "when my master joined the insurgents, I escaped to the officials, "reported what had occurred and worked for them." T'ang Yü (湯 玉) deposes, "when my "master joined the insurgents I proceeded to the officials in order to report the occurrence, and was "called upon by the authorities to labour for them without wages." Wang T'ing-kuei (王 廷 貴) deposes, "my master became an insurgent; I refused to go with him, and ran away to the "Government officials, one of whom I served as cook." Li K'ang-wên (李 康 穩) deposes, "when "my master joined the insurgents I went of my own accord to a dépôt and laboured there." Liang A-chao (梁 阿 照) and 1 other depose, "my master joined the insurgents; I declined to "go with him, and the administrator conducted me to the dépôt." Ch'ên A-hsiu (陳 阿 秀) deposes, "our master joined the insurgents but we all dispersed; I, however, was arrested by the "authorities and placed in a dépôt." Chiang A-lin (姜 阿 麟) deposes, "when my master joined "the insurgents I ran away, and was seized and confined in a dépôt." Wu A-jung (吳 阿 容) deposes, "I was carried away by the insurgents, but in a few days I succeeded in escaping, and "was subsequently conducted to a dépôt." Chang Shêng (張 生) deposes, "after I had served "for four years, the plantation was set on fire by the insurgents. I ran away, was arrested and "placed in jail."

Thus, the probability is that the Chinese are unwilling to take part in aiding the insurrection; minute details could only be ascertained by reference to sources of information,—the camps of the insurgents,—which could not be reached.

XXXV

HAS COOLIE LEGISLATION IN CUBA BEEN AFFECTED BY THE REBELLION? HOW DOES IT, AS THEREBY AFFECTED, AFFECT CONTRACT COOLIES, AND WHY? IF A TEMPORARY PRECAUTION MERELY, HAS THE GOVERNMENT HAD JUST CAUSE TO TAKE THE PRECAUTION, OR IS ITS ACTION SIMPLE AND INDEFENSIBLE TYRANNY? TO WHAT EXTENT IS SUCH SPECIAL LEGISLATION IN OPERATION, AND WHAT DO THE BETTER CLASS—*e.g.*, THE MONEYED CHINESE IN THE CITIES—SAY OF IT?

No changes proposed or effected in the system of Government applied to the Chinese, have been explicitly admitted to have been the result of the insurrection, with the exception of the cessation of the introduction, which was recommended in 1870 on the plea that they impeded the pacification of the island; and in the following year the suggestion was withdrawn, as "owing "to the progress effected in the pacification of the island, measures formerly desirable had become "needless." The Rules of September 1872, devised by the Central Commission with the sole object of retaining Chinese in Cuba and inducing them to renew their engagements, contain no provision indicating any apprehension of participation by them in the insurrection, and the fact derived from the Tables of the same Commission, that out of 1,932 labourers despatched to the Trocha—the point the closest in proximity to the insurgent districts—1,827 were Chinese, is clear evidence that no precautions in regard to them were deemed necessary. Moreover, if their presence called for such precautions, why do the proprietors of the island still desire to bring them to it in large numbers? It is thus apparent that no such suspicions are entertained in regard to them.

In Cuba there exists no better class of Chinese; all receive the treatment of slaves, and however much legislation may degenerate "into simple and indefensible tyranny," protest is impossible, and, deprived of every means of escape, the men who have completed the years of service for which they contracted, as well as those who have not, have simply to submit. Avarice induces the merchants and planters to disregard such provisions as were framed for the protection of the Chinese, and a similar cause induces the guards and police not to overlook the enforcement of a single clause of those of the opposite nature. Such a clause is the 16th Article of the Rules of 1868, defining the manner of registration of domiciled Chinese. It is to the effect that during the second fortnight of February, the deputed officers shall visit their residences, and shall personally inspect and call for the production of their Letters of Domicile and Cedulas, and that the former documents shall be retained by the inspecting officers, and the latter returned to the holders, sealed and endorsed "Registered." The Decree of the Captain General dated December 1871 contains similar instructions; the officers designated are to direct one or more of their subordinates, accompanied by the residents in the vicinity, to visit the dwellings of, and personally inspect the Chinese in question; the Letters of Domicile and Cedulas of the latter are to be examined with the most scrupulous care and the descriptions of personal appearance which they contain are to be compared with the actual appearance of the holders; and the adoption is authorized and enjoined of every precaution that may appear necessary in order to ascertain the genuineness of each document, &c. This system of inquisition, producing a perpetual dread, is applied not only to those who, because they failed to obtain certificates of completion, or because they arrived after February 1861, never received cedulas, but to the men who years ago enjoyed the good fortune of securing freedmen's papers.

The petition of Chien Shih-kuang (簡 仕 光) and 96 others states, "the police, knife in " hand, burst open our doors, search our chests and boxes, and take away whatever of value they " see. We may call in vain for any aid from our neighbours, and if we attempt resistance we are " at once charged with crime and conveyed to prison," and ("in the 10th year of T'UNGCHIH the " planters and corrupt officials") "marshalled troops and effected a general seizure of Chinese, " depriving us of our freedmen's papers, and placing us all in jail." The petition of T'ang Lien-shêng (唐 聯 陞) and 106 others states, "if the applicant succeeded in obtaining a Letter of " Domicile, and intended to remain in the island, he had to procure an additional document, a " cedula which cost ten dollars more or less, which has to be changed annually, and of which the " loss or delay in renewal provokes severe penalties. Again, a journey from one town to another " necessitates a pass, and a physician cannot practice, or a beggar ask for food, without a similar " document, the issue in each case requiring the payment of a fee, whilst application for authori-" zation to open a shop of any class involves greater delay and larger outlay. When these " documents have been received the inspection of them is constantly demanded by any guard " whom we may meet, or by the police who search our houses; the papers are then alleged to be " fictitious, and are torn up and we are dragged away to prison or to the dépôt. We there are " laden with chains on the neck and feet, and compelled to labour on Government works." The petition of Chu Chi-hsün (朱 箕 訓) and 10 others states, "the police and guards day and " night enter our houses and accuse us of opium smoking or of possessing no papers, whilst their " real object is the robbery of our money and our property. Whether we hold papers or not we

" are dragged away to officials or to a dépôt to work on roads, and are subsequently fined $ 10 to
" $ 20 and are not released until we can induce a foreigner to become bail." The petition of
Chao K'un (趙 昆) and 97 others states, "the police and various official underlings, constantly
" in search of gain, feed upon us more ravenously than a silkworm does on leaves; they
" constantly enter our apartments, search over our beds, accuse us of a breach of law, basing
" the charge on the possession of any article on which they lay their hands, and then rob us of
" all we have, furniture or money." Têng A-ssŭ (鄧 阿 四) declares in his petition, "in October
" last year, I was employed on a sugar plantation, when the guards visited it and accused me of
" having forged my papers, and, alleging that I had not completed my term, conducted me before
" the authorities. I was placed in jail, and was deprived of all I had on me, worth about $ 70;
" besides, $ 200 in paper, and two horses belonging to me were taken away by the officials." The
petition of Tai Jih-shêng (戴 日 生) and 1 other states, "in cities, too, our countrymen are
" exposed to the exactions of the police. Those who do not hold papers are arrested and must
" yield to extortion, whilst even the possessors of them are subjected to penalties." Ho Fu-t'ang
(何 福 堂) declares in his petition, "I find all my movements restricted, as on the railways we are
" asked to produce our cedulas and if unable to do so are arrested and punished." Yü A-hsia
(余 阿 洽) declares in his petition, "those who formerly obtained cedulas dare not go beyond the
" limits of this city lest they be arrested by the foreign guards." Fan Tsu-hsing (范 足 興)
declares in his petition, "when one of us possessing a cedula and a little money prepares to
" return to China, the circumstance is soon discovered by the police and other small officials, and
" his papers are seized and torn up, and he himself is accused of being a deserter. He is tied up
" and tortured, robbed of his money and effects, and if he tries to offer any protest or explanation
" is severely beaten. Many have been thus killed."

XXXVI.

WHAT IS THE HEALTH OF THE COOLIE?

It may be admitted that the greater portion of the Chinese employed as cooks and
domestic servants received sufficient food, and are comparatively physically vigorous; but in the
larger number of instances the men seen on the plantations and in the dépôts showed, in their
features and their spiritless demeanour, the privations and hardships which they were enduring;
and not a few of those who now gain their living independently, still suffer from maladies, the
result of their years of exhausting suffering.

The petition of Chien Shih-kuang (簡 仕 光) and 96 others states, "we see almost half of
" our companions die, and we who survive are either mutilated or internally injured." Lin A-i
(林 阿 亦) deposes, "my chest was injured by blows on the plantation, and I still suffer
" constantly from the pain." Kuo A-jung (郭 阿 榮) deposes, "the administrator and the over-
" seer constantly dealt me thrusts with sticks, or kicked me, and I now still suffer from internal
" bleeding." Lü A-wu (呂 阿 武) deposes, "the master directed negroes to hold me down and
" dealt me more than 80 blows with a rattan rod, and inflicted injuries which caused me to vomit

"blood and from this malady I am still suffering." Ch'ên A-shun (陳 阿 順) and Yang Chin (楊 錦) depose that on the plantation they were injured by blows and that they still vomit blood. Huang A-chang (黃 阿 章) declares that he suffers from a similar malady; and Ch'ên A-yang (陳 阿 養) deposes, "a few days after my arrival, I received such blows and thrusts from "sticks that I still constantly vomit blood." Chu K'ai-tzŭ (朱 開 自) deposes, "I was allowed "no bed and compelled to sleep on the ground, and the humidity having induced a disease of "the back I am now forced to beg for food." Shên A-ts'ai (沈 阿 才) and one other depose, "when I arrived I possessed strength, but I have been so constantly beaten that I am now "entirely debilitated." Hu Kêng-hsiu (胡 庚 秀) deposes, "my health has been entirely "destroyed by the hardships I endured on the plantation." Wêng A-i (翁 阿 宜) deposes, "I suffer "from rheumatism in my feet and hands, and the malady is the result of the labour imposed "upon me." P'an Yo-hêng (潘 岳 衡) deposes, "my foot is diseased, the result of wounds "caused by chains." Lin A-mei (林 阿 美) deposes, "my left foot is diseased, the result of an "accident when at the Trocha. Maimed as I am, I am still compelled to labour." P'ang A-tien (龐 阿 電) deposes, "the wounds I received have maimed me for life." Liu Kuang-ts'ai (劉 光 采) deposes, "I was decoyed here and wept every day, and to this and to bad treatment I attribute "the disease of my eyes." Hu A-t'ai (胡 阿 泰) deposes, "I received internal injuries from the "flogging with sticks, and I am now constantly sick."

XXXVII.

How are the sick cared for?

Many of the hospitals existing in each Cuban city possess extensive accommodation, are arranged not without a regard to elegance, and are surrounded by, or surround gardens and shrubberies, are completely fitted with bedding and other appointments, and are well provided with attendants, and although not specially constructed for Chinese, the latter enjoy in them all the advantage that they afford.

The infirmaries on the plantations are also clean, and are, in some cases, under the care of surgeons, but according to the statements collected by the Commission the proportion of Chinese permitted to enter them is small.

The petition of Lai Chih-chih (賴 質 直) and 3 others states, "if we are sick and cannot "work we are beaten." Li Ying-sung (李 英 松) states in his petition, "I was, if sick, struck with "the closed fist, kicked, or even when greater severity was displayed stabbed or flogged almost "to death." Ch'ên Tê-ming (陳 德 明) declares in his petition, "if sick, we were not allowed to "rest in the hospital, and when we applied for admission we were beaten, chains were placed on "our feet, and our wages were withheld." To the same effect are the following extracts from depositions. Lin Lung (林 龍) and 17 others declare that when ill they were not permitted to report themselves sick; Liao Ying (廖 應) and 15 others declare that they were flogged for reporting themselves sick; Yang Chin (楊 錦) and 9 others declare that they were not permitted to report themselves sick, and that if they did so, their feet were chained; Chou Liu (周 六)

and 2 others declare that, when sick, they were not allowed to enter the infirmary, that they were chained, beaten and forced to continue labour; Ch'ien A-jung (錢阿榮) deposes, "when ill I was not allowed to cease labour; I was beaten and forced to resume "work." Ts'ui An (崔安) deposes, "for reporting myself sick, I was twice chained "and beaten." Ch'ên A-jung (陳阿榮) deposes, "during three years my eyes were diseased, "but I was never permitted to report myself sick." 'Han Chin (韓錦) deposes, "several "times when reporting sick, I was placed in irons and beaten. Once I was flogged so severely "that I vomited blood, and I was besides kept in chains during seven months." Li A-lai (李阿來) deposes, "when I reported myself sick I was constantly beaten. I was accused of "pretending to be ill." Ch'ü Tan-k'o (屈且亮) deposes, "labourers who reported themselves "sick on account of sores on the feet were told by the master that such ailments could not be "regarded as sickness, and he also, seizing a stick, beat them indiscriminately." Ch'ên A-chin (陳阿金) deposes, "when I was sick and reported the fact to the overseer he accused me of "speaking falsely, and ordering four men to hold me down removed my trowsers, and flogged me "so severely that my flesh became lacerated. I then had to labour in irons, and at night, when "I returned, my wounds were rubbed with salt and lime-juice, causing a pain that almost killed "me." Li A-'hui (李阿會) deposes, "when, on the plantation, I was incapacitated for work "by sickness, four negroes were directed to hold me prostrate, whilst I was being flogged on my "naked person. Afterwards when ill in the Dépôt my elbow was broken by an overseer." Chou A-ting (周阿丁) deposes, "two men who suffered from sores on the head and were inca- "pacitated for severe labour asked to be permitted to perform a lighter class of work, and for so "doing the administrator chained their feet and beat them almost the death." Hsieh A-hsüan (謝阿選) deposes, "I have seen men flogged, forced to work in chains during the day and "placed in prison for reporting themselves sick; others too, natives of Tungkwan (東莞), I "saw who, having been flogged for reporting themselves sick, hanged themselves through fear "of being confined in the stocks." Wu Lien-shêng (吳聯勝) deposes, "I saw a sick man "who was unable to go out to labour, killed by the overseer." Huang A-tou (黃阿斗) deposes, "I saw a native of Hiangshan (香山), who had been severely beaten by the administrator "for reporting himself sick, hang himself on the same evening; I also was the witness of "the murder of a native of Hunan (湖南), by name Li (李), who had been flogged for "reporting himself sick. I saw, too, the suicide by drowning of a man named Chêng (鄭) who "when sick had been dragged out and flogged; and I know that two men, one a native of "Swatow, the other a native of Kwangtung, died in the infirmary from starvation." Wang A-shêng (王阿盛) deposes, "when repairing a cart-road my leg was fractured, and the surgeon "found it necessary to furnish me with a wooden limb. The master relieved me from all severe "labour but the administrator on one occasion ordered me to move some heavy stones, and as I "was unable to do so broke my wooden leg, and also, by a blow, removed a portion of my ear." Liang A-jên (梁阿壬) deposes, "when on the plantation we reported ourselves sick, a negress "was told to make water, and if we consented to drink it our statement was admitted, but if we "refused we were compelled to continue labour." Ch'ên A-fu (陳阿福) deposes, "one of my "arms was broken by the injury. The fracture was cured, but I was punished by the deduction "of nine months' wages." Li Cho (李卓) deposes, "for reporting myself sick the administrato "beat me, and chained my feet during three days, and withheld from me wages during eight "months." Huang A-man (黃 阿 滿) deposes, "when sick the surgeon incited the dogs to bite, "and beat us with rods." Yü A-t'ien (余 阿 田) deposes, "when so seriously sick that I was "unable to move, the surgeon in the first instance beat me before admitting me into the "hospital." Liu A-yao (劉 阿 耀) deposes, "when sick I was locked up in the infirmary, and "sometimes during a few days received no food whatever; but the surgeon never visited me." Yüan A-an (袁 阿 安) deposes, "when so sick that I vomited blood, the surgeon would not admit "me into the hospital." Kao A-tai (高 阿 代) deposes, "when I was sick, I received no medical "care."

XXXVIII.

WHAT IS THE RATE OF MORTALITY?

The census effected under the supervision of the Central Commission of Colonization applies to a period commencing in the 6th moon of the 27th year of TAOKWANG and terminating at the 7th moon of the 11th year of T'UNGCHIH. The statistics show that during five years of this period —from the 28th year of TAOKWANG until the 2nd year of HIENFÊNG inclusive—no vessels conveying Chinese reached the island, and that during the 20 remaining years 114,081 landed, of whom, on the completion of the census, there remained 58,400.

Another Table prepared by the Commission shows the departure during 1872 and the first nine months of 1873 of 235 Chinese, being an annual average of 134. Assuming—to aid the calculation—that 571, the number arrived in the reign of TAOKWANG, were all enabled to leave, and bearing in mind that the departure of any men comprehended in even the first subsequent importations—those of the 3rd year of HIENFÊNG—could not commence before the 11th year of HIENFÊNG—producing at the above average, a total of departures for that and the eleven following years, of 1,608,—the entire number departed amounts to 2,179; and a deduction of these and of the surviving population shows that the deaths reached the aggregate of 53,502, in which, also, are not comprised the deaths during the voyages, which up to the same date—T'UNGCHIH 11th year 7th moon—exceeded 15,000. All these, too, were young men, and their fates certainly merit compassion.

The facts of the Tables of the Central Commission only specifying the population surviving in the 11th year, and of no information being attainable, as to that successively existing at the end of each of the antecedent ones, and as to the augmentation effected during each, preclude any minute reply to the query.

XXXIX.

WHAT HAVE BEEN THE CAUSES OF DEATH?

The excessive heat of the climate, the severity of the labour, and the scantiness of the food, have been the causes of a great mortality, through sickness; but the deaths from other causes have likewise been numerous. Yüan Kuan (袁 觀) states in his petition, "the new

" administrator was cruel as a wolf or a tiger and his heart was as venomous as that of a snake.
" A certain Ch'ên A-tsao (陳阿灶) not being able to endure the ill-treatment jumped into a sugar
" caldron; Lien A-hsing (連阿興) suffering from a bad leg and unable to work, on being forced
" to labour hanged himself; Liu Pai-jên (劉百忍) was flogged by the administrator till he spat
" blood and died; Hung A-fu (洪阿富), being unable to do the work allotted to him, ran away,
" was brought back and at night was killed by the administrator; Chang A-ping (張阿丙), being
" sick and unable to work, poisoned himself; Chou Shih-lan (周石蘭), 15 days after arrival, was
" flogged by the administrator so severely that he died." Lin A-yu (林阿有) deposes, "last
" year, Tsêng A-chi (曾阿基) was murdered, a crime for which no punishment could be
" obtained." Ch'ên A-chi (陳阿吉) deposes, "on the plantation I saw three men commit
" suicide, on account of a severe flogging which had been inflicted on them." Ch'ên Lin (陳林)
deposes, "of ten men who were with me three killed themselves by hanging." Chou Liu (周六)
deposes, "on the plantation ten men hanged themselves." Wên Ch'ang-t'ai (文長泰) deposes,
" I saw nine men hang themselves, one man throw himself into a sugar caldron, and 12
" men die from the results of wounds—these festered and bred maggots." Ho Hsi (何錫)
" deposes, "with me were 20 men; of these two hanged themselves, and four cast themselves
" into a well." Liang En (梁恩) deposes, "with me were 15; of these four hanged them-
" selves, one named Liang Pai-shêng (梁百勝) after being wounded on the head and body
" by the administrator, was attached by the latter to his horse's tail and dragged back to the
" quarters. He proved to be then dead, and his body was cast upon the dung-hill." Ch'ên
" A-ying (陳阿應) deposes, "I have seen many hang themselves. In the boiling house I
" have seen two who hanged themselves by one rope—others I saw who had died in a similar
" manner in the privies and dormitories." Jung A-ts'ai (容阿彩) deposes, "a man who ran
" away and was captured was beaten by the administrator with a thick stick so severely that he
" died." Wên A-chao (溫阿照) deposes, "I saw a man named A-lai (阿來) killed through
" blows inflicted with a stick and a knife when in chains; I saw also another named A-san (阿三)
" hang himself." Fêng A-hsiu (馮阿秀) deposes, "I saw five men hang themselves." Wu
A-ch'ing (吳阿清) deposes, "of 50 men who were with me, only 25 survive. There were
" suicides by drowning, hanging and cutting of the throat." Li Hui (李惠) deposes, "I saw two
" Shuntêh (順德) men, by name Ch'ên (陳) and Liang (梁), who found the chastisements unendur-
" able, poison themselves with opium. I saw also a Hakka hang himself." Lo A-fa (羅阿發)
deposes, "I saw the administrator strike two men dead with a knife, and I also saw two men
" who found the ill-treatment unendurable, hang themselves." Li Cho (李卓) deposes, "at the
" end of the eight years I had seen six or seven men killed by violence, 13 men hang themselves,
" and three men poison themselves." Lin A-i (林阿亦) deposes, "with me were 20 men, of
" whom, finding the ill usage unendurable, two poisoned themselves, five hanged themselves and
" four cut their throats." Lo A-ch'ang (羅阿昌) deposes, "with me were 24 men, of whom two
" hanged themselves." Lin A-t'ai (林阿泰) deposes, "I saw four men hang themselves to-
" gether, of whom two died. The cause was that they found the ill-treatment unendurable."
Liang A-lin (梁阿林) deposes, "I saw three men hang themselves, ten die from wounds and
" four poison themselves with opium." Wên Man (溫滿) deposes, "I saw on the plantation the
" suicide of two men by hanging; one was named A-ch'ih (阿遲) and the other A-kuan (阿官).

"Both killed themselves on account of finding the ill usage unendurable." Ch'ên A-yang (陳 阿 羕) deposes, "I saw a Cantonese, by name A-lu (阿 陸), cut his throat in the plantation "jail, and I saw another Cantonese hang himself." Lo A-chi (羅 阿 紀) deposes, "with me were "80 men; within a few years four hanged themselves, three poisoned themselves with opium, and "the master reported all the deaths to the officials as the results of sickness." Ch'ên Chün-k'ai (陳 均 開) deposes, "I witnessed the suicide by drowning of Yeh A-ts'ai (葉 阿 才)." Li Wên-ts'ai (李 文 財) deposes, "on the plantation I saw two men hang themselves, three men throw "themselves into wells, and other three poison themselves with opium. I also saw two "others who were sick, and were flogged in order to force them to work, die on the spot." Jung Chou-kuan (容 周 寬) deposes, "I saw a man hang himself, on account of inability to "endure the ill usage." Wu Chin-kuei (武 進 貴) and two others depose that they saw two men die from thrusts with a stick, and other two from the effects of wounds inflicted. Ts'ai A-ping (蔡 阿 丙) deposes, "I saw four men hang themselves, unable to endure the ill usage, one jump "into a well, and three die whilst in chains from wounds." Chang A-hsi (張 阿 喜) deposes, "I saw a native of Shuntêh (順 德), by name Huang (黃), hang himself after the administrator had "beaten him with such severity that his legs were lacerated." Li Yu (李 有) deposes, "I saw a "native of the Hwa (花) district, by name A-kuei (阿 桂), hang himself, because he found the "treatment unendurable, and the food insufficient." Li Ho (李 河) deposes, "I saw a native of "the Sinhwei (新 會) district, by name Ch'ên A-kuang (陳 阿 光), 20 years old, hang himself on "account of finding the chastisements unendurable. I saw also two other men, natives of the "same place, Li A-wei (李 阿 魏) and Ch'ên A-chên (陳 阿 振), commit suicide in a similar "manner." Shih A-kou (石 阿 狗) deposes, "I saw four men who found the usage unendurable "hang themselves. They did so on one cord." Ch'ên A-shun (陳 阿 順) deposes, "I saw three "Chinese killed by violence on the plantation. No report was made to the officials. The bodies "were buried; and the matter was ended. I also saw four men hang themselves when wounded, "owing to the usage being unendurable." Lin A-pang (林 阿 榜) deposes, "I have seen some "20 men commit suicide by hanging themselves and by jumping into wells and sugar caldrons." Liang A-jên (梁 阿 壬) deposes, "I saw the suicide by hanging of one man, who found the usage "unendurable." Ch'ên A-yin (陳 阿 音) deposes, "I saw the suicide by taking opium of Huang "A-fa (黃 阿 發), who had been so severely wounded that he was incapacitated from labour. I "saw the death by hanging of a Tungkwan (東 莞) man, named A-ho (阿 和), who had been "wounded by blows." Ch'ên Shui (陳 水) deposes, "I saw on the plantation one man jump "into a well, and one man hang himself." Yu A-shih (游 阿 式) deposes, "with me were "16 men, of whom eight are already dead." Ho A-chi (何 阿 基) deposes, "I saw a man "who being sick had been refused permission to rest, attempt to hang himself, and after "being rescued jump into a well." Su A-fa (蘇 阿 發) deposes, "on the plantation I saw "three men flogged in such a manner that on the following day they were dead." Ch'ên A-shun (陳 阿 順) deposes, "on the plantation one man was killed by a blow from a knife, "dealt by the manager of the plantation shop; the latter was not arrested. Other two died "from the effects of blows dealt by the administrator, but as the latter presented the officials "with money no proceedings were taken." Ch'ên A-êrh (陳 阿 二) deposes, "on the plantation "I saw eight men drown themselves and four men hang themselves, owing to their finding the

" labour and the chastisement unendurable."   Ch'ên A-pao (陳 阿 保) deposes, "on the plantation
" two Cantonese who could not endure the chastisement hanged themselves, and of 31 of my
" gang, two hanged themselves, and three swallowed opium, owing to their finding the ill
" treatment unendurable."   Li Shun (黎 順) deposes, "one of the men with me, a native of
" Hweichow (惠 州) killed himself on account of the cruelty."   Han Yen-p'ei (韓 炎 培) deposes,
" of 50 men with me three drowned themselves and two hanged themselves, on account of finding
" the cruelty unendurable, and 13 died from the effects of wounds."   Ch'ên Chung-hsiu (陳 忠 秀)
deposes, "with me were 22 others, of whom two hanged themselves, and two poisoned themselves
" with opium, owing to finding the cruelty unendurable.   Besides four died from the effects of
" wounds."   Yang Shih-fêng (楊 石 鳳) deposes, "with me was a native of Polo (博 羅), by
" name Hsien Shih (洗 士); he was so wounded by blows that the pain was unendurable.   The
" surgeon gave him some aperient medicine, which he vomited, and he afterwards hanged
" himself.   A native of Kweishan (歸 善), by name Ch'ên A-ts'ai (陳 阿 才), after being flogged,
" was ironed on both feet and forced to work, and fell into a lime-pit, in which he died.   The
" deaths from wounds and in the hospital, of which I have been a witness, have exceeded 100."
Li Hsin (黎 信) deposes, "I saw a native of Hweichow (惠 州), by name Lin A-ssŭ (林 阿 四), hang
" himself, being unable to endure the pain resulting from a flogging.   The 20 men of the same
" gang laid a charge before the officials, but the latter gave no heed to the complaint; and the
" master having brought them back, placed them in irons, so that the accusation could not be
" renewed."   Li A-wu (李 阿 伍) deposes, "I saw three men drown themselves, and five hang
" themselves, on account of the cruelties to which they were being subjected."   Chêng A-chu
(鄭 阿 柱) deposes, "I saw Li A-san (李 阿 三) killed by blows because being sick he was unable
" to move certain bundles of cane.   I also saw two men hang themselves, and one man jump into
" a well."   Huang A-yung (黃 阿 榕) deposes, "on the plantation, I saw Ch'ên A-kou (陳 阿 狗)
" and Hsien Yü-tsai (鹹 魚 仔) hang themselves, being unable to support the chastisement.   One
" hanged himself on a tree, the other in the dormitory."   Chiang A-lin (姜 阿 麟) deposes, "I saw
" one Cantonese hang himself, and four men poison themselves with opium."   Yu A-ssŭ
(游 阿 四) deposes, "I saw one of my gang, a native of Fukien, by name Ch'ên A-kou (陳 阿 狗),
" so beaten with a stick, for weakness in the legs, that he died in seven days.   I also saw the suicide
" by hanging of three natives of Nanhai (南 海)."   Liu A-jui (劉 阿 瑞) deposes, "I saw two
" men hang themselves."   Ch'ên I (陳 翼) deposes, "I saw three men hang themselves and one
" drown himself."   Chêng A-t'u (鄭 阿 土) deposes, "I saw ten men so wounded by blows that
" in a few days they died, and other four who were unable to endure the cruelty hang them-
" selves."   Liang A-hsin (梁 阿 新) deposes, "on the plantation, I saw three men who were
" unable to endure the cruelty cut their throats."   Chang Erh (張 二) deposes, "of those with me,
" two drowned themselves and three swallowed opium."   T'an Yu (譚 友) deposes, "I saw a
" native of Sinning (新 甯), by name Huang A-yang (黃 阿 羕), killed by blows dealt by the
" administrator."   Wu A-i (吳 阿 義) deposes, "on the plantation I saw one man drown himself,
" three men poison themselves with opium and one man hang himself."   Liu A-ssŭ (劉 阿 四)
deposes, "I saw the death in the infirmary of ten men, who had been wounded; it took place
" within one or two days after infliction of the blows.   I also saw the suicide of a native of
" Fukien, who was driven to the act by the cruelty."   Sun Kuan-fu (孫 觀 福) deposes, "of those

"with me, two hanged themselves and one poisoned himself with opium. They did so because "they found the cruelty unendurable." Yeh A-san (葉阿三) deposes, "I saw a Cantonese "poison himself with opium." Ho A-pa (何阿八) deposes, "I saw the master kick, so "that he died, a man who reported himself sick and whose statement was not accepted. "The matter was in no way investigated by the officials." Liu A-ch'ang (劉阿長) deposes, "I saw a Cantonese hang himself on account of the cruelty. No enquiry was made by "the officials." Lin A-mei (林阿美) deposes, "I saw three Cantonese hang themselves." T'ang Chan-k'uei (唐占魁) deposes, "of those with me in the bakery, one man unable to "endure the blows hanged himself." Lo Yung-shêng (駱永勝) deposes, "during the eight "years I saw a Cantonese throw himself into a well, a Fukienese throw himself into a sugar "caldron, and a native of Swatow cut his throat. Besides eight Cantonese hanged themselves." Ch'ên A-'huan (陳阿煥) deposes, "with me were 100 men, of whom 50 hanged themselves." Ch'ên A-fu (陳阿福) deposes, "with me were 25, of whom three hanged themselves." Yü Ming-hsing (余名興) deposes, "I saw two men cut their throats? One was named A-k'ai (阿開) "and the other Chiu Chio-chih (九角紙), but the wounds were afterwards healed. I also saw "three men hang themselves, and one man kill himself by wounds inflicted on his private parts." Huang A-ying (黃阿英) deposes, "I saw one man, a native of Kaochow (高州), hang himself." Lu Chung (盧鍾) deposes, "of those with me, one threw himself into a well, and two poisoned "themselves with opium." Wang Tzŭ (王滋) deposes, "I saw two men commit suicide." Ch'iu Yüan (邱元) deposes, "of 20 men with me, three committed suicide." Ch'ên Han-pin (陳漢彬) deposes, "of those with me two committed suicide, and one was killed by the administrator by a "blow from a knife." Han Chin (韓錦) deposes, "with me were 30 others, of whom, in the eight "years, two hanged themselves, two drowned themselves, and one poisoned himself with opium." Li Pan-chang (李班章) deposes, "I saw two men commit suicide by hanging, and one man drown "himself." Liang A-yin (梁阿陰) deposes, "of those with me, eight hanged themselves, and two "drowned themselves." Li A-ta (黎阿達) deposes, "of those with me, one man after having been "wounded by blows, entered the infirmary, and died there in one day." Li A-'hung (李阿鴻) deposes, "I myself saw one man killed by blows." Liang Tao-'han (梁道漢) deposes, "of 12 with "me, two poisoned themselves and one hanged himself." Li Yu (李游) deposes, "I saw 20 men "commit suicide." Kuo Ching-fang (郭景芳) deposes, "I saw two men poison themselves with "opium, and three hang themselves." Li A-fu (李阿福) deposes, "I saw four men hang them- "selves on account of being flogged with severity." Tsêng A-shih (曾阿十) deposes, "I saw a "native of Nanhai (南海) killed by blows. He vomited blood, but the chastisement was not "stopped." Ch'ên Tê-chêng (陳得正) deposes, "I saw five men hang themselves." Chêng Chiu (鄭九) and 14 others depose, "I saw Li A-êrh (李阿二) struck, fall into the water, and "in it die by drowning." Ho Ch'iu-shih (何秋史) deposes, "I saw two men cut their throats; "one died and the other was cured." Huang A-chang (黃阿章) deposes, "I saw two men who "had been wounded by blows dealt by the administrator removed to the infirmary, in "which they died on the next day. I also saw six poison themselves with opium, and three "hang themselves." Wang T'ing-kuei (王廷貴) deposes, "of those with me five hanged them- "selves." Chu Ts'un-fang (朱村房) deposes, "my brother, by name Chu Mei-hsiang (朱梅香), "placed on a waggon a smaller than ordinary quantity of sugar-cane, and in reply to an overseer

' explained that the oxen were thin, and not able to move a heavier load. The overseer became
" very angry, said he would not permit Chinese to argue with him, and seizing a stick, inflicted
" heavy blows. This occurred about 4 P.M. and at 6 P.M. my brother was dead. I also saw six
" men hang themselves." Ssŭ T'u-hsing (司徒性) deposes, " of 43 with me, 29 committed
" suicide." Liao A-ping (廖阿餅) deposes, " I saw four men hang themselves and one man
" drown himself." Li Jun (李聞) deposes, " I saw four men struck dead by the master, who
" suspected them of mutiny. I also saw a Hakka, by name Lin Ch'iao (林橋), drown himself."
Tsêng A-yang (曾阿養) deposes, " I saw a native of Hweilai (惠來), named Li Lien-hsiu
" (李聯秀), poison himself with opium as he was unable to endure the chaining and flogging."
Pai Mien (白棉) deposes, " of ten men with me, one poisoned himself with opium." Wu I
(吳義) deposes, " I saw ten men hang themselves." Yeh Ch'üan (葉全) deposes, " I saw
" a native of Tungkwan (東莞) poison himself with opium." Yu A-chü (游阿巨) deposes,
" I saw three men poison themselves with opium, and two men hang themselves through
" being unable to endure the cruelty." Ho A-ch'iu (何阿求) deposes, " of those with me
" one man poisoned himself with opium." Li A-lai (李阿來) deposes, " two men who had
" been beaten severely died from the effects." Ch'iu Mu (邱木) deposes, " I saw two men
" hang themselves." Li Chia (李嘉) deposes, " I saw three men hang themselves, and five
" men poison themselves with opium." Liang A-k'o (梁阿売) deposes, " I saw three men
" hang themselves, and three men poison themselves with opium. Last year, in the second
" month, the administrator struck dead three men by blows from a stick." Ch'ên A-ch'ing
(陳阿慶) deposes, " I saw two men cut their throats, two men die from the effects of wounds
" inflicted two days before, and two men hang themselves. No official came to enquire into
" the matter. We were not able to leave the plantation, and did not know where any officials
" were to be found." Chang A-chao (張阿照) deposes, " A man with me, a native of Ho-
" yüen (河源), by name Wên T'ing-jang (溫廷讓), unable to endure the chastisements,
" poisoned himself with opium." Lin A-kuei (林阿貴) deposes, " I saw three men hang them-
" selves, three poison themselves with opium, and six die from the effects of blows, one or two days
" after their infliction." Yeh Ying-pao (葉應寶) deposes, " I saw one man poison himself with
" opium and one man drown himself." Li K'un (李昆) deposes, " a man with me, by name
" A-yü (阿遇), unable to endure the chastisements drowned himself." Wên A-lai (文阿來)
deposes, " of ten men with me, one drowned himself, and three hanged themselves." Liang A-lien
(梁阿連) deposes, " of those with me, one hanged himself and three poisoned themselves with
" opium." Lo A-tê (羅阿德) deposes, " I saw the master of the plantation kill one man by blows."
Chên A-hung (陳阿洪) deposes, " of 13 men with me, seven were killed by blows." Têng A-mu
(鄧阿木) deposes, " of three men who came with me, one, a native of Hoshan (鶴山), by name
" Huang A-liu (黃阿六), and another named Wu A-chiu (伍阿九), poisoned themselves with
" opium." Yüan A-ts'ung (阮阿聰) deposes, " of those with me two, unable to endure the
' chastisements, jumped into a well." Wang Ta-ch'êng (王大誠) deposes, " I saw a man killed by
' blows on the plantation." Tsou A-êrh (鄒阿二) deposes, " of ten men with me, one man
" drowned himself, and three died from the effects of wounds caused by blows." Chung A-tai
(鍾阿代) deposes, " I saw three men hang themselves who were unable to endure the chastise-
" ment." Liang A-san (梁阿三) deposes, " I saw a man by name Hu (胡), unable to endure

"the chastisement, hang himself." Li Shun (李 順) deposes, "of those with me, I saw 11 commit "suicide." Ho P'ei-ch'i (何 沛 麒) deposes, "I saw one man hang himself, one man leap into "a well, and another, an old weak man who had allowed a certain field implement to fall into a "pool, killed by blows dealt by the administrator." P'ang A-tung (龐 阿 東) deposes, "of those "with me, one hanged himself, and another died from the effects of a severe flogging." Lai Ying-lai (賴 英 來) deposes, "I saw three poison themselves with opium, and two men drown "themselves." Chang Hui (張 會) deposes, "I saw two men hang themselves, and one man "poison himself with opium." Huang A-hsing (黃 阿 杏) deposes, "of 40 men with me, three were "so severely beaten that one died on the spot, and the two others afterwards, in the infirmary." T'ang Shih-chu (唐 石 柱) and 1 other depose, that on the premises of the Railway by which they were employed they saw two men poison themselves with opium, and one man hang himself—the suicides being due to their inability to support the ill usage. Ho A-wei (何 阿 魏) and 1 other depose, that they saw two men poison themselves with opium. Liu Wu (劉 五) deposes, "I saw three men "hang themselves, one man poison himself with opium, and a third, who had been beaten by an "overseer, jump into a well." Li Shan (李 山) deposes, "I saw three men poison themselves with "opium, and other three hang themselves." Wu A-yao (伍 阿 耀) deposes, "of 20 men with me, "three poisoned themselves with opium." Chu A-fu (朱 阿 福) deposes, "I saw a native of "Hiangshan (香 山), by name Ch'ên A-wang (陳 阿 旺), so severely beaten that he drowned "himself. Besides there were other seven who committed suicide." Kuang K'uan (鄺 寬) deposes, "on the plantation three men hanged themselves, and three men poisoned themselves with "opium." Wang Ching (王 敬) deposes, "I saw three men drown themselves." Ch'ên Yu (陳 有) deposes, "I saw two men hang themselves, and three men drown themselves, on account of their "being unable to endure the cruelty." Têng Shêng (鄧 勝) deposes, "I saw six men poison "themselves with opium." Li Ts'ai (李 才) deposes, "of those with me one man hanged himself "on account of having been severely beaten by the overseer." Chung Lai (鍾 來) deposes, "an "old man who could not move a heavy weight was killed by blows dealt by an overseer." Liu A-shih (劉 阿 石) deposes, "a native of Hweichow (惠 州), by name Chu A-mu (朱 阿 木), was so "severely chastised by an overseer that he drowned himself." Huang Hsing (黃 興) deposes, "I saw three newly arrived Chinese killed by blows from the overseer, who declared that they "could neither speak nor work." Lin Tzŭ-yu (林 滋 有) deposes, "I saw a native of "Yangkiang (陽 江) hang himself with a handkerchief, being unable to endure the hard-"ship." Liang A-shêng (梁 阿 盛) deposes, "I saw a Cantonese, by name Li (李), hang himself "because he had been chained and confined in the prison though guilty of no offence." Liang A-shêng (梁 阿 盛) deposes, "I saw a Cantonese, by name Ch'ên A-kuang (陳 阿 光), hang himself "when wearing chains, through inability to endure the ill treatment." Huang A-t'i (黃 阿 體) deposes, "I saw three men wounded by blows and removed to the infirmary; in it they died "on the following day." Huang A-ch'ang (黃 阿 昌) deposes, "I saw Wang A-kuang (王 阿 光) "hang himself after having been ironed and severely beaten." Ch'ên A-hung (陳 阿 紅) and 3 others depose, "I saw a man named A-chi (阿 紀) so severely struck on the neck "by the negro overseer that he died in three days." Chou A-hsing (周 阿 興) deposes, "I saw a "native of Hweichow (惠 州), by name Chang (張), poison himself with opium, through inability "to endure the ill treatment." Chiang Li-shih (蔣 禮 實) deposes, "I saw three men hang "themselves." Lü A-liang (盧阿良) deposes, "of the men with me, a native of Kweishan "(歸善), by name A-yin (阿寅), was killed by blows, another, a Hakka, by name Ma Tsai (馬仔), "hanged himself, and a third, A-t'ou (阿透), poisoned himself with opium." Chang Chêng-kao (張正高) deposes, "I saw Wang A-chiang (王阿江) hang himself in his chains, on account of "the frequency of the floggings inflicted. Of those with me seven men, who had been gravely "wounded by blows, died from disease thus produced." Lin Kuei-hsing (林貴興) deposes, "I saw a native of Polo (博羅), by name Huang (黃), killed by blows." Ho A-ch'êng (何阿成) deposes, "I saw a man jump into a sugar caldron, two men hang themselves, and another wearing "chains throw himself into a well." Hsiao To (蕭多) deposes, "of those with me, one man "hanged himself, as he was chained and constantly beaten." Lo Fu (羅福) deposes, "of those "who came with me, one man hanged himself, and another died from the effects of a severe "chastisement." Liu A-sung (劉阿松) deposes, "of those with me two hanged themselves, and "two poisoned themselves with opium." Wên Erh-chang (溫二章) deposes, "I saw one man "poison himself with opium, and one man hang himself, being unable to endure the hardships." Lai A-hsi (賴阿携) deposes, "I saw six men hang themselves." Yeh Jui-chang (葉瑞章) deposes, "I saw a native of Sinhwei (新會) killed by blows dealt by the administrator." Chiang A-t'êng (江阿騰) deposes, "I saw 12 men hang themselves." Huang Ch'ên-fu (黃陳福) deposes, "I saw one man killed by blows." Ch'ên Hua (陳華) deposes, "on the plantation I "saw a native of Sinhwei (新會), by name Huang A-fang (黃阿芳), who worked in the sugar "storehouse and who was detected asleep, beaten and bitten to death by dogs incited to attack "him. Another man poisoned himself with opium." Liao Chün (廖均) deposes, "I saw a "native of Nanhai (南海), by name Lin (林), hang himself." Huang Chien-hsing (黃建馨) deposes, "of those with me, three men committed suicide." Liu Chin-hsiu (劉錦秀) deposes, "I saw two men hang themselves." Ch'ien Yu (錢有) deposes, "I saw 28 men hang themselves "through inability to endure the cruelty." Wên A-an (溫阿安) deposes, "I saw three men "drown themselves." Hung A-i (洪阿異) deposes, "I saw the Cantonese Liang A-hua (梁阿華) and 11 others poison themselves with opium." Hsieh A-hsing (謝阿興) deposes, "I saw a native of Hweichow (惠州), by name Lin A-fa (林阿發), and a native of Hiangshan "(香山), by name A-man (阿滿), killed by blows. Another man, too, who was placed in foot "irons, wounded on the legs by blows, and deprived of food, hanged himself." Chou A-chiu (周阿九) deposes, "of 20 men with me, six died from blows which caused wounds and vomiting "of blood." Liang A-hua (梁阿華) deposes, "of the 42 men with me, two threw themselves into "the mountain ponds, two were killed by blows dealt by the administrator, and one by blows "inflicted by the surgeon." Tsêng A-ming (曾阿明) and 3 others depose, "of 13 men with me, "six died from the effects of wounds and bad medical treatment." Ch'ên A-shên (陳阿深) deposes, "I saw one man who had been wounded by blows die on the following day, one man who was beaten "and cruelly used drown himself, and two hang themselves." Ho A-hsien (賀阿先) deposes, "I "saw a native of Hweichow (惠州), named Liu A-hsiu (劉阿秀), so wounded by blows dealt with "a stick that he died on the following day." Ho A-chien (何阿堅) and Têng San (鄧三) declare that they each saw on plantations two men hang themselves, who were unable to endure the cruelty. Mai A-an (麥阿安) deposes, "I saw, on the plantation, two men hang themselves. "Their terms of service had expired and they were not permitted to leave." Huang-A-yu

(黃阿友) deposes, "I saw a man struck on the neck with a stick. He was injured, and died in a "few days. I also saw other two men hang themselves." Huang Yang-shun (黃楊順) deposes, "on the plantation I saw two men drown themselves, two hang themselves, and three poison "themselves with opium." Hsü Kuan (徐觀) deposes, "the overseer kicked a man and inflicted "wounds from which he died. I also saw three men commit suicide." Ch'ü Jung (區榮) deposes, "in the sugar warehouse eight men hanged themselves." Chang Ssŭ (張四) deposes, "of those "with me two men committed suicide." Ch'ên Ping (陳炳) deposes, "I saw five men commit "suicide, of whom three poisoned themselves with opium; the two others killed themselves when "in the stocks. Last year a native of Shuntêh (順德) was struck by an overseer with a stick on "the ribs and died on the same evening." Hsü Pai-hao (徐百好) deposes, "on the plantation "I saw two men commit suicide, and another was so severely wounded by lashes with a whip "that he died." Liu A-yao (劉阿耀) and 1 other declare that two days before they made their depositions two men hanged themselves, the cause being inability to endure the cruelty. Liang A-chang (梁阿掌) deposes, "I saw one man hang himself and 14 men poison themselves with "opium. These were all Cantonese." Lai A-ssŭ (賴阿四) deposes, "I saw the Cantonese "A-t'ien (阿田) hang himself on account of having been severely flogged. Two others also "poisoned themselves with opium. These were all Cantonese." Ch'ên Kuan-chih (陳觀植) deposes, "I saw two men who were chained together leap into a sugar caldron." Chao Ch'ang (趙長) deposes, "I saw a man commit suicide." P'an Wên-tao (潘文道) deposes, "of those with "me two men committed suicide." Chung Liang-ch'ên (鍾亮臣) and 1 other depose, "I saw a "native of Fukien, by name Lin Sung-ming (林松明), poison himself with opium in the fields, "being unable to support the cruelty." Kuan Hsien (關賢) deposes, "I saw a man "hang himself in the infirmary who had been placed there after being flogged." Ho A-wên (何阿文) deposes, "I saw three men commit suicide." Liang A-kuan (梁阿關) deposes, "of those with me two hanged themselves, and one who had been severely flogged "died from the effects." Hsü Shao-lin (徐紹麟) deposes, "my brother, by name Hsü Shao-jung "(徐紹榮), drowned himself, because he was unable to endure the flogging." Huang A-mu (黃阿穆) deposes, "of those with me more than 100 died from blows." Ch'ü Tsu-k'ang (區祖康) deposes, "of those with me one man hanged himself." Shên Yao-chung (沈耀忠) deposes, "I saw two men killed by blows and three men kill themselves voluntarily by casting "themselves under wheels." Shên Chin-kuei (沈金奎) deposes, "of three men with me, one, a "native of Kiangsi (江西), by name A-man (阿滿), died from blows." Yüan A-an (袁阿安) deposes, "of those with me two hanged themselves, being unable to endure the cruelty. A native "of Sinhwei (新會), by name A-ping (阿炳), also cut his throat, but the wound was cured." Têng A-hsing (鄧阿星) deposes, "I saw a native of Nanhai (南海), by name Lin (林), hang "himself." Chu A-jui (朱阿瑞) deposes, "I saw a man killed by blows; another man committed "suicide by jumping into the furnace, and a third whose ribs had been fractured by blows, died "in the infirmary on the following day." Mo A-kang (莫阿岡) deposes, "I saw three men who "had been wounded by blows hang themselves, and other three for a similar reason poison them- "selves with opium." Ho A-fa (何阿發) deposes, "I saw Chang A-wang (張阿旺) hang him- "self on account of the cruelty to which he was subjected, and two others, natives of K'iungchow "(瓊州) poison themselves with opium." Yang A-chi (楊阿紀) deposes, "a sick man who was

"not permitted to enter the infirmary, poisoned himself with opium and died on the same day."
Mai T'ai-ch'ang (麥泰常) deposes, "of those with me two hanged themselves, and one cut his
"throat." Liu A-kuei (劉阿貴) deposes, "of those with me six hanged themselves on account
"of the severity with which they had been flogged." Tu I (杜義) deposes, "I saw an old man die
"from a fracture of the ribs caused by a blow dealt by an overseer. He died at once." Li Erh
(李二) deposes, "I saw a native of Nanhai (南海) hang himself on account of the cruelty."
Liang Man (梁滿) deposes, "I saw a native of Ch'aochow (潮州), by name Ch'ên Li
"(陳禮), hang himself, on account of the insufficiency of the food and the constant
"flogging." Ts'ai A-t'êng (蔡阿勝) deposes, "I saw two men hang themselves, two men
"poison themselves with opium, and another leap into the sugar caldron." Liu Ying-fa (劉應發)
deposes, "I saw a Cantonese, by name Lin T'ien (林添), drown himself, being unable to endure
"the flogging." Shên Yang (沈仰) deposes, "I saw a native of Changchow (漳州), by name
"Hsieh, (謝), so severely beaten that, after vomiting blood, he died. A native of Ts'üanchow
"(泉州) also, by name Ts'ai (蔡), poisoned himself with opium." Ch'ên I-yu (陳乙有)
deposes, "I saw one man cut his throat; the wound however was healed. Other three men
"hanged themselves." Hsieh A-tung (薛阿東) deposes, "on the plantation I saw a Fukienese,
"by name Ch'ên A-lai (陳阿賴), hang himself." Hu A-ssŭ (胡阿四) deposes, "I saw one
"man unable to endure the cruelty drown himself." Ko A-ch'ing (柯阿慶) deposes, "I saw
"one man die from injuries caused by kicks inflicted by the administrator on the preceding day."
Wu A-ch'êng (吳阿成) deposes, "I saw the manager of the shop on the plantation kill by blows
"with a stick a man named Ch'ên A-fu (陳阿福). Another, by name Yang A-k'un (楊阿坤),
"was so severely flogged by an overseer that he died on the following day." Ch'ên Lung
(陳龍) deposes, "two newly arrived men, natives of Fukien, hanged themselves." Yü A-p'ing
(余阿平) deposes, "on the plantation only a few days ago two men hanged themselves." Hu
A-t'ai (古阿泰) deposes, "I saw 3 men die from wounds caused by blows. Another man,
"a native of Hoyüen (河源), by name A-i (阿義), drowned himself." Liu A-hsiu (劉阿秀)
deposes, "of 25 men with me six who were not allowed to report themselves sick and were also
"severely beaten, died." Chu A-shan (朱阿山) deposes, "of 23 men with me two hanged
"themselves, and one man poisoned himself with opium." Ch'ên P'ing-an (陳平安) deposes,
"of 34 men with me, two hanged themselves." Liang Lien-ch'ing (梁連慶) deposes, "on
"the plantation there were suicides on account of the cruelty; two men drowned themselves,
"and two hanged themselves." Liang P'ing-an (梁平安) deposes, "I saw three men
"hang themselves, four men poison themelves with opium, and three men throw themselves
"into the sugar caldrons." Liang Piao (梁標) deposes, "in the baker's shop I saw
"one man poison himself with opium." Liang A-hsiu (梁阿秀) deposes, "I saw a
"Hakka poison himself with opium." Yeh A-hsi (葉阿錫) deposes, "I saw a native
"of Hweichow (惠州), by name Wan A-fa (萬阿發), hang himself, being unable to endure
"the cruelty. I saw also Wan A-hsing (萬阿興) and his brother jump together into
"a well." Kuo A-jung (郭阿榮) deposes, "I saw a man who was working in irons pushed
"down, and wounded by a white man. He desired to proceed to the infimary, but was observed
"and beaten with great severity by the same white man, and in a few days he died." Ch'ên Shou
(陳受) deposes, "I saw one man killed by blows." T'an Ch'ang-hsiu (譚長秀) deposes, "I saw

"a man hang himself." Fêng Erh (馮二) deposes, "I saw a native of Tungkwan (東莞) poison "himself with opium." Ch'ü A-ch'iu (區阿求) deposes, "I saw a man so severely beaten, that "he died in a few days from the effects of the blows." Liu Hsin-fa (劉新發) deposes, "of those "with me one man hanged himself." Liang Ting (梁丁) deposes, "Li A-ch'iu (李阿求), a "native of Ch'aochow (潮州) being old and unable to move the refuse cane, was struck by an "overseer in the ribs, and in consequence died." Chêng A-chi (鄭阿吉) deposes, "I saw a "native of Hiangshan (香山), by name Chêng (鄭), hang himself. A man named A-fu (阿福) "poisoned himself with opium. The cause of both suicides was inability to endure the cruelty." Liang T'ing-po (梁廷鉑) deposes, "I saw one man vomit blood, and die in consequence of "thrusts with a stick, dealt by the administrator. Two others died in the infirmary from the "effects of grave injuries inflicted by the administrators." Chi A-lê (紀阿樂) deposes, "I saw "seven natives of Shanghai commit suicide. Of these, two being unable to endure the chastise-"ments poisoned themselves with opium, three drowned themselves, and two hanged themselves. "Of six Fukienese, also, four hanged themselves together, one poisoned himself with opium, and "one threw himself into a sugar caldron. Severe injuries were the causes of all these suicides." Chou A-tung (周阿東) deposes, "I saw eight Cantonese commit suicide owing to inability to "endure the cruelty. Besides four men, who after being wounded by blows, were forced to "labour, died within three days from the infliction of the injuries." Ho A-kêng (何阿庚) deposes, "I saw four men hang themselves in a chamber, and three men hang themselves on "trees; these had been unable to endure the cruelty."

XL.

WHEN A MAN DIES, HOW DOES THE EMPLOYER ARRANGE HIS AFFAIRS? IS THERE ANY
DIFFERENCE IN THE TREATMENT OF MEN WHO DIE DURING OR OUT OF
AGREEMENT TERM?

Chinese procuring a Letter of Domicile and a Cedula, are in the enjoyment of a small amount of independence, but the refusal of these documents during recent years, the withdrawal of others previously issued and the successive renewal of contracts enforced by the master or the dépôt on all who through either the refusal or the withdrawal, are unprotected, causes the fact of death taking place after the completion of the agreement, to create no difference in the arrangement by the employers of the affairs of the remainder.

The following extracts from the depositions furnish information as to the manner of this arrangement. Chou Jun-ch'ing (周潤晴) deposes that the unbaptised are not admitted into a cemetery. Hsü Li-shêng (徐立生) and 98 others depose that Chinese receive neither coffin nor grave, and that their bodies are cast out anywhere. Ch'ên Tê-lin (陳德林) and 2 others depose that when buried they are not placed in coffins, and that their clothing is removed. Kuo A-mei (郭阿美) and 1 other depose that they made the coffins (used on the plantation where they served) and that these were provided for negroes but not Chinese. Huang Chieh (黃揩) and one other depose that their employers used one coffin, which was brought back after the bodies had been carried to the hills and buried. Li A-chiu (李阿九) deposes that Chinese are not placed in coffins, and that after the lapse of a few years their bones are burnt into lime. Lo-A-chi (羅 阿 紀) deposes that the bodies are placed in a shallow hole, that in the course of time the bones are turned up by the spade, and piled up in little heaps, dissolve under the sun and rain; he also remarks that as the charred bones of oxen are required for the refining of sugar, the mixture of those of men would produce an even purer whiteness.

Again the petition of Jên Shih-chên (任 世 貞) and 2 others contains the following statement: "we have been here 17 and 18 years, and are so environed by the devices of the "Commission of Colonization and others interested that egress is hopeless. We are old and "weak and it is only uncertain whether we shall die in a dépôt or in a fresh place of service, or "cast out as useless by the roadside; but it is certain that for us there will be neither coffin nor "grave, and that our bones will be tossed into a pit, to be burnt with those of horses and oxen "and to be afterwards used to refine sugar, and that neither our sons nor our sons' sons will ever "know what we have endured."

XLI.

WHAT IS THE CHINESE POPULATION OF CUBA?

The census prepared by the Central Commission of Colonization shows that at the commencement of the 7th month of the year before last there were in Cuba 58,410 Chinese, and the Tables received from the British Consulate General specify 11,332 as the number which subsequently quitted China up to the 3rd month of this year. From the latter figures have to be deducted 907 deaths on board ship, reducing the number landed to 10,425; and as there is no record of the mortality since the completion of the census the only estimate that can be offered of the existing population is 68,825.

XLII.

HOW IS IT DISTRIBUTED?
a. SUPPORTING THEMSELVES,
b. WORKING OUT CONTRACTS,
c. WAITING TO GO ELSEWHERE,
d. IN PRISON.

Those supporting themselves,—that is, who, formerly having obtained certificates of completion from their employers, and having been baptised, procured Letters of Domicile and Cedulas, were enabled to engage in a small trade or to gain their livelihood by free service, and are described in the Census Table as "naturalized" or "subjects of foreign powers,"—may be estimated as forming $\frac{2}{10}$ths of the population; but it must not be forgotten that even these have undergone hardships and have been and are subjected to extortion, and that at present the issue of passports and a departure to their country are attended by many difficulties.

Of those working out contracts it is needless to speak; and the freedom of the men whose agreements were completed during more recent years is so completely restricted by the enforced renewal of contracts, that the "going elsewhere" is an impossibility for them, and that no distinction can be drawn between them and those whose original engagements are still in force. The depositions and petitions all agree that it is desired to render them prisoners for a lifetime, and that they have to abandon all hope of a return home, and these two classes form 7 or 8 tenths of the entire number.

The proportion in jails, consisting of those sentenced, of those who have been long detained without trial, and of men who, on the termination of their engagements, were confined without any cause, does not exceed a few hundreds.

XLIII.

Have any Chinese become wealthy? Socially, what is their status? To what extent does the Government recognize them?

The smallness of the proportion that has ever received Letters of Domicile and Cedulas; the liability of the holders to the withdrawal of these documents, a measure which at once prevents the engaging in any independent business, and the constant extortions practised by every class of the inhabitants, preclude any hope of the acquisition of wealth being entertained; and the enquiry has shown, that among the Chinese in question, there are no men of opulence. By officials the Chinese are regarded as appertaining to a category very different to that under which their own countrymen are recognised as falling; and this view is shared by the people generally. Thus the petition of Kao Lao-hsiu (高老秀) and 16 others states, "the shops, too, " of those of us engaged in a small trade at any of the towns, are daily entered by the inhabitants " who take away what suits their fancy without even offering payment, and if we ask for it we " receive only blows. They care not if they kill us, and a single individual commencing an " assault is aided by ten others, whilst all complaints to the officials are totally unheeded. Thus " we have only to fold our arms and submit." The petition of Lin A-yüan (林阿源) and 3 others states, "the foreigners—black and white—make purchases from us on credit, or promise " payment at the end of the month, but when the time comes they are so unprincipled that not " only they refuse us our due, but, besides, beat us. At other times after having sold us an " article, they induce an accomplice to come to our premises to claim it as his, and to accuse us " before the *tipao* (Capitan de Partido) of theft. The officer makes enquiry, declares that we " deal in stolen goods, places us in fetters, and sends us to jail. We complain to the manager " of the market, but either he is not willing to interfere or if he speaks to the officer, the latter " does not heed him, and we eventually have to pay a fine." The petition of Hsien Tso-pang (洗佐邦) and of 13 others states, that they all without reference to their abilities or positions in their own country were treated as common labourers and slaves; they add, "in the streets we " are constantly exposed to insult, to being struck by stones, and unless we submit in silence

" we are soon assaulted by a mob and are finally dragged off to jail. If a Chinese desirous to
" effect a purchase tries to bargain, he is at once abused, but a Spaniard or Cuban entering
" the shop of a Chinese wounds or even kills the latter if he attempts to ask for payment."
The petition of Chien Shih-kuang (簡仕光) and 75 others states, "though those employed in
" the cities may suffer a little less, they are treated by the inhabitants worse than slaves." The
petition of Chu Chi-hsün (朱箕訓) and 9 others states, "when we go out or make any sales or
" purchases, three or five of the inhabitants will together assault us with stones, rotten eggs or
" some other offensive missile, wounding us on the head, face and body, and breaking whatever
" we may be carrying; indeed sometimes wounds so serious as to have fatal results, are thus
" received. The neighbours in such cases never interfere, and the police, if appealed to, accord
" nothing but abuse. They ask why such as we, having neither fathers, nor mothers, nor families
" should throw ourselves in a tiger's path? Vicious men armed with knives or firearms
" constantly rob us of whatever we may have on our persons, and wound us with their weapons,
" regardless whether we live or die." The petition of Ch'iu Tê-i (邱得意) states, "on the
" streets, too, boys constantly throw stones at us, without any attempt at prevention on the part
" of the Government, and the underlings of the officials arrest us on fictitious charges, and drag
" us before the authorities, who close our mouths and impose fines."

　　Chou A-chiu (周阿九) in his deposition declares, "I keep a shop for the sale of
" sweetmeats. I am subject to wrong, as I am forced to sell on credit, and never permitted to ask
" for payment; if I do so I am beaten. For what passers by, too, may choose to pick up and
" take away, I dare not ask any payment. Against all the acts of malice from which we suffer
" here at the hands of the white men we cannot utter a remonstrance." Han A-hsing (韓阿興)
deposes, "I carry on a small business in selling sweetmeats. I earn sufficient to support myself.
" If I laid by any money the people of the country would come and extort it from me.
" Every day men enter my shop, pick up and take away something, never enquiring the
" price, and strike me if I ask for payment." Liang Tao-han (梁道漢) deposes, "I
" keep a small shop for the sale of spirits and rice. The white men constantly subject
" me to extortion, buy on credit and refuse payment." Yeh Yu (葉由) deposes, "I sell
" vegetables. The people of the island buy on credit and strike me if I ask for payment.
" On the street they constantly pelt me with stones." Lin Ch'üan (林泉) deposes, "here Chinese
" are treated most injuriously. Debts due to them are not paid, and a request for settlement is
" replied to by blows. If we walk in the streets stones are cast at us, and the officials look on
" with indifference." Chou Ch'ên-tung (周陳東) and 4 others depose, that on the streets the
boys—white and black—cast stones at them. Hung A-pan (洪阿扳) deposes, "the people are
" bad. They constantly stone the Chinese." P'an A-pao (潘阿保) deposes, "on the streets the
" white people constantly pelt me with stones." Wu A-ch'ing (吳阿清) deposes, "the white and
" black men whom we meet on the streets all cast stones at us. They also rob us of our property,
" and look upon us as pigs or dogs." Kuo Chan (郭占) deposes, "Spaniards who meet us on
" the streets constantly kick us and no one interferes." Li A-pao (李阿保) deposes, "on the
" streets we are scoffed at and abused. This occurs perpetually." Ch'ên A-fa (陳阿發) deposes.
" it is the custom of this country that the police, who carry swords, arrest all Chinese wearing
" good clothes whom they may meet. They charge them with being gamblers. The officials in

"no way interfere, and an outlay of money is the only way of arrangement." Li Yu (李有)
deposes, "the inhabitants treat the Chinese with great injustice. The innocent are dragged away
"to the dépôts, and are not released until they disburse money." Pai Yung-fa (白永發)
deposes, "the Chinese here suffer greatly, and are treated worse than the negroes." Li A-tung
(李阿東) deposes, "my master treats the Chinese worse than the negroes. The Spaniards
"devote themselves to the traffic of decoying and selling us, as they consider us slaves for a life-
"time." Ch'êng Chang-ming (程章明) deposes, "because they look upon us as horses or dogs,
"they think that we should be slaves for a lifetime." Tsêng A-shih (曾阿十) deposes, "the
"Chinese here are treated worse than fowls or dogs." Ch'ên A-fu (陳阿福) deposes, "Chinese
"here are treated like fowls or dogs, and I long for death." Chi A-lê (紀阿樂) deposes, "the
"administrator constantly says that Chinese are like fowls and dogs, and when they die others
"can be bought." Ho Fu-hsing (何復興) and 9 others depose, that the sufferings of the Chinese
are matters of public notoriety, that they are treated worse than beasts. Ch'ên Shui (陳水) and
1 other depose, "Chinese are now in Cuba treated worse than formerly. The negroes also at
"present strike us more violently."

XLIV.

ARE CHINESE FOUND IN POSITIONS OF TRUST? POSITIONS REQUIRING INTELLIGENCE, CHARACTER
AND ATTENTIVENESS? ARE THEY FAIRLY PAID AND PROPERLY TREATED, OR THE
REVERSE?

The larger proportion of the Chinese in Cuba are Cantonese. With this exception natives
of Fukien, Hukwang, Kiangsu and Chêhkiang are the most numerous. Besides, there are natives
of every province, and even Bannermen.

Out of these, during the course of the enquiry, were met civil and military officials and
literary graduates (hsiu-ts'ai) mixed up with the general body of common labourers. They had
been decoyed and sold like the remainder, for, as is remarked in the petition of Chang Luan
(張鑾) and 30 others, "the intelligent as well as the vicious are caught in these nets and fall
"into these snares;" and among the several tens of thousands in the island, there undoubtedly
must be men gifted with "intelligence, character and attentiveness." One treatment however is
applied to all, the treatment of slaves, and to them ability is a useless possession.

Wages, also, are paid in accordance with a fixed system, usually $3 during the first year
and $4 during the remaining seven, and whatever augmentation may be granted on the com-
pletion of the term of original engagement is not a recognition of the existence of exceptional
capacity. No method of giving effect to any such recognition is included among the provisions
of the rules which govern the Chinese in Cuba.

XLV.

AS COMPARED WITH THEIR FORMER CONDITION IN CHINA, WHAT IS THEIR CONDITION IN CUBA?
MORE COMFORTABLE, MORE PROSPEROUS, OR THE REVERSE? DO THEY REGRET
HAVING GONE TO CUBA? DO THEY WISH TO GET AWAY? CAN THEY GET AWAY?

Lin A-yung (林 阿 用) deposes, "on account of the condition of affairs at Cuba I do not desire to remain." Fêng Hui (馮 會) deposes, "the food is insufficient and the labour arduous; "my repentence is without limits." Li A-lung (黎 阿 隆) deposes, "in China I worked daily "during 8 hours, here I have to labour during 20." Liu A-fu (劉 阿 福) deposes, "though "I hold a Letter of Domicile and Cedula, and work independently, I am constantly subjected to "outrage. Here we are regarded as appertaining to the same class as the negro, indeed some- "times these latter are treated better than we are." Li Hsi-pao (李 錫 寶) deposes, "we are "struck without cause; such usage would not be endured in China a single day." Chao A-ling (趙 阿 凌) and 14 others depose that they think the existence of a beggar in China preferable to theirs in Cuba. Ho A-chi (何 阿 基) deposes, "Chinese are treated like the black slaves. I prefer "returning to China to beg, to remain here to be ground and broken." Liu Shêng-lin (劉 聖 麟) deposes, "although my master is good, the labour I have to perform is ten thousand times more "grievous than that of China." Chang Lin-an (張 林 安) deposes, "the men in China who suffer "the extremest hardships, suffer less than those here." Li A-yao (李 阿 耀) and 185 others all declare in their depositions that they desire to return to China. Ch'ên Hsio-chou (陳 學 周) deposes, "through the aid of friends I was able to redeem myself and in two years saved sufficient "for the cost of my passage back. I then met certain officers who had been sent to arrest all "Chinese, and I was seized, placed in prison and there forced to labour. My padrino or godfather "upon this, by an outlay of $150, was permitted to bail me, and I thus avoided being again "sold to the mountains as a slave, but I lost all my property." Wang Hsiang (王 向) deposes "I now possess $200; if the dépôt would grant my release I would return to China.

XLVI.

HAVE THE MEN MARRIED? WHAT WIVES? WHAT IS THE CONDITION OF THEIR WIVES AND
CHILDREN, AND WHAT FUTURE HAVE THE CHILDREN BEFORE THEM?

The 35th clause of the Spanish Royal Decree of 1860 is to the following effect: "Immi- "grants may marry with the consent of their employers."

"If this consent is refused and the immigrant is of age, he may either redeem himself in "accordance with the provisions of clause 43, or may seek another employer who will fulfil these "provisions for him."

The 43rd clause is thus worded: "Every immigrant can at any time redeem himself by
" paying the following amounts:—

" 1. The amount originally paid for his acquisition.

" 2. The amount due as indemnity for the cessation of work during contract hours, or
" from any other cause.

" 3. The highest estimate passed by experts of the increased value of the services of
" the immigrant since his acquisition.

" 4. Compensation for the loss that may ensue from the difficulty of replacing the
" labourer.

" The immigrant cannot make use of this right of redemption during the sugar season or
" at the time of execution of any of the pressing labour permitted even on the festivals of the
" church."

From these extracts the difficulty of effecting redemption becomes apparent.

Some years ago two Chinese having completed their term of contract, having obtained
Letters of Domicile and Cedulas, and having won prizes in a lottery, married Chinese women. They
and their wives are still in the island, being unable to pay the cost of passage home.

Chêng A-lai (鄭 阿 來), a native of Ch'aochow (潮 州), the only man among the tens of
thousands of Chinese who have landed in Cuba who is reputed to have amassed any considerable
sum of money, married a white woman. He subsequently twice endeavoured to leave the island,
but was on each occasion arrested. He is now dead and no portion of what he possessed was
remitted to China.

At present there is another by name Chang Ch'ang-kuei (張 長 貴) who has married a
a white woman and who earns by his labour sufficient for his support. His deposition was taken
and in it he states that he was disliked on account of his marriage, and speaks of the hatred
entertained towards him for other reasons, and of the injury done to him by the *tipao* (Capitan
de Partido).

Besides, a few others, by name Ho Hsi (何 錫), Chuang Wên-ming (莊 文 明), Wu A-
ling (伍 阿 靈), Ch'ên Hsiu (陳 秀), Ho Tan-kuei (何 丹 桂), &c., &c., have married mulattoes
and negresses. But the aggregate of these cases is very small.

Of the children it can only be said that they are brought up by their parents.

XLVII.

IN CERTAIN LAWS SAID TO HAVE BEEN PROPOSED FOR TEMPORARY ENFORCEMENT AND CONSE-
QUENT ON THE REBELLION, THE WORDS OCCUR " AT THE EXPIRATION OF THEIR
" CONTRACTS, COLONISTS WILL REMAIN UNDER THE GUARDIANSHIP OF THEIR LATE
" PATRONS," AND " IN CASE THE COLONIST SHOULD NOT DESIRE THIS, HE WILL BE
" PLACED IN THE MUNICIPAL DEPOSIT." WHAT IS " GUARDIANSHIP," AND WHAT IS
A " MUNICIPAL DEPOSIT " ?

Changes in the regulations applicable to Chinese in Cuba have been of frequent occurrence, but no rules are stated to have been framed in consequence of the insurrection. The

necessity of either a renewal of contract or of labouring on public works was laid down as long ago as 1860, in articles 7 and 18 of the Decree of that year.

(*Note by translator :—*

> The term "temporary guardianship" referred to in the query is used in the Decree of the Colonial Government, a portion of the purport of which is quoted under query 25, and which is more fully described in the memorandum concerning Legislation. The guardianship meant temporary continued use of the services of the Chinese in question, on condition of the employer guaranteeing their appearance whenever it might be called for, and their retention in one locality until "the Government can ascertain whether they are deserters or whether they have "been guilty only of the fault of neglect to re-contract themselves in a regular "manner."

> As shown in the memo. referred to, the guardianship ceased on the 14th September 1872, and was replaced by the re-contracting prescribed in the Regulations of that date.)

"Guardianship" by the original employer, being prolonged service for his benefit, was not likely to be acceptable to those interested. As shown by the petition of Jên Shih-chên (任 世 貞) and two others, the enforcement of contracts for eight years entered into for five, is regarded as a wrongful exaction of three years' labour, and a few other extracts will prove the feelings of dislike in regard to any such prolongation entertained by the Chinese, and the prejudicial nature of such a tutelage when imposed. Thus Tsêng A-shih (曾 阿 十) deposes, that 40 men who had completed their contracts were forced to labour in chains ; P'ang A-tung (龐 阿 東), that at the end of the eight years if a new contract was refused, they were beaten and chained ; Lin Tzŭ-yu (林 滋 有), that a native of Nanhai (南 海) who declined to renew his contract was so injured by thrusts with a stick in the chest inflicted by the administrator that he died in a few days ; and Liang A-shêng (梁 阿 盛), that a Cantonese, by name A-chi (阿 寄), who declined to renew his contract was so injured by thrusts that he died in a few days.

The institution known as the "dépôt" is named in the depositions in various ways, but these different appellations, ten in number, have reference to one establishment. This originally was created for the detention of runaway slaves, and its jurisdiction was subsequently extended to the similar cases of Chinese. To the latter were added, later, all not possessing Letters of Domicile and Cedulas, whether the absence of these documents be due to refusal of them, or loss, or withdrawal by violence ; and the general cessation of their issue which has taken place of recent years has rendered liability to such arrest universal. The Chinese who declines to renew his engagement with his original employer, and who, despite the chains and the whip, in so many cases resorted to, persists in his refusal, is delivered to the dépôt to labour on Government work without remuneration until through its intervention a new contract is enforced,—a process constantly repeated and calculated of course to prevent any return home and any attempt to gain a livelihood independently, and resulting in exposing to the danger of being handed over to the cruelties of the plantation,—the extremest,—men who, hitherto employed in other services, have escaped them.

The petition of Li Chao-ch'un (李肇春) and 166 others states, "our countrymen who "have completed their first contracts must enter the dépôt, and they have either to in it work "in irons and without wages, or are hired out to labour in any part of the island, a servitude "without limit and which may last till death. The original employer or any other may "also make an agreement with the official, under which he will pay $ 10, or over $ 10, a month, "for the services of each Chinese he selects in the dépôt, and we are bound by the conditions "of this contract, though the authorities receive the greater portion of the wages and only some "$ 4 a month reach our hands. The contracts issued to us at Macao are in most instances kept "by the master. If a death occur, the employer may, after agreement with the officials, visit the "dépôt and point out such or such a man as the signer of the dead man's engagement. "The dépôt was formerly a house of detention for deserters, but at present many of our "countrymen who never ran away and who regularly completed their time of service are "forced to enter it, and whilst in it are compelled to carry earth and hew stones, working "in chains, some wearing even two or three, under overseers who with whip and knives "drive them to labour. The sole object of these cruelties is to oblige them to enter into "new contracts with the wealthy proprietors and to thus fetter themselves again for a certain "number of years, and when the new engagement is over, they are sent back to the dépôt "and successively dealt with in the same manner. Is it not real slavery for life to which "Spaniards condemn us? All these measures are devised to retain us here till death, to prevent "our ever again seeing our country." The petition of Hsien Tso-pang (洗佐邦) states, "these "dépôts are in no way different from prisons, and many of us who years ago fulfilled our contracts "are liable to removal to either one or the other on a charge of desertion. Such are the devices "for the retention of the Chinese in this island, for the execution by them of Government work "without wages, and for the deriving profits from the fees payable when fresh contracts are "entered into." The petition of Ch'ü Ping-nan (區炳南) and 22 others states, "the dépôts "established for the Chinese are filled by the acts of the police officers, who visit at night the "residences of the freedmen, demand the production of their papers, arrest on the plea of opium "smoking or gambling those who present them, and on the plea of desertion those who fail to do "so; and all thus seized have to work with foot irons in the dépôts." The petition of Ch'ên Ku (陳古) and two others refers to their countrymen being dragged away by the police to the endless servitude of the dépôts. The petition of T'ang Chan-k'uei (唐占魁) and 8 others states, "in "all the towns of the interior dépôts now exist, and our countrymen when their original engagement "is at an end are placed in them whence they are either taken away to the mountains or are "coerced into renewing their contracts; whilst in the dépôts they are fed like fowls or dogs, "chastised and forced to labour like oxen or horses." The petition of Chao K'un (趙昆) and 97 others states, "when the officials have refused the papers we are at once arrested and confined in "the dépôts where chains on neck and feet and the whip are also in use. The stronger may be "able to work again in a plantation, but the older, after toiling like oxen or horses, are allowed "to die like useless insects." The petition of Chêng Hsing (鄭性) and 5 others states, "at the "end of the eight years, too, we were delivered by our employer to officials who forced us to "repair roads, attached chains to our feet and placed us under the orders of overseers who "constantly struck us." The petition of Lai Shêng (賴勝) and 9 others states, "when taken to

" the dépôts we are employed in the fatiguing labour of repairing or cleaning the roads and are
" given no wages. The food there too, is insufficient." The petition of Ch'iu Pi-shan (邱 碧 山)
and 34 others states, "confinement, chains and hard labour—the treatment in fact of criminals—
" is that accorded in the dépôts; the cruelties which we there endure differ in no way from those
" practised in the plantations. The object in view in subjecting us to these wrongs is to retain
" us as slaves for life." The petition of Wu A-kuang (吳 阿 光) states, "we all are confined in
" chains in the dépôts, compelled to execute unpaid labour and even escorted to the place of
" work by an armed guard. Unless guaranteed by a Spaniard, Chinese may wear chains until
" the day of their death. I myself was in irons for years and my feet are in consequence maimed,
" rendering me a cripple for ever, and mutilated." The petition of Lo A-pao (駱 阿 寶) states,
" after my eight years, the master being bad refused to give me a cedula. I went away to work
" elsewhere, but having no papers was found and seized by the guards and brought to this
" dépôt. I have now been in it four or five years, receiving no wages." The petition of Ch'ên
Yü-shu (陳 玉 樹) and 4 others states, "those who had the patience to complete their eight
" years, thinking that their position would then be improved, were, under the system devised
" by the officials, either obliged to bind themselves by a new contract or were sent to the
" dépôt, from which there is no outlet." The petition of T'ang Chan-k'uei (唐 占 魁) and 106
others states, "originally the slaves of only one individual, we are now, through the dépôts,
" in the servitude of the entire population, a servitude, too, that can end only with death."
Chang K'ai (張 開) deposes, "having lost my cedula, I was sent to the dépôt where I laboured
" for eight years without wages." Huang A-mu (黃 阿 木) deposes, "the dépôt hired me out
" as a seller of water at monthly wages of $ 20 of which $ 15 were retained by the officials of
" the dépôt." Liu A-t'ang (劉 阿 唐) and 4 others depose, that they were hired out at monthly
wages of $ 15 of which $ 10 were retained by the officials. Liu A-hsing (陸 阿 杏) deposes,
" I was hired out by the dépôt to a plantation at monthly wages of $ 20 of which $ 10 were
" retained by the officials." Li A-tê (李 阿 德) deposes, "I was hired out by the dépôt at
" monthly wages of $ 11 of which $ 10 were retained by the officials. I subsequently was
" transferred to a manufacturer of machinery at monthly wages of $ 17 of which the officials
" retained $ 12." Chang Luan (張 鑾) deposes, "I am hired out by the dépôt, leaving it in
" the morning and returning at night. Of the wages paid only $ 4 are delivered to me, the
" balance is retained by the administrator." Lin A-tê (林 阿 得) deposes, "many are hired
" out by the dépôt, the wages being all retained by the latter. Nine men who were with me
" are now hired out to a plantation." Li A-pao (李 阿 保) deposes, "the dépôt is cramped
" and filthy and we all sleep on the ground like pigs in mud, and though we number more than
" a thousand have all to wash ourselves in a trough a few feet long." Li Hsi-pao (李 錫 寶)
deposes, "in the dépôt I saw a native of Shuntêh (順 德) over 60 years old whose arm had
" been fractured by blows and subsequently cured. I also saw there a native of Canton more
" than 40 years old and whose back bones had been injured by blows inflicted on account of his
" walking slowly." Ho A-shan (何 阿 善) deposes, "in the dépôt the negro overseer strikes
" most frequently the men advanced in age. Wang Ta-ch'êng (王 大 誠) deposes, "at the
" Trocha, when clearing the mountains, my leg was broken by a tree. I was conducted back to
" the dépôt where, after the fracture had partially healed, I was knocked down by the adminis-

'trator, the fall causing the injury to resume its original proportions." Ch'ên A-pao (陳 阿 保) deposes, "ten old men who were cripples were sent away to the country two days ago on account "of the visit of the Commission being expected. My brother who, holding a cedula, "is unjustly confined in the dépôt, was also sent away." Yu A-ssŭ (游 阿 四) and 8 others depose, "we originally slept on the ground and our feet were in consequence swollen. On "the visit of the Commission being expected, wooden beds and clothing were issued." Li A-nêng (李 阿 能) deposes, "these new clothes were issued yesterday; the men in chains were also "released yesterday." Lin A-kou (林 阿 狗) and 21 others depose, "when the visit of the "Commission was expected clothing was issued to us." Lin Êrh (林 二) deposes, "when the "visit of the Commission was expected rations of rice and new clothing were issued." Liu A-hsi (劉 阿 喜) deposes, "when the visit of the Commission was expected rations of rice were issued."

XLVIII.

HAVE THE CHINESE EXAMINED TALKED FREELY?

ꓛ men examined in the dépôts, prisons and plantations were selected by the Commission from a number who, in the first instance, were designated by the functionaries of the respective establishments. Besides, on the plantations, in most instances the enquiry had to be conducted under the eyes of the administrator or overseers. Their presence tended to produce intimidation and reticence; nevertheless some did not hesitate to recapitulate their sufferings, to boldly exhibit their scars, and to hold forward the raw bananas, dried beef and maize which were their food.

The purport of the several depositions, too, constitutes a reply to the point raised in the query.

[The author of the Report interprets the query to possibly refer to the permitted attitude of Chinese under examination by Cuban authorities, as well as to their demeanour during the interrogation by the Commission, and consequently appends the following extracts :—]

Shên San-wên (沈 三 穩) deposes, "a negro who had committed a theft having accused "me of being an accomplice, I was imprisoned and sentenced to seven years' confinement. "During the trial the official would not allow me to enter into any details. The term for "which I was sentenced has expired but I am still in prison." Lai A-hsi (賴 阿 携) deposes, "a native of Polo (博 羅), by name Huang A-kuang (黃 阿 光), having been beaten and "forced to work in chains hanged himself during the night. We laid a charge before "the neighbouring officials. They, however, gave no heed to our complaint and the body was "buried without any enquiry being made. We, 23 in all, in view of this wrong renewed the "accusation before an officer of higher rank. The administrator followed us and reached the "office at the same time as we did. A prolonged conversation took place between him and the "official, at the conclusion of which the latter enquired who of us were willing to return to the "plantation, giving an assurance that we would not be chastised; and he added that those who

" refused would be sold to other plantations.   Ten accepted the second alternative ; I and 12 others
" went back to the plantation."   Kuan A-hsi (關 阿 喜) deposes, " our master having dealt a blind
" man blows with his fist and wounded his head, we laid a charge before the officials.   The latter
" however refused to accept our. complaint and placed us in prison."   Han Yen-p'ei (韓 炎 培)
deposes, " on my asking the administrator for eight months' wages (due me) he beat me. · I
" preferred a charge before the officials ; when the latter sent for him he declared that I had stolen
" straw from the stable, and I was at once imprisoned."   The petition of Tsêng Jui-t'o (曾 瑞 託)
and 4 others states, " after the 7th year of HIENFÊNG, the officials, corrupted by the planters,
" endeavoured to coerce all of us, irrespective of the date of arrival or the possession of papers, to
" enter into fresh contracts, disregarding all remonstance."

XLIX.

HAVE THE SPANIARDS OFFERED ALL NECESSARY FACILITIES ?

With one exception, the Commission is indebted to the instructions issued by the late
Captain General, Lieut. General JOVELLAR, for its admission into the dépôt, prison, hospital and
barracoon of Havana, into the dépôts, prisons and hospitals of the other towns visited, and into
the plantations at which it prosecuted its enquiry.   At the time of quitting Havana for the interior,
letters addressed to the Sub-Commissions of Colonization established in the chief town of each
jurisdiction, were received from Señor ZULUETA, then Governor now Mayor of Havana, and
President of the Central Commission of Colonization.   The exception indicated was Las Cañas,
the plantation of Señor POEY, visited by the Commission on the invitation of the owner.

At the other plantations the Commission was only received after arrangements had been
entered into between the local official and the proprietor.

Whilst the interrogations were proceeding, representatives of the Government occasionally
were present, but they in no way interfered.

No other facilities were afforded by Spaniards of any class.

L.

HAS THERE BEEN ANY INTERFERENCE OR INTIMIDATION ?

The proceedings of the Commission within the dépôts, prisons and hospitals of Havana
and the other cities were attended by no difficulties ; but the depositions show that in the first
of these establishments in expectation of the visits rations of rice, new clothing and even beds,
were supplied to the occupants.

The hours of visiting the plantations were settled in advance by the· local officials, and by
them the Commission was occasionally accompanied.

To the proprietors of some plantations the Commission is indebted for the providing of
carriages and hospitality, but the request that the common labourers should be produced for

interrogation was constantly met by the excuse that they were at work in the fields, and the cooks and other domestic servants, in all an inconsiderable number, were offered in their stead, and when after a long delay a few of the class desired were brought forward, it was urged that their absence was productive of harm and that the examination should in consequence be as brief as possible. Ordinarily, too, the administrators and overseers stood by whip in hand; but fortunately they attempted no more overt intimidation. It is right however to place on record that on the plantation "Armonia" in the Matanzas jurisdiction the administrator, though he had consented to the examination of thirty labourers, dispersed with blows and kicks, after ten had been questioned, the remainder who were awaiting interrogation, and only after a prolonged discussion promised to bring forward a few others on the following morning—a promise fulfilled by the production at 4 A.M. of a small number, who, also, had to be questioned with the utmost haste.

The following extracts from petitions supply additional information. Liang A-tê (梁阿德), in service at Matanzas, declares, "I last night intended to in person lay my story before the "Commission, but I was dragged back and placed in irons by my employer, and I am in conse-'quence compelled to hand in this written statement." P'an To-li (潘多利) and 2 others in service in the neighbourhood of Cardenas declare, "hearing of the inquiry which you are institut-"ing we intended to in person present our statement, but our employer said he would only allow "(other) eight men to visit you, and as his severity is great we did not dare to disregard the "order and therefore transmit this written petition."

True translation.

(Signed)   A. MACPHERSON,

(Signed)   A. HUBER,

Commissioners of Customs.

PART THREE
Memorandum and Regulations

THE first Regulations regarding the importation of Chinese into Cuba, to which reference has been possible, are those contained in the Royal Decree dated 22nd March, 1854, and published in Havana on the 10th May of that year. The 56th article of the Decree declares that the Rules previously existing are abrogated, but no record of the latter has been found. The Decree of 1854 was cancelled and superceded by that dated 7th July and published 4th August, 1860, which is still in force, and a full translation of which is appended. The first Decree entitled " Regulations " for the introduction into, and government of immigrants in, the island of Cuba," refers to Spanish, Chinese and Yucatanese, and, although it remained in force six years, is stated to be applicable during only two years. It is divided into three Sections, headed respectively, (1) " Concerning the introduction of immigrants;" (2) " Concerning the obligations and rights of " immigrants and their employers;" (3) "Concerning the disciplinary jurisdiction of employers." There is, in addition, a separate and concluding clause headed " General Provisions. " The second Decree is denominated " Regulations for the introduction of Chinese labourers." The titles of the three Sections are preserved, and the heading " General Provisions " enlarged into a Section.

The first Section of the earlier Decree contains only 15 Articles, that of the latter contains 30; the difference between the two consists altogether in additions and amplifications, the only clause found in the 1854 Decree and omitted in that of 1860, being one providing for the compulsory introduction of a certain number of women; and the additions and amplifications apply solely to the relations between the Colonial Government and the importers of labourers, with the exception of two clauses rendering necessary on the expiration of the immigrant's original and all subsequent contracts, either his acceptance of a fresh one, or departure from the island, or temporary service in government works. The 2nd and 3rd Sections in both Decrees are word for word alike, save that in the first Decree the two Sections extend to 51 Articles, and in the second to only 48, the three omitted clauses being,—one providing that the immigrant cannot claim from employer, government, or importer, the cost of a passage back to his country unless his contract expressly specifies the privilege; a second providing for the abrogation of previous Rules; and a third removing every disability from the immigrants who had fulfilled their original contracts. Of the 4 Articles found in the 4th Section of the 1860 Decree, but one, that providing for an annual census of the immigrants, occurs in the Decree of 1854. It will be observed that the other three Articles provide that a Chinese is unable to surrender any of the privileges bestowed on him by law, that government possesses the right of stopping immigration on giving 8 months notice, and that the Decree of 1854 and all antecedent Regulations are cancelled.

The Decree of 1854 thus had conferred upon Chinese, whose original contracts had been duly completed, the rights enjoyed by other aliens. These rights resolved themselves into the liberty to take out a Letter of Domicile, a document issued for 5 years, and which, it is alleged, contained a clause to the effect, that on the expiration of that term the holder must be naturalized and embrace the Roman Catholic faith or quit the island,—a clause which, it is stated, was easily evaded by a brief absence and an application for a new Letter on return. In the case of the Chinese, however, it would seem that acceptance of the new religion was almost invariably a necessary preliminary to the obtaining of the document, and that, without taking any further steps, or surrendering the Letter of Domicle, they, at the close of the 5 years, were regarded as naturalized. These inferences may be drawn from the 75th clause of the Instructions of 1868 calling for the production of Letters of Domicile accompanied by Certificates of Baptism, from the 16th and 83rd clauses of the Instructions, and from the depositions. These also show that the convert desirous of being baptized required the services of a Spanish subject, to act for him in the capacity of Godfather or Padrino; and that, at the time of application for the Letter of Domicile, the presentation of a certificate that the term of contract had been completed to the employer's satisfaction was indispensable. The possession of the Letter of Domicile enabled the holder to obtain a Pass requiring annual renewal, termed Cedula de Vecindad, without which, at every step, arrest was, and is, possible and probable.

For the sake of clearness, it is well to state here that a Cedula is issued to employers for each Chinese contracted to them; these, however, are simply proofs that the employer has reported to the authorities each contract which he has acquired, and in no way increases the security of the immigrant. Protected, on the other hand, by that which he himself obtained and held, the Chinese could open a shop, form with others of his countrymen a gang of independent workmen, and accept whatever employment suited best his interests.

His position was radically changed by the Decree of 1860. Its Articles 7 and 18 applicable to all landed after the 5th February, 1861, deprived him of what a few months after his arrival he found to be the chief recompense of his years of bondage. During these he could only by the most rigid self-denial save a sum barely sufficient for the expenses of his return to China, the costly voyage to New York, San Francisco and Hongkong; but if at their close allowed to use his natural sagacity and the knowledge he had acquired of the language and the habits of the people, he could soon earn a far larger amount. This no longer was lawful. If he refused to accept whatever terms those who well understood his needs chose to tender, he must reach his home as destitute as when he quitted it, after, if prompt departure were beyond his means, in addition toiling for government an indefinite time. Eight years afterwards the results of this change necessitated further legislation, and on the 31st December, 1868, were made public "Instructions for the application of the Regulations for the introduction of Chinese immigrants, "for their good government, and for their police supervision." The objects of these Instructions are, in the preamble, stated to be the extinction of abuses, which had arisen through disregard of the provisions of the 1860 Decree, and the establishment of perfect order in all matters connected with Asiatic immigration. They contain 83 Articles which prescribe,—

1st, The preparation of a census of all Chinese in Cuba, to be completed during the following February, and to be divided into—

    1°. Table of those serving under contracts;

    2°. Table of deserters still at large;

    3°. Table of deserters detained in the dépôts; (houses of detention for captured deserters and non-recontracted Chinese; originally established for runaway slaves;)

    4°. Table of those who having completed their contracts are detained in the dépôts, pending departure or recontracting;

    5°. Table of those confined in the various prisons;

    6°. Table of domiciled or free Chinese.

2nd, Measures for afterwards tracing the movements of Chinese.

3rd, Measures for the treatment of deserters and of those who desire to recontract or to leave the island.

The Articles appertaining to the first category are 23 in number, but as Tables 1—5 were necessarily to be framed by the deputed officer in concert with employers, and by the authorities of the dépôts and prisons, from the records of the various establishments, the execution of the task could in no way affect or molest the individual regarding whom the information was required, and it was only the domiciled Chinese who were unavoidably brought in contact with the registering officers. The Article, No. 16, defining the manner of the registration, is to the effect, " that during the second fortnight of February the deputed officer shall visit the residences of the " domiciled Chinese, and shall, before registration, personally inspect them, and call for the " production of their Letters of Domicile and Cedulas, that the former document shall be retained " by the inspecting officer, and the latter returned to the holder, sealed and endorsed, ' Registered.' " Another Article, No. 80, prescribes the arrest of all presenting Cedulas originally issued to other individuals. The census, thus commenced, was, however, never carried out. This is evident from the preamble to the Colonial Decree of 1871, which repeats the order for its enforcement, and from the wording of the order of the Colonial Government, dated February 3rd, 1872, in which the census of Chinese, then in course of preparation, is spoken of as the first executed

The Articles falling under the second category are 16 in number, and, with the exception of one, No. 31, directing domiciled Chinese to apprise the proper authorities of all changes of residence, are confined to the ordering of certain records and reports to be regularly made and kept by distinctly specified functionaries. Two are still of interest as being, with article 62 of the Rules of 1873, the only Regulations existing, having reference to steps to be taken in cases of death. The first, No. 27, is to the effect that employers shall report such deaths to the local officials, and shall deliver to them the contract and Cedula of the deceased for transmission to the chief authority of the district, by whom they are to be cancelled. The other, No. 30, refers to domiciled Chinese, and is similar in purport; it does not, however, specify by whom the report of death is, in the first instance, to be made.

The 44 Articles appertaining to the third category, with two exceptions, are practically to be found either embodied in or appended to the Rules of 14th September, 1872, and 7th May,

1873, which with the Decree of 1860 form the code now in force, and translations of which are attached.

The first exception is Article 55, which declares that Chinese desirous of quitting the island, but not possessing the necessary funds, shall, if after working one year for Government the sum to their credit is insufficient, be sent away at the cost of the dépôt. This provision, though never absolutely rescinded, is wholly in abeyance. The other clause was not included in the Rules of 1872, and was cancelled before the issue of the Rules of 1873. It, No. 71, lays down that Chinese who arrived before the 15th February, 1861, but who had omitted to apply for their Letters of Domicile, had, by their neglect, forfeited their right to the privilege. It was cancelled by an order of the Colonial Government dated 13th February, 1873, in "consideration of reasons " of expedience and justice which counselled the change.

The Instructions of 1868 seem to have failed to establish the perfect order hoped for, as in July and August, 1870, the Cuban authorities complained to the Spanish Government, that the development of agriculture and commerce and the pacification of the island were impeded by the immigration of Chinese, and urged its prompt cessation, and the necessity of the immediate departure of those in the island not engaged in the agricultural tasks for which they had been introduced, and stated that free labour would be found in abundance and was preferred by the planters. In reply to this appeal there was published at Havana, on the 13th June, 1871, a Royal Order, dated the 27th April of that year, declaring immigration suspended, in accordance with the provisions of 1860, and authorizing the deportation of all Chinese, without distinction, who, on the expiration of their original or subsequent contracts had not, according to the provisions of the laws, entered into fresh ones, who were devoting themselves to objects alien to that for which they had been brought to the island, or who had become elements of disorder; it was added, that the deportation of vagabonds and paupers was to be effected at the expense of the Government. The Colonial Government, however, did not avail itself of the assent thus accorded to its wishes. On the contrary, on the 18th October a Decree was issued explaining that the progress made in the tranquillization of the island rendered needless steps previously desirable, and that Chinese were permitted to remain in Cuba subject to the provisions theretofore in vigour, and calling upon all who had not yet done so, to at once act in accordance with these; that is to say, that immigrants who had arrived before the 15th February, 1861, should be careful that their Cedulas were in order, and that those of later arrival should either recontract or depart within two months. On the 13th December another Decree of the Colonial Government, of a different tone and of a more stringent nature, appeared. It recalls the facts, that of 6,948 immigrants landed from 1861 to 1863, whose contracts for eight years expired between 1869 and 1871, a large portion had evaded the law, and that in addition there existed a number of deserters whom it devolved on the Government to send back to their employers, so that the latter might be indemnified for the labour of which they had been deprived; it adds that the measures dictated in the Instructions of 1868 had been found inadequate, and that exceptional steps became indispensable, where the task to be undertaken was that of teaching obedience to the law to a multitude of individuals scattered over the island, who, whether they were engaged in agriculture, or manufacture, or domestic service, were sources rather of disorder than of peace and prosperity. This Decree contains 26 Clauses, and 1 Supplementary Article containing provisions of temporary application. The first 9 clauses repeat and amplify the Rules for the preparation of the Census Tables contained in the Instructions of 1868. The Articles Nos. 8 and 9, concerning the registration of domiciled Chinese, are characterized by increased stringency. The officers designated are to direct one or more of their subordinates, accompanied by two residents in the vicinity, to visit the dwellings of, and personally inspect the Chinese in question; the Letters of Domicile and Cedulas of the latter are to be examined with the most scrupulous care, and the descriptions of personal appearance which they contain are to be compared with the actual appearance of the holders· the adoption is authorized and enjoined of every precaution that may appear necessary in order to ascertain the genuineness of each document, and the legality of the manner in which it has been obtained by its possessor; documents even which withstand such tests are to be regarded and endorsed as still "subject to the revision of the Colonial Government," and resort, when judged needful, is ordered to the arrest prescribed in clause No. 30 of the 1868 Instructions. The remaining clauses meriting special notice provide that all other Chinese not employed on estates or in commercial establishments, or in private residences, are immediately to be arrested and confined in the dépôts; that all Chinese so employed, but not formally recontracted, are to remain under the temporary guardianship of the individuals in whose service they may be, until the Government can ascertain whether they are deserters, or whether they have been guilty only of the fault of neglect to recontract themselves in a legal manner; that a contract is to be entered into between these guardians and each Chinese thus placed under their care; that the contract is to be worded according to the specified form, to the effect that monthly wages of $ 12 are to be paid, $ 4 of which are to be handed to the workman and $ 8 to the Government for retention until the former's antecedents can be verified, for surrender to him if it be found that he is simply a non-recontracted, or for delivery with him to his original acquirer if he is proved to have resorted to flight; that the working collectively in gangs of even legally free Chinese is prohibited; that Chinese who, whilst the Census is being carried out, complete their first contracts are to have the option of remaining under the guardianship of their master or of entering the nearest dépôt; and that during the same period no papers of any class whatever are to be issued to Chinese, save Passes for those serving under original contracts whom their masters may desire to transfer from one locality to another.

These provisions were, of course, equivalent to the compulsory detention in the island of all Chinese then in it, and their stringency was relaxed in favour of those who had legally completed their contracts and desired to quit Cuba, by an order of the Colonial Government of the 16th January, 1872; but on the following 5th February this relaxation was withdrawn, and the withdrawal was reiterated in another order dated 17th May, and the issue of Passports was only sanctioned by an order dated 3rd July, 1872. On the 18th July, also of that year, the direct payment to immigrants serving under the temporary guardianship of their original employers was permitted. The state of tutelage in which so many Chinese were placed only ceased on the 14th September. An announcement to that effect and of the substitution of recontracting in accordance with prescribed formalities was appended as a Supplementary Article to the Regulations made public on that date. In another Decree, also dated 13th December, the Colonial Government, "considering necessary the creation of a Board, which, from the special

" qualifications of its members, may offer guarantees of success to the system prescribed as to " be adopted in regard to the Chinese already in the island, and to immigration generally," orders the constitution of a Central Commission of Colonization. This Commission is to consist of a President, 12 members, and 12 members substitute—who, apparently, only possess a vote in the absence of the members proper. Two-thirds of the members are to be planters. The presence of 5 voters is to form a quorum. The President and members are to be nominated by Government, and are to receive no salaries, and the expenses are to be defrayed out of the fees payable by the employers of labour, who, under the other Decree of the same date, retain or recover the services of Chinese. The Commission is empowered to act as the chief adviser of the Colonial Government, and as, under it, the chief administrator in all matters connected with immigration. Two days later a third Decree nominated the President and members. On the 19th May, 1872, the creation of Sub-commissions in every town which was the residence of a Governor or of a Lieutenant-Governor, and of a Delegate, under the orders of the Sub-commission in each district of such government, was ordered by the Colonial Government; and on the 10th September instructions for the guidance of these framed by the Central Commission and approved by the Colonial Government were made public. Though not distinctly specified in the above order, it is evident from the Regulations of May, 1873, that a Sub-commission for Havana was also constituted. The Chinese, however, had become desirous either of securing for their interests special representation or of availing them elves more extensively of a protector, which, though by no means free from disadvantages, eman ed at least from a source that was not affected by the influences which operated on planters, and on all who benefitted directly or otherwise by the cheapness of labour. Certain Chinese domiciled in Havana and possessed of some means, induced the Colonial Government to sanction, by a Decree dated 20th March, 1872, the appointment of a foreigner resident in that city, as Chief Agent, and of Sub-agents in the cities of the interior, to act as representatives of Chinese, in cases where interference became necessary to prevent the suffering of wrong through ignorance of the laws and language, and the bad faith of those with whom they were dealing. This scheme, commenced with very fair prospects of success, resulted in failure, owing to the withdrawal in the following July of the permission accorded, on the ground of abuses alleged to have been committed by the Sub-agent at Cardenas; but it is right that this Commission should place on record the fact that Chinese of every class speak in the highest terms of the honour, integrity and justice of the gentleman selected as Chief Agent. Again, a law dated 4th July, 1870, relative to foreigners residing in Spanish Colonies regularized and improved the position of these, and directed the issue of Cedulas de Estranjeros,—a document free from the restrictions with which the old Letter of Domicile was burdened,—to all registered in the books of their Consulates, and in those of the Colonial Government; and application by the Consulates was one of the methods indicated for effecting the latter registration and obtaining the Cedula referred to. The Consulate of Portugal, as indicated in the 56th article of the 6th section of the Macao Emigration Regulations, had long assumed the right to act as protectors of all Chinese embarked at Macao, had endeavoured, with imperfect success, to maintain a system of, on the arrival of a ship, inspection, registration and collection of fees, and had not unfrequently obtained for these alleged Portuguese subjects Letters of Domicile, and many Chinese, under the pressure of the Decree of 1871, entertained hopes that through the new law this external aid might be more easily resorted to, and the disabilities to which they were subjected more generally evaded. In an order, however, dated the 9th December, 1872, the Colonial Government decided that Chinese holding Cedulas as of Portuguese nationality, did not, if they had arrived after February, 1861, escape the application of the Decree of 1868,—*i.e.*, a fresh contract or departure; and in a later Order of the 16th of the same month, it announced its approval of the views expressed by the Commission of Colonization, that such Cedula could only be obtained by Chinese who had landed before February, 1861.

On the 20th June, 1873, the Colonial Government, in accordance with orders received from Spain, created the appointment of a paid Inspector of Chinese Immigration. The duties of this functionary are defined to be " the personal investigation of the treatment received by Chinese " during the voyage, the ensuring that all concerned obey strictly the Regulations and Provisions " in vigour relative to such immigration, and the inexorable enforcement by either administrative " or judicial means of the law, when any violation of it or abuse is encountered."

In the meantime the members of the Central Commi sion of Colonization had entered on the task of codifying and improving according to their own views the existing legislation. The results are the Regulations of the 14th September, 1872, (at first objected to by the Spanish Government as unnecessary,) and the Regulations of the 7th May, 1873, made public by order of the Colonial Government, and which, as before stated, combined with the Royal Decree of 1860, form the Code applicable to-day in Cuba to Chinese who have arrived, or may arrive under contract.

ROYAL DECREE OF 1860.

SECTION I:

Concerning the introduction of Chinese immigrants.

1.—The admission of Chinese immigrants into the island of Cuba is only authorized in accordance with the provisions of these Regulations.

2.—Every importer of Chinese must appoint a consignee in Cuba. The latter must be a proprietor of known standing resident in the island, or a firm established in it. Companies formed by shareholders cannot act as consignees; even those established in Havana and empowered by their statutes to introduce immigrants must designate a consignee as above defined.

3.—The consignee will be held responsible for those represented, in the event of any failure taking place in carrying out the provision of these regulations, without prejudice to the responsibility still attached to the master and officers of the vessel.

4.—The consignee must, in the first instance, report to the Captain General the name, capacity, crew and master of any vessel chartered for the purpose of conveying immigrants. He must at the same time report the number of Chinese whom he proposes to import in such vessel. The Captain General will publish these details in the *Havana Gazette*, and will, by the first mail, communicate them to this Government.

5.—The cognisance and authorisation of the Consul of Spain or of his agent, according to the locality of contracting a shipment, are indispensable preliminaries to the reception of the Chinese in Cuba. The Consul and his agents are directly responsible that such shipments are effected in accordance with the provisions of these Regulations.

6.—Every contract should specify and contain:—

1. The age, sex, and district of the Chinese contracted.
2. The term of contract.
3. The wages, and the nature, quality and quantity of the food and clothing which the immigrant is to receive.
4. The obligation of supplying the immigrant with medical aid during sickness.
5. Whether wages cease during a sickness not the result of labour or of any act for which the employer is responsible.
6. The number of hours of labour obligatory each day; and a declaration that if the employer is empowered to increase these during certain days, such increase must be compensated for by a proportionate decrease on other days.
7. The obligation on the part of the immigrant of making good to the employer such hours of labour as the latter may have lost by his fault.
8. The obligation on the part of the immigrant of submitting to the discipline of the plantation, manufactory, or other establishment to which he may be assigned.
9. A clause conceived as follows:—
    "I, _N. N._, fully aware that the stipulated wages are much less than those earned "by free labourers on the island of Cuba, agree to them because I consider that "this difference is comp e sated for by the other advantages which my employer "has to confer upon me, and which are those specified in this contract."
10. The signatures of the contracting parties, or in default of that of the immigrant, those of two witnesses.

7.—In addition to these particulars, an essential condition and clause of every contract entered into with a Chinese is, that on termination of his engagement he will not be able to remain in Cuba unless contracted afresh, as apprentice, or workman, agricultural labourer, or domestic servant, guaranteed by, and under the responsibility of his employer, and that failing such recontract, he will be forced to quit the island within two months from the termination of his contract.

8.—Contracts entered into with Chinese will be prepared in quadruplicate, and of these a translation in duplicate will be prepared by the interpreter of the Consulate.

9.—A list in quadruplicate of the Chinese embarked on board each vessel is to be prepared and signed by the person in charge of the shipment. This must specify sex, age and personal appearance, and must be delivered to the Consul of Spain, or his agent. The four copies will be endorsed by the Consulate, by which one copy also will be retained; of the other three one copy is to be returned to the shipper, one is to be transmitted directly to the Government of Spain, and one is to be forwarded to the Captain General of Cuba.

10.—Minors can only contract themselves with the consent of the person under whose charge they are.

11.—Immigrants are to be embarked in the proportion of one person for every two tons of fit accommodation remaining, after deduction of the space occupied by the cargo.

12.—It is besides obligatory on the importer,—

1. To provide the vessel with a quantity of water and sound food proportioned to the number of individuals who have to be embarked, and to the distance to be traversed.

2. Adopt the precautions necessary for maintaining on board the cleanliness and ventilation indispensable to the health of the passengers.

3. Carry a surgeon and medicine chest when the number of passengers exceeds 40.

4. Submit to whatever guarantees and police regulations may be in force at the port of Cuba which the vessel may enter.

13.—In order to ensure attention to these Regulations the immigrant can only be introduced by the port of Havana, except when shipwreck or other unavoidable accident renders compulsory entrance into and disembarkation at another port.

14.—The Consul of Spain in China will apprise in a circumstantial manner, directly and by the shortest route, both his Government and the Captain General of Cuba of the departure of each vessel conveying labourers to that island.

15.—Within 24 hours after arrival of such a vessel, its consignee must deposit in the Spanish Bank of Havana $ 50 for each Chinese embarked, without prejudice to the general provisions of the 3rd Article. This sum will be devoted to the immediate execution of any salutary measures which the state of the Chinese may reclaim, and to the immediate supplying them with proper lodging and assistance, in the event of neglect in either of these respects by the consignee, and to the payment of any pecuniary indemnities to which the Chinese may be entitled on account of occurrences either at time of embarkation, or during the voyage, or on arrival; and to, after these outlays have been defrayed, the payment of whatever penalties the actual importers have rendered themselves liable to. This deposit or the balance will be refunded to the consignee as soon as he is declared relieved of the responsibility thus imposed on him.

16.—When it appears from examination of the papers that the mortality of the Chinese during the voyage has exceeded six per cent., an enquiry into the cause will be instituted; and according to the report which ensues the Captain General, in consultation with the Board of Health and of Trade, will inflict a proportionate fine, or will transfer the matter to the tribunals.

17.—Within 24 hours after arrival or issue of bill of health, the consignee will tender a list of the immigrants originally embarked, noting on it those who have died during the voyage and the causes of death. The Captain General on receipt of this list, and after adoption of the precautions which he may deem necessary for the prevention of fraud, will permit landing.

18.—Two months after the termination of his engagement, the Chinese must either have renewed his contract as apprentice, or workman, or agricultural labourer, or domestic servant, or have quitted the island as prescribed in Article 7; and this provision becomes successively applicable to him on the completion of each engagement into which he enters, and in the event of his not fulfilling it, he will be employed on public works until, after deducting the cost of maintenance, the sum accumulated to his credit is sufficient to defray the cost of passage to the locality which he may select, or which, if he fails to do so, the Captain General may designate for him.

19.—Repeated abuses on the part of the actual importers, or the manifest insolvency of the consignee or his representative, will result in the authorisation for the continuance of the traffic being withdrawn. When such insolvency occurs, the Captain General will direct the actual importers to nominate within two months another consignee, and in the event of their failing to do so, their declarations of charter will be rejected, and such importations as may arrive for them will be regarded as undertaken in defiance of the provisions of these Regulations.

20.—Neglect to nominate a consignee or to declare in advance the charter of the vessel and the probable number of Chinese to be conveyed, the omission of the authorisation by the Consul of Spain or his agent of the contracts, shipments, and manner of equipment of the vessel, and the judgment of the tribunals in the grave cases which demand their interference, will result in the forfeiture by the importers of their rights over the Chinese introduced.

21.—When such forfeiture takes place, the Captain General will arrange for the landing and lodgment of the Chinese at the cost of the consignee, and will leave them at liberty to contract themselves as mechanics, labourers, or domestics, adopting at the same time the measures that may protect them most effectually against the disadvantages of their position.

22.—If within two months after landing, such Chinese have not succeeded in obtaining employment or have at any time shown a desire not to contract themselves on the island, the Captain General will exact from the consignee a sum sufficient to defray the costs of the re-exportation of the entire number, and will arrange for its being carried out in the securest manner possible, consulting, as far as he can, the wishes of the Chinese.

23.—Importers of Chinese can cede them to others engaged in similar undertakings, to plantations or to families, on whatever terms they may deem expedient, provided always that the acquirers bind themselves to fulfill the conditions of the contract and the provisions of these Regulations. This power of transfer will also be retained by such acquirers, subject in a like manner to being rendered void of any changes effected in the conditions of the original contracts.

24.—Importers and acquirers must report to the Captain General the number of immigrants whom they transfer and receive within 24 hours after the completion of the transaction. These reports must state the name, sex and age of the Chinese, the vessel in which they arrived, and the locality in which they are to reside.

25.—These transfers will be recorded in the Books of the Political Secretariat.

26.—The locality of residence of Chinese can not be changed without previous communication with the Government.

27.—Vessels conveying Chinese females are exempted from the payment of tonnage dues on the space occupied by these.

28.—Violations of these Regulations not specified in the foregoing clauses, by the importer or the consignee will be punished by the Captain General in consultation with the Royal Tribunal by the infliction of fines of not less than $ 1,000 and not exceeding $ 5,000; or if the violation has affected the safety and good treatment of the Chinese, of not less than $ 2,000 and not exceeding $ 10,000.

29.—Appeal to this Government is permitted regarding fines so imposed and the decisions of the Captain General when applying these regulations to particular cases.

30.—Without prejudice to the other cases specified in these Regulations, the Captain General in all those in which he imposes the fines prescribed, will hand to the Attorney General a minute of the circumstances, so that that functionary may, if he considers it his duty, instruct his deputy to, in the name of the Chinese, take legal action against the importers.

SECTION II.

Concerning the reciprocal obligations of immigrants to their employers.

31.—The Captain General of Cuba shall be the natural protector of Chinese immigrants, and shall exercise this function in the various governments by means of his delegates, the Governors and Lieutenant-Governors, who in turn will be aided by the Captains of districts. The latter officers shall, in every case, act under the direction of the Governors.

32.—In their relations with the Tribunals of Justice, immigrants will be defended, in the lower, by the Attorneys of the Courts of Justice of the Peace, and in the higher, by the Attorney General.

33.—The deputed protectors will watch over the good treatment of the immigrants and the fulfilment of the contracts entered into with them. They will propose to the Captain General such measures as they may deem advisable for the well-being and amelioration of those committed to their care, and will settle in a simple and informal manner any questions which may arise between the latter and their employers.

If these questions, however, involve any point of law, the protector will be aided by an assessor, and will convey his decision in the form of a verbal judgment, after hearing the statement of both parties.

If the matter is one of greater importance, it will be decided in accordance with the law by those on whom the duty devolves, and following the procedure established for the tribunals in question.

34.—It is understood that immigrants, when signing and accepting their contracts, renounce all civil right which may not be compatible with the accomplishment of the obligations to which they engage themselves, unless it be a right expressly conferred upon them by these Regulations.

35.—Immigrants may marry with the consent of their employers.

If the consent is refused and the immigrant is of age, he may either redeem himself in accordance with the provisions of clause 42, or may seek another employer who will fulfill these provisions for him.

36.—Immigrants will exercise over their offspring and wives all paternal and marital rights, in so far as these are compatible with the position under the law of the latter.

37.—The position of children born whilst the mother is serving under contract will be the same as that of the mother; but after they have completed their eighteenth year they will be free, even though the mother still continues under contract. Minors living with their mothers at the time of contract shall be dealt with according to the terms agreed to by the contracting

If no stipulation on the subject has been entered into, they shall be entirely free, but will, nevertheless, be entitled to receive, until the age of 12, from the employer of their mother such food, lodging and clothing as are enjoyed by the latter.

38.—Children born whilst the mother is serving under contract shall possess the same rights, so long as their position is analogous to hers; but it is obligatory that they shall render to their employers whatever services their age may permit of.

39.—Married immigrants can only be ceded to those who are willing to, at the same terms, acquire the wives and the children under 12 years.

No employer shall oblige either the husband and wife, or the mother and children under 12, to habitually live apart.

40.—Immigrants may acquire properties, and may dispose of what appertains to them either by gift or by sale, so long as such acts do not involve engagements, expressed or tacit, incompatible with the provisions of their contracts.

41.—Immigrants represented in the manner prescribed in Article 32, may publicly prosecute their employer. In actions against parties other than their employer they will be represented by the latter, if willing to undertake the task. Should the employer decline to do so, or should his interests in a dispute between the immigrant and a third party be opposed to those of the immigrant, the latter will be represented in the manner prescribed in Article No. 32.

42.—Immigrants who have entered into contracts before they have completed their 20th year, shall possess the right of cancelling these when they have attained to their 25th year. Those who have entered into contracts after the completion of their 20th year, shall possess the same right on the expiration of the 6th year of contract.

Employers shall likewise possess the right of cancellation when the 25th year of age and the 6th of contract, as above defined, have been completed.

The immigrant however cannot avail himself of the privilege conferred upon him by this article until by his labour, or in some other form, he has indemnified his employer for whatever he may owe him.

43.—Every immigrant can, at any time, redeem himself by the payment of the following amounts:—

1. The amount originally disbursed for his acquisition.
2. The amount due, either as indemnity for cessation of work during contract hours, or from any other cause.
3. The highest estimate formed by experts of the increased value of the services of the immigrant since his acquisition.
4. Compensation for the loss that may ensue from the difficulty of replacing the immigrant.

The immigrants can not make use of their rights of redemption during the season of cutting the sugar-cane, or at the time of execution of any of the pressing labours permitted even on festivals of the church.

44.—When an employer treats an immigrant cruelly, or fails to carry out his engagements towards him, the latter shall resort to the designated protector who shall order the cancellation of the contract, if, after hearing both parties, he is convinced of the justice of the complaint. In such case no indemnity shall be allowed for the sum expended in the acquisition of the immigrant, and the cancellation shall be enforced without prejudice to the civil or criminal actions at law, to which either party may see fit to resort.

45.—During days or hours of leisure, immigrants may work for their own profit within the establishment or plantation where they reside, or outside the limits of these if the permission of the employer be in the first instance obtained. On the same occasions, they may also engage in such amusements as are reputable and do not affect the disciplir⌐ of the establishment or estate.

46.—The immigrant shall dispose freely of what he may desire from his own property, or from his labour during days and hours of leisure, but he cannot engage in any permanent business against the desire of his employer.

47.—When an immigrant desires to part with property belonging to himself, he shall apprize his employer of his wish, and shall give him the preference as purchaser.

48.—Unless the contrary be expressly stipulated, the immigrant shall dispose of all tue fruits produced on any ground ceded to him by his employer for cultivation during the days and hours of leisure.

49.—Immigrants cannot quit the estate or establishment on which they are serving without the written permission of their employer or his representatives. Those who are met without this document shall be arrested and conducted, at the cost of their employer, to the locality which they had quitted.

50.—Should an employer be prevented by circumstances from supplying to immigrants food of the description, and clothing of the form and quality stipulated in the contracts, he shall be at liberty to furnish food and clothing of a different description, form and quality, but the quantity prescribed must be adhered to. If immigrants object to such substitution they shall have recourse to their Protector, who shall give a decision on the subject, conciliating as much as possible the interests of both parties, but, in any case, adopting a course which shall be in harmony with the essential rights of the immigrant.

51.—Whatever may be the terms of the stipulations of the contract regarding the medical aid to be supplied to the immigrant, such aid shall include, not only the attendance of a physician but also the medicines and nutriment which may be prescribed by him during sickness and convalescence.

52.—Labourers shall work for their employers on all days other than festival days, during the number of hours stipulated in the contracts. For the interpretation of this clause, the expression "days other than festival days" shall be held to include all days on which the teaching of the church does not prohibit labour, as well as days on which, despite the celebration of the festival, work shall be permitted by the ecclesiastical authorities.

53.—Under no circumstances, and notwithstanding any stipulations to the contrary, shall employers exact from immigrants, on an average, more than 12 hours' work.

54.—When a contract empowers the employer to distribute in the manner most convenient for his interests, the number of hours agreed upon with the immigrant, in accordance with the provision of paragraph 6 of Article 6, it shall be understood that no more than 15 hours can be exacted in one day (of 24 hours) and that the immigrant shall enjoy either during the day or night at least 6 consecutive hours of rest. If the right of distribution be not mentioned in the contract, the employer shall not be able to exact a number of hours greater than that specified in that document.

55.—The immigrant shall execute whatever tasks his employer may assign to him, unless the nature of the work which he is to perform, or of that which he is not to be called upon to execute, is specified in the contract. When such stipulations have been entered into, the labourer may decline to diverge from them. An employer may also hire out to a third party the services of his immigrants, so long as the contract contains nothing opposed to such a course, and so long as the services exacted are not contrary to its provisions.

56.—During the sickness or convalescence of an immigrant he shall not be forced to labour until the medical attendant certifies that he can resume work without endangering his health.

57.—Employers shall pay the stipulated wages in the form and in accordance with the conditions agreed upon in the contracts.

58.—Immigrants shall receive their entire wages whilst sick or recovering from maladies induced by any act of their employer, or arising from any cause which he might have prevented. This right, however, shall not extend to other maladies, unless it be so prescribed in the contract.

59.—Even when the contract provides for the payment of full wages during all maladies, the stipulation shall not be considered applicable when the ailment is the result of acts intentionally committed by the immigrant himself.

60.—The classification of maladies necessary for the operation of the two preceding clauses shall be effected by the physicians of the plantation or establishment, or in default of these, by two nominated by the employer. Should the immigrant decline to accept their decision he may have recourse to the deputed Protector, who shall order a second examination by two physicians, one designated by him and one by the employer, whose decision must be submitted to without further appeal. If the physicians thus nominated fail to agree, the Protector shall designate a third, whose judgment shall be final.

61.—Immigrants shall indemnify, by prolongation of their contract services, their employers for the days or hours during which they have by their own fault ceased work. For the days of labour thus wasted no wages shall be issued to the immigrant, unless the contract contains an express provision to the contrary.

The provision of this Article shall be inforced without prejudice to the liability of the immigrant to other penalties to which, by the offence in question, he may subject himself.

62.—In order to facilitate the execution of the provisions of the first paragraph of the preceding Article, the owners or administrators of plantations or other establishments employing Chinese immigrants shall keep records of the daily labour of these, and of the sums paid to them, so that at any time an account may be rendered of the amount to the credit or debit of each of the immigrants, and so that the latter may know for what term their contracts are to be prolonged.

63.—These accounts shall be made up and the result communicated to the immigrants at the close of each month, so that if any objection occurs to him he may raise it at once, and may resort to the Protector in the event of dissatisfaction with the decision of the employer.

64.—The provision—which each contract ought, as provided in Article 6, paragraph 8, to contain—as to the obligation of the immigrant to submit to the discipline of the estate or establishment in which he is employed, as well as all other provisions prescribing obedience on his part to the orders of his employer, shall be interpreted with the reservation that the rules and orders which the immigrant is expected to observe shall not be contrary to other conditions of the contract, or to any of the provisions of these Regulations.

65.—On the escape of an immigrant from the plantation or establishment in which he is employed, his employer shall report the fact to the local authorities, in order that the necessary steps may be taken for his arrest.

The employer shall refund, at once, the expenses of capture and restitution, but he shall possess the right of indemnifying himself by subsequent deduction of half the wages payable.

66.—Employers shall have immigrants instructed in the doctrines and morality of the true religion, without, however, resorting to means other than persuasion and argument, but if any one shall manifest a desire for admission into the Catholic faith, the fact shall be communicated to the ecclesiastic of the parish, so that the necessary steps may be adopted.

67.—When an immigrant receives an injury or offence affecting his person or interests (but not constituting a crime of which the law of its own accord takes cognizance), either from a man who is free or from an immigrant in another service, his employer shall make enquiry, and shall, should he consider the complaint a just one, endeavour to procure from the culprit or his employer in a friendly and extra-judicial manner the rightful reparation, and shall, if this intervention be unsuccessful, either appeal to the proper authorities or request the Government Attorney to do so on his behalf.

If he deem the grievance unfounded he shall inform the immigrant of his views, and shall urge him to abandon the complaint; and the immigrant, if still dissatisfied, must then in person have recourse to the Attorney in question. When disputes arise between two immigrants in the same service, the employer or his representative will decide the question in the manner that appears just.

Appeal against this decision may be made to the Protector or his delegate, who shall deal with the matter in the manner prescribed in Article 33.

68.—Importers or employers who fail to act in accordance with the obligation and formalities prescribed in this and the preceding sections, shall incur a fine proportionate to the gravity of the offence, to be imposed by the Executive, without prejudice to their liability under criminal or civil law, which shall be enforced in the proper manner by the Authorities.

SECTION III.

Concerning the disciplinary jurisdiction of employers.

69.—Employers are empowered to exercise disciplinary jurisdiction over immigrants in virtue of which they shall be able to inflict the following penalties :—

1°. Arrest from one to ten days.

2°. Loss of wages during the same term.

The first of these may be imposed without the second; but the latter cannot be resorted to unless the first has been enforced.

70.—When an employer imposes either of these penalties, he shall within 24 hours report the fact to the Protector of Chinese, in order that the latter may, should he deem it expedient, acquaint himself with the details of the offence, and may alter the sentence if it appears to him unjust.

Any employer neglecting to report within the time specified, shall be fined by the Executive a sum not less than $ 25, and not exceeding $ 100.

71.—Immigrants shall, in any case, possess the right of making complaint to the Protector regarding any wrong done to them by their employer, whether such wrong consists in the infliction of punishment without sufficient cause, in the imposition of unauthorized penalties, or in the breach of any of the provisions regulating his treatment of them.

If the Protector finds the employer guilty of a crime recognized by law, he shall denounce him to the proper tribunal; if the offence is of a more venial character, he shall simply impose a fine not exceeding $ 100.

72.—In order to ensure the fulfilment of the provisions of the preceding Articles, the Protectors shall, either in person or by their delegates, visit when they see fit, the estates and establishments on which Chinese are employed, and shall collect from the latter whatever information may be necessary.

73.—The representatives of employers are empowered to exercise a similar disciplinary jurisdiction, the employers being held pecuniarily responsible, without prejudice to the liability under criminal law, of their subordinates.

74.—The offences for which the specified penalties may be imposed, are:—

1°. Insubordination towards employers or managers of manufactories, etc., or towards any representative of the employer.

2°. Refusal to work or want of punctuality in the execution of the tasks assigned.

3°. The commission of assaults producing injury not rendering necessary suspension of work by the person injured.

4°. Flight.

5°. Drunkenness.

6°. Violation of the rules established by the employer.

7°. Any offence against morality, so long as it is not one of those which require the intervention of a prosecutor, or so long as, being of that class, the party injured refrains from complaint.

8°. Any other act intentionally committed, and causing injury or loss to another person, but not constituting a crime of which the laws can take cognizance.

75.—This disciplinary jurisdiction shall be exercised by the employer, without prejudice to the right of appeal to the tribunals that may be claimed by the person injured.

76.—In all cases of liability under criminal or civil law in which the competence of employers to act as judges ceases, the ordinary tribunals shall be resorted to, before which immigrants shall be represented in the manner prescribed in these Regulations.

77.—When the penalties specified in the 69th Article prove insufficient to prevent the commission by an immigrant of analogous or other offences, the employer shall have recourse to the Protectors, who will direct, if the act constitutes a crime under the law, the punishment of the offender in accordance with its provisions or, in the contrary case, an augmentation of the disciplinary penalties.

78.—When immigrants on an estate mutiny, or offer an active and united resistance to the orders of their superiors, the employer may have recourse to force in order to subdue them, and he shall at the same time at once communicate with the Protector of Chinese, so that the latter, if the gravity of the incident requires it, may arrange for the punishment of the offenders in the presence of their fellow labourers.

Section IV.

General Provisions.

79.—All renunciation by Chinese of the provisions in their favour prescribed by these Regulations shall be null and void.

80.—The Captain General shall adopt the necessary measures in order to ensure that each year, during the month of January, a census of Chinese immigrants shall be prepared. This census must specify the name, sex, age, condition and nature of labour and duration of contract of each individual, as well as the name, profession, and residence of the employer. The Captain General shall also transmit to the Minister charged with the administration of Colonial affairs a précis of the census tables. This précis shall show the entire number of immigrants classified by sex; by age, distinguishing between those under 15, those over 15 and under 50, and those over 50; by condition, distinguishing between the unmarried, the married, and the widowers or widows; by occupation, distinguishing between those employed in agriculture, manufacturing, or domestic labour; by the districts in which they reside; and by the duration of their contracts, distinguishing between the contracts of less than 5 years, of from 5 to 10 years, of from 10 to 15 years, and of from 15 years upwards.

81.—The Government reserves the right of at any time suspending and prohibiting the introduction of Chinese labourers into the island of Cuba. The resolution it may arrive at on this question shall be made public in the *Madrid* and *Havana Gazettes,* and the term on the expiration of which importation must cease, shall begin from the date of publication in the latter.

This term shall not be less than 8 months, and all importations taking place after it terminates shall be regarded as appertaining to the category of those specified in Article 20. It must be understood by importers that the fact of their engaging in the traffic is a recognition by them that its suppression or prohibition confers upon them no right to compensation.

82.—The Royal Decree dated 22nd March 1854, and all other anterior provisions relative to this subject are abrogated.

REGULATIONS OF 14TH SEPTEMBER 1872 CONCERNING THE RE-CONTRACTING, &C., &C.,
OF CHINESE IMMIGRANTS.

1.—Every Chinese immigrant arrived after 15th December 1861, the date on which the Royal Decree of 1860 came into force, is compelled to leave the island on the completion of his contract, or, should he desire to remain, to re-contract himself in the capacity of immigrant, labourer, or workman, according to the provisions of Article 7 of the above-quoted Royal Decree, of Articles 51 and 52 of the Instructions of 1868, and of the Decree of 18th October 1871.

Article 51 of 1868 simply prescribes the enforcement of Article 7 of 1860.

Article 52 is to the following effect :—

" Immediately after a Chinese who has completed a contract and who has not made
" a fresh agreement with his employer, has entered a dépôt, the facts of his being
" open to engagement shall be made public in the local journal, or, in the
" absence of such journal, notices to the same effect shall be posted in the most
" populous localities of the district. A similar notice shall be inserted in the
" official journal of the Government and in that of either Santiago de Cuba,
" Puerto Principe or Havana, according to the department to which the
" jurisdiction appertains."

The portion of the Decree of 18th October 1871 referred to, lays down that such re-contracts must be entered into with persons of recognized responsibility, and directs adherence to the spirit of Articles 46, 47, 48, 49, 62, 63, 64, of 1868, the purport of all of which is contained in Articles 13, 14, 18, 19, 20 of the present Regulations.

2.—The immigrant who, on the completion of his contract, desires to leave the island, shall be removed to the dépôt of the chief town of the Government, so that his embarcation within two months may be effected, as laid down in Article 7 of the Royal Decree of 1860 and in Article 54 of the Instructions of 1868; and if, at the close of this term, he has not prepared the sum required for the cost of passage, or if, although promising sufficient funds, he has not taken his departure, he shall be liable to be re-contracted, so that the municipalities may be spared the outlay involved by a large assemblage in the dépôts of such immigrants, and so that other evils arising from such assemblages, together with those resulting from the withdrawal from active labour of a number of Chinese, may be avoided. The latter, in this manner, will themselves reap advantage whilst benefitting by their labour agriculture and manufactures.

Article 54 of 1868 simply provides that, if the labourer fails to specify the district to which he desires to proceed, the Captain General shall do so on his behalf

3.—If the dépôt in which, as prescribed in the preceding Article, the immigrant is placed is distant from a sea-port, or if being a sea-port it offers no facilities for the transportation of the labourer to the locality to which he desires to proceed, he shall at once be sent to the dépôt of. Havana, whence his departure from Cuba will be effected.

4.—Deserters not claimed by their employers within a term of 11 months, calculated from the date of entering the dépôt, shall be held liable to a new contract, the operation of the original one being suspended, as laid down in Article 46 of the Instructions of 1868.

> Article 46 of 1868 is the same as the above; it simply adds that the immigrant is to remain in the dépôt until the new contract is made, and that on the completion of the 11 months he is to be transferred from Registration Table 3—"Deserters "detained,"—to Registration Table 4—"Chinese detained pending re-contracting."

5.—Chinese having completed penal sentences, shall, if their original contracts have expired, or if they are not claimed by their employers, be transferred to the dépôts. They shall then be liable to a new contract unless the Colonial Government sees fit to order their deportation from the island, or their sentence prescribes such deportation.

6.—Immigrants whose services have been from any reason whatsoever renounced by their employers, shall be subject to a new contract from the time of their entering the dépôt or from the time of their arrest, if they are seized as deserters after the renunciation has taken place.

7.—Applications for the recontracting of Chinese shall be made to the office of the Captain General, and shall, in accordance with the principles of the Decree of 13th December 1871, be handed by the latter to the Central Commission of Colonization. The Commission, by means of its special qualification and in accordance with its functions of aiding the administration in the application of the legislation, which has had for its object the improving of the morality and the regularising and utilizing of Chinese immigrants, shall report on the applications submitted to its consideration, so that under no circumstances the rights of the immigrants who, by no fault of their own, do not possess the funds necessary to enable them to quit the island may be disregarded.

8.—When, in consideration of the applicant possessing the necessary qualification of standing and respectability and in consideration of the dépôts containing a sufficient number of Chinese in a position to enter into fresh contracts, the Commission reports favourably regarding an application, the Captain General will, if he agrees with the views there expressed, instruct the Commission to, with due regard to existing rules for the enforcement of which it is responsible, prepare a deed or minute of cession of the Chinese whose services are applied for.

9.—It is indispensable that the willingness of the Chinese, whose liberty and rights are guaranteed by law, to enter the service of the employer who is desirous of hiring him be specified in this deed of cession, and the Government will regard as null all contracts made under deeds in which the consent is not expressed.

10.—In order to ensure the genuineness of this assent, the Commission of Colonization shall appoint a delegate who, in the dépôt and in the presence of the applicant or his representative, shall obtain it from the Chinese, and shall record it in a separate minute, which shall be signed by him, the applicant, and the officer of the dépôt, and which shall be attached to the deed of cession. These deeds, the list of the Chinese recontracted, and the contracts in quadruplicate, prepared as directed in these Regulations, shall then be transmitted to the office of the Captain General, so that the latter may give directions for the delivery, under receipt, of the immigrants in question.

11.—When Chinese detained in the dépôts of the chief towns of the Government are recontracted, the nominated delegates (the Sub-Commissions) shall take charge of the execution of the provisions of Articles 9 and 10.

12.—No Chinese can be recontracted for less than 6 years or for more than 8 years, and any agreement not in accordance with this provision shall be obligatory on neither the employer nor the immigrant.

> This Clause was cancelled by the substitution of two years as the minimum by an Order of the Colonial Government, dated 29th March, 1873.

13.—Deserters not claimed by their employers within 11 months, as specified in Article 4, shall only be recontracted for 6 months, at monthly wages of $4. These contracts shall include every obligation of the original contract, and may be successively renewed, but they must all contain the following Clause, as prescribed in Articles 46, 47 and 48 of the Instructions of 1868:—

> "The Chinese, *N. N.*, declares that he has deserted from the estate of his employer,
> " *D. N. N.*, (or of whose name he is ignorant,) and he hereby agrees to, should the
> " latter claim his services, indemnify him—on the termination of the present
> " contract—for the period intervening between his desertion and return."

> For Article 46, 1868, *vide* Article 4; Articles 47 and 48 of 1868 are similar to the above, with the exception that the wages are not specified.

14.—On the termination of their new agreement, deserters claimed by their original employers shall be compelled to serve the latter for a period sufficient to terminate their original contracts, as laid down in Article 49 of the Instructions of 1868; and this obligation shall also be applicable to cases of abandonment of fresh or renewed contracts.

> Article 49 of 1868 is similar to and contains only the first paragraph of the above.

15.—It is compulsory on all employers of deserters, under Article 13, to permit the inspection of the latter, during the day-time and in the localities where they may be occupied, by any individual duly authorized by the Inspector of Vigilance or Captain of District of his place of residence, and provided that the inspection takes place before the employer or his representatives or, in the event of their absence, before the person of most responsibility present on the plantation or other place of service, as on no pretext shall the inspection be delayed or prevented. The functionaries referred to shall issue at once, on application, and gratis the authorizations in question. In these shall be specified the name and condition of the person applying and of those, not to exceed two, accompanying him. It is however distinctly understood that these authorizations can only be applied for by proprietors of plantations or commercial or industrial establishments, or by heads of families who can prove by a reference to Registration Table 2 that Chinese have abandoned their service; representatives of such proprietors, &c., &c., shall also, on presentation of the cards of the former, be permitted to effect the inspection.

16.—The authorization thus issued shall be available for use in all parts of the island, and the bearer shall receive from the Inspectors of Vigilance and Captains of Districts in their various jurisdictions whatever aid is required of them.

The authorizations shall be void, and must be returned to the functionary by whom they were granted, on the expiration of three months from the date of issue.

17.—Employers desirous of renewing original contracts shall, three months before their maturity, make application to the office of the Captain General, and if their application be assented to, the recontracting may be proceeded with without any preliminary delivery of the immigrant to the dépôt, but in strict accordance with all other formalities, more especially with that specified in Article 9.

> This Article is modified by an Order issued by the Colonial Government on the 20th May 1873, which permits the verification of the assent of the Chinese in question to take place in the country districts before the Delegate of the Sub-Commission of the Government, instead of in the chief town before the Sub-Commission itself, as specified in Article 11.

18.—The labours of Chinese recontracting shall only be utilized for the benefit of their employers. The latter shall under no circumstances permit such Chinese to engage in other distinct occupations, or exact from them fees or compensation of any description, as already laid down in Article 62 of the Instructions of 1868.

> Article 62 of 1868 is exactly similar to the above.

19.—Employers are not permitted to transfer such recontracts, or to hire out the immigrants to other individuals, as already laid down in Articles 42 to 63 of the Instructions of 1868; only in the event of death of the employer the contract may pass to his heirs with his other rights and property

> Article 63 of 1868 is exactly similar to the first paragraph of the above.

20.—Any violation of the preceding (two) Articles shall be punished by a fine of $500 for each Chinese so transferred or hired out, in addition to the cancellation of the contract and the removal of the Chinese to the dépôts.

> Article 64 of 1868 is similar to the above; only the fine specified in it is from $200 to $1,000.

21.—The new contract shall be written on paper of 8vo. size, and must be granted in the presence of the Governor or Lieutenant-Governor, who, in the capacity of Protector of Chinese, shall exercise care that the provisions of the Regulations are exactly observed.

> The Order referred to under Article 17, sanctioning the recontracting in the country district of certain Chinese before the Delegate of the Sub-Commission, prescribes in such cases the transmission of the contract by the latter to the Governor for signature.

22.—These contracts, prepared in quadruplicate and signed by both parties and by the chief local Authority, shall be transmitted through the office of the Captain General to the Central Commission of Colonization, to be recorded by it. Unless this last condition is fulfilled the contracts become void.

23.—On the completion of this formality, one copy shall be retained by the Commission and one by the office of the Captain General. The remaining two shall be handed to the immigrant and his employer.

24.—To each recontract, whether the immigrants appertain to the class of those who have duly fulfilled previous contracts or to the class of deserters, the employer shall pay a fee of $4.50. These sums cannot be deducted afterwards from the immigrants' wages. They shall be devoted by the Central Commission to the defraying of its office and other expenses, and a monthly account of such outlay shall be handed to the office of the Captain General.

Employers recovering possession of deserters shall, in addition to refunding the expense of capture, pay a like sum, and these amounts shall also, to the extent necessary, be devoted to the purpose specified in the preceding paragraph.

> This Article is modified by an Order of the Colonial Government dated 29th March 1873, substituting for the first paragraph a payment of $ 10 for each year of the new contract, to be paid in one amount, in advance, at the time of issue of the contract; and a payment of $ 5 for each deserter's 6 months' contract.

25.—Sections 2 and 3 of the Royal Decree of 1860, defining the mutual obligations of immigrants and their employers, and the disciplinary jurisdiction of the latter, shall be applicable to the new employers and to the recontracted immigrants.

26.—The recontracted immigrant shall be subject, during the period of his engagement, to the rules observed in the commercial or industrial establishment, plantation or private residence in which he is serving.

27.—Immigrants shall, by prolongation of their contracts, indemnify their employers for the days or hours during which by their own fault they have ceased work. For the days of labour thus wasted no wages shall be issued to the immigrant, without prejudice to the other penalties to which he may be liable as provided in Article 61 of the Royal Decree of 1860.

28.—In the event of sickness, an immigrant shall receive the medical attendance, the supplying of which is obligatory on his employer; but no wages shall be issued until he is able to recommence labour. The time during which he is absent from work shall not be deducted from the period specified in the contract, and will have to be made good if the cessation of labour is due to a sickness or to a cause voluntarily originated by himself, or which could not have been prevented by his employer. If however the sickness arises from a cause for which the employer is responsible, the wages shall continue to be paid and the period of absence shall be deducted from the contract term.

29.—During sickness immigrants shall be placed in quarters suitably arranged with reference to their state, and they shall there receive such aid in the form of medicine and medical attendance as may be necessary.

30.—The immigrant shall be supplied with food similar to that furnished to other workmen or labourers of his class employed in the commercial or industrial establishment, plantation or private residence where he is serving. Yearly also, in the months of January and July, he shall receive two suits of clothes consisting of a palm-leaf hat, a shirt and trousers of cotton fabric, shoes of twined hide, and in January, in addition, a woollen jacket and a blanket.

31.—The contract shall be made out in Spanish, and in it the immigrant shall declare his acceptance of the wages stipulated—although they may appear lower than those earned by other labourers—in consideration of the exceptional advantages secured to him.

32.—The employer must present to the Authorities of his place of residence the contracts and cedulas of all Chinese recontracted to him, and with these documents he shall deliver the list of the names of the immigrants as prescribed in Article 8 of the Instructions of 1868. The Authorities, after making the necessary entries in Registration Table No. 1 ("Chinese serving under contract"), and after having entered, sealed and returned the contracts and cedulas as prescribed in Article 9 of the Instructions referred to, shall transmit the list, through the office of the Captain General, to the Central Commission.

> Article 8 of 1868 applies to the census then ordered, and directs that contracts and cedulas of immigrants serving under contract, and a list of them according to a model given, shall be furnished to the local Authorities.

> Article 9 directs the comparision of the list with the contracts and cedulas, and the sealing and returning of the latter to the employer.

33.—Employers who do not desire to renew the engagement of immigrants who have been recontracted to them, shall report the fact of completion of contract to the local Authorities and shall, on the day following completion, deliver the immigrant to the dépôt of the chief town of the Government. Any neglect of these provisions shall be punished by a fine of $ 25, unless it can be shown that sickness on the part of the immigrant rendered such delivery impossible.

34.—At the time of delivery to the dépôt, the employer shall hand the contract and cedula of the immigrant to the chief local Authority, affixing to each document a note signed to the effect that the contract was duly completed and that the immigrant was handed to the dépôt.

This note shall be endorsed by the local Authority specified, who shall also, through the proper channel, transmit the documents in question to the Central Commission.

35.—The copy of the contract held by the immigrant shall also be delivered to the Commission.

36.—The Commission shall make public periodically a list of immigrants awaiting recontracting in the various dépôts.

37.—All immigrants arrived after the 15th February 1861, who shall be found employed, without being in due form contracted, on a plantation or in an industrial or commercial establishment or private residence, shall be conducted to the dépôt of the chief town of the Government, so that they may be recontracted in the manner prescribed by these Regulations, or be delivered to their proper employers if discovered to be deserters.

38.—The proprietor of such plantation, establishment or private residence shall be fined a sum of $ 500, without prejudice to his other legal responsabilities, for each Chinese thus employed. The date of infliction of these fines, and the cause of their infliction, shall be made public in the Official *Gazette*.

39.—All persons receiving into their service immigrants contracted to other employers shall be subject to a like penalty.

40.—The fifth part of such fines and of those imposed under Article 20 shall be paid by the Treasury to the Government official or police officer who has detected the offence, or to the private individual who has denounced it. A full report of the details shall be made to the office of the Captain General, to which at the same time shall be remitted half the amount of the fine, on receipt of which, orders for the payment within three days of the rewards above indicated shall be issued.

41.—The official of the districts in which the commission of the offence above referred to has been denounced and verified, shall be removed, and shall, in addition, be subject to any other action to which inquiry may give rise.

REGULATIONS of 7th May, 1873.

Section I.

Concerning the organisation of Central and Municipal Dépôts.

1.—In accordance with the provisions of the 8th paragraph of the 5th Article of the Decree of 13th December 1871, establishing the Central Commission of Colonisation, two central dépôts are established at Havana,—one for the Chinese coolies arrived after the 15th February 1861, and obliged by Article 7 of the Royal Decree of 1860 to renew their completed contract or to quit the island,—the other for deserters, who have to be either sent back to their employers or provisionally contracted.

> Paragraph 8 of Article 5 of the Decree of 1871 above referred to, assigns as one of the duties of the Central Commission the proposal of measures for the concentration at Havana of all the Coolies sent away from the Central and Eastern Departments.

2.—The central dépôts shall be under the exclusive charge of the Central Commission, and shall be free from all interference on the part of the municipality.

3.—The cost of the lodging, food, clothing and custody of the Chinese in the dépôts shall be defrayed out of the special revenue of the Commission.

For each Chinese contracted in accordance with the Regulations of the 14th September 1872, shall be paid, in advance, in one sum, by the contractors at the time of contract, $10 for each year during which the contract is to be in force; and for each deserter secured for his employer shall be paid by the latter—in addition to whatever amount may be due to the person effecting the arrest—the $4.50 originally prescribed in the Temporary Provision of the Decree of December 1871 (and again ordered in Article 24 of the Regulations of September 1872).

> The collection of $5 for each deserter's 6 months' contract (*vide* note to Article 24 of the Regulations of September 1872) has not been countermanded, and the omission of this provision in these Rules appears to be accidental.

4.—Deserters on admission into the central dépôt may be hired to persons of position and character in accordance with provisions to be specified below, in order that the remuneration obtained for their labours may be devoted to the defraying of any outlay incurred in excess of the receipts defined in the preceding clause.

5.—Such deserters, however, can not be hired out singly, whether for work in the cities or in the country. They shall only be leased in gangs of not less than 10, which shall be subject to the discipline in force on the plantation or in the commercial or industrial establishment where they are employed, and by which they are to be guarded, supplied and generally cared for.

6.—After the lapse of 11 months from the time of entering the central dépôt, a deserter can not be hired out, but must be recontracted for 6 months in due conformity with the provisions of Articles 46 and 49 of the Instructions of 1868 and of Articles 13 and 16 of the Regulations of September 1872.

7.—Employers of deserters shall, on recovery of the latter, simply pay the amounts defined in Article 3, as the expenses of transmission to and residence in the central dépôt are to be defrayed out of the revenues of that establishment.

8.—The financial administration of the central dépôts shall be confided to the Central Commission of Colonisation, which shall be careful to give effect to the final clause of Article 9 of the Decree of 1871 establishing the Commission. The staff of the central dépôt, of every class, shall be under the control of the Commission.

> The clause of Article 9 of the Decree of 1871 prescribes delivery to the Central Government of monthly accounts of receipts and expenditure.

9.—The administration of the central dépôts shall exact only the authorised fees. It shall be responsible for the escape of Chinese, when it can be proved that such incidents were due to defective vigilance and to neglect in the execution of its functions. The administration will nominate the employés of the central dépôts, and will be responsible for their good conduct. It will also frame rules for the internal government of these establishments, and will give due effect to the provisions regarding their administration contained in the present Regulations.

10.—In addition to the central dépôt, local dépôts for deserters are established in the chief towns of each Government. These shall be under the charge of the municipality, and subject to the supervision of the Sub-Commissions of Colonisation. Deserters shall be detained in these dépôts only one month, on the expiration of which they shall be transmitted to the central dépôt as hereafter prescribed.

11.—In these municipal dépôts of the chief towns, the Sub-Commissions shall, in addition to the function indicated in the instructions addressed to them on the 9th August 1872,—viz., that of recording and reporting the admissions and discharges,—undertake the arrangements for the speedy and economical transport to the central dépôt of deserters not claimed within one month after admission; and they shall also carefully guard against any delivery of Chinese by official order, when the formalities prescribed in the present Regulations have not been complied with.

> The instructions above referred to call for no notice more particular than that to be found among the explanatory remarks with which this memorandum commences.

12.—In order to ensure the observance of the provisions of the preceding Article the Superintendents of prisons and of the municipal dépôts of Havana and the chief towns, shall inform the local Sub-Commission of all admissions and discharges, and their causes, in order that the latter may supply to the Central Commission the details required for the preparation of its statutes and for the due order and administration of the central dépôt.

13.—Deserters during the months of detention in the municipal dépôts shall only be employed, duly guarded, on municipal works, and the Authorities shall be held responsible if it is ascertained that their labour is devoted to other objects.

SECTION II.

Concerning the detention in the Central Dépôt of Chinese awaiting recontracting.

14.—Chinese of the class referred to in Article 1 who, having completed any contract, are either unwilling or unable to procure its renewal, shall be delivered (by their employers) to the local Authorities.

The expired contracts and çedulas must be handed in at the same time.

15.—Chinese who have been recontracted since the 13th December 1871, and in recontracting whom the requirements of the Rules of September 1872 have not been fulfilled, as well as all others removed from the previously existing dépôts since December 1871, without the cognizance of the Central Commission—with the exception of those to whom the order of the Colonial Government of the 29th October applied—shall be either delivered to the central dépôt or surrendered to the Authority of the locality.

> The Order of 29th October 1872 refers to the unauthorised removal of Chinese from dépôts spoken of in the above Article, orders their return, and excepts only a very small number in regard to whom "the Colonial Government has granted "special concessions."

16.—Chinese arrived after the 15th February 1861, who have not duly recontracted with the proprietors of the plantations or commercial or industrial establishments or private residences where they may be found, or who have not been duly entered on the registration tables, shall be removed to the central dépôt at the cost of their employers, in order that they may be recontracted in the proper form, or, if ascertained to be deserters, may be surrendered to their legal masters in accordance with the provision of Article 37 of the Regulations of September 1872; and this removal shall not affect the liability of those concerned to the imposition of the fine prescribed in Article 38 of the said Regulations.

17.—Any recontracted Chinese found labouring independently, or who is hired out or in any manner transferred by his contract employer, shall likewise be brought at the cost of the latter to the central dépôt, in accordance with the provisions of Article 62 of the Instructions of 1868 and of Articles 18 and 39 of the Regulations of September 1872; and both contract employer and the Chinese shall be liable to the fines laid down in Articles 20 and 38 of the Regulations just referred to.

18.—All Chinese arrived after the 15th February 1861 wrongfully in possession of papers of freedmen shall be conducted to the central dépôt, with a view to their being recontracted, after the date of their arrival and the illegality of the manner in which they obtained such papers have been verified.

19.—When, as provided in the preceding Articles, Chinese are sent either to the central dépôts or different local Authorities, their original and subsequent contracts and the cedulas held for them by their employers, must in due course be transmitted to the Central Commission.

20.—Within 10 days after the delivery, as above provided, of a Chinese to any local Authority, he shall be forwarded by the latter to the central dépôt at the cost of his employer when such a course is prescribed; or at that of the Central Commission when payment from any other source has not been definitively indicated. The transport shall be effected in the most convenient and economical manner.

21.—Any neglect to conform to the preceding Article shall be reported by the Sub-Commission of the chief town or Delegate of the District, and shall be punished by the immediate removal of the official complained of.

22.—Chinese entering the central dépôt on completion of their original contracts, shall declare whether they are in possession of the funds necessary to enable them to quit the island, and whether they desire to obtain passports, and shall, when expressing the desire, be allowed two months in order to effect their departure. If however any Chinese within this term has not proved satisfactorily that he duly fulfilled his original contract, the provisions of Article 4 of these Regulations shall be applied to him, without prejudice to the continuance of the enquiry as to the fact of such fulfillment.

23.—The Chinese referred to in this Section shall, on admission into the central dépôt, be entered in Registration Table No. 4,—" Chinese who, having completed contracts, are detained " in dépôts pending departure or recontracting,"—and a minute shall be made of the entrance of each individual, to which shall be attached his expired original contract and his employer's certificate of its completion.

24.—When by the production of these latter documents the fact of completion of the original contract has been duly ascertained, the Chinese shall be at liberty to recontract himself in accordance with the provisions of the Regulations of September 1872; but if, after the lapse of a sufficient time, the necessary proof has not been furnished, he shall be liable to the application of Article 4 of these Regulations.

25.—Chinese who have completed their original and subsequent contracts, and who desire to quit the island, shall receive Passes to enable them to proceed to Havana in order to procure Passports in the manner prescribed in the Order of the Colonial Government of the 13th July 1873, and shall deliver the original contracts and the certificates of expiration to the Central Commission. Those residing in Havana shall be conducted by their employers before the Central Commission, to which at the same time the above specified documents must be delivered; failing the production of these or of the guarantees spoken of in the said Order, the Passport shall be refused.

>   The Order of the 13th July is similar in purport to the above, but it adds that the
>   guarantee must be satisfactory to the Central Commission.

26.—All Chinese detained in the central dépôt pending recontracting, shall possess the right of applying to the Captain General for an inquiry into the date of their arrival, with a view to the amelioration of their position under law. During such inquiry however, and until the accuracy of their statement has been proved, they shall continue to be subject to the provisions of these Regulations.

Neither the Central Commission, nor any of its subordinates, shall in any way prevent recourse to the right just specified, but on the contrary shall afford to the Chinese in question facilities for justifying the correctness of their claims.

SECTION III.

Concerning Deserters.

27.—Chinese failing to prove the due completion of their contracts shall, as well as those who have abandoned their employers, be regarded as falling under the provisions of these Regulations applicable to deserters.

28.—A deserter captured in any part of the island shall be detained during three days by the Authorities of the locality where his arrest is effected. The fact of the arrest shall, if it has taken place in a country district, be made public by notices posted throughout the district, and if, after the expiration of the term specified, no application has been made by the employer, the deserter shall be removed to the chief town of the Government, to be held at the disposition of the Governor.

29.—All Captains of Districts, or Inspectors or Superintendents of Vigilance in these, into whose hands deserters fall, shall report the fact to the Governor and to the senior member of the Sub-Commission of Colonization at the chief town, and if within the three days during which the seizure is made public, an application, supported by production of the original contract or recontract of the Central Commission,—on which should appear the endorsement of date of flight prescribed in Article 11 of Instructions of 1868,—is made by the employer, the deserter shall be delivered to him. The functionary who effects the delivery shall also, in conformity with Article 24 of the Instructions of 1868, note on the contract or recontract the date of seizure, and this note shall be signed by him and the employer. He shall further collect from the latter the sum payable to the person who effected the seizure, and the prescribed fee of $4.50, and shall transfer the entry from Registration Table 2 ("Deserters") to Table 1 ("Serving under contract"). The fee shall be remitted to the Governor, and a report of the circumstances shall be made to the Sub-Commission at the chief town.

> Article 11 of 1868 is to the effect that for the preparation of Census or Registration Table 2, "Deserters," employers shall fill up a certain form, and shall hand it and the contracts and cedulas of the deserters to the local authorities, who shall return to the employers the latter two documents after endorsing in the contract the date of flight.

> Article 24 prescribes a report to the local Authorities of the recovery of a deserter, and the presentation with it again of contract and cedula; and that the Authorities shall endorse on the contract the date of recovery and the obligation of making good the duration of the fugitive's absence.

30.—The delegates of Sub-Commissions in the country district are charged with the supervision necessary for the exact fulfillment of the provisions of the preceding Article, and shall report to the Sub-Commission in the chief town all infractions of it that may take place.

31.—On the expiration of the term of three days, no application having been made by the employer, the deserter shall, as directed in Article 28, be sent to the chief town, to be then held at the disposition of the Governor; and a report of the fact of removal shall at the same time be made to the senior member of the Sub-Commission.

32.—In all cases of seizure of deserters, the official to whom they are in the first instance delivered shall prepare for transmission to the local Governor a minute of whatever information he has elicited in regard to the deserter (and this minute shall be accompanied by a copy of the report made to the Sub-Commission). If the Governor is thus enabled to ascertain the name and residence of the employer interested, he shall at once communicate with the latter, and shall note on the minute he has received the fact of his having done so.

33.—If, thus apprised, the employer shall make application within the term of one month, to which the detention of the deserter in the chief town is limited, the latter shall be delivered to him on the due fulfillment of the formalities indicated in Article 29. If the month has elapsed without such application having been made, he shall be forwarded to the central dépôt at the expense of the Commission of Colonization. No excuse or pretext shall relieve the Governors from their responsibility for the strictest observance of this rule.

34.—The minute containing the result of the enquiry instituted regarding a deserter, shall be forwarded to the President of the Central Commission, who shall be careful that the removal to the central dépôt of the Chinese referred to is—if it does not take place in due course—promptly enforced.

35.—During the month of detention thus to be passed in the municipal dépôt of Havana or of a chief town of another Government, deserters shall be supported by the respective municipalities, as prescribed in Article 10 of these Regulations, and may be employed in the public works of the locality. They shall not, however, on any plea be loaned, hired or contracted to private employers.

36.— During this term of one month, each Sunday deserters shall be assembled in the dépôt from 6 A.M. until 6 P.M. and then inspection by employers shall be permitted. On such days also deserters, whilst at work or resting, may in a like manner be inspected with a view to recognition; and in addition their presence in the dépôts shall be made public by means of notices in the local journals, and of a list posted at the gate of the dépôt containing such details as may appear likely to facilitate identification. On receipt of an application for delivery from an employer the formalities prescribed in Article 29 shall be observed.

37.—Any Chinese met outside of the plantation or commercial or industrial establishment where he is employed, without the written permission of the owner or his representative, prescribed in Article 49 of the Royal Decree of 1860, shall be seized by the official of the locality, and shall be forwarded at the cost of his employer to his place of service, if the latter lies within the district where the seizure is effected, in accordance with the provisions of Article 37 of the Instructions of 1868.

The purport of Article 37 of 1868 is similar to that of the above.

38.—The offences of sheltering a deserter in a private residence or on a plantation, or of, by means of fictitious documents, registering him as in legal service or as free, shall be punished by the infliction of a fine of $ 500 for each individual so sheltered or registered, without prejudice to the criminal liability before the Court of Justice of the guilty individual, in accordance with the provisions of Article 36 of the Instructions of 1868. In such cases the deserter shall be at once removed to the central dépôt.

Article 36 of 1868 is similar to the above.

39.—For the prevention of the offences just referred to, the Sub-Commission and Delegates, and any private individual who may desire to co-operate with them, shall resort to whatever methods of inquiry their zeal or interest may suggest to them, and shall denounce to the Central Commission the cases of which they become aware.

40.—All Chinese found on any estate or in any establishment labouring collectively in a gang under a head or a contractor in violation of the first paragraph of the Temporary Provisions of the Decree of the Colonial Government of 1871, and of the Order of the 13th May of last year shall, with the head of the gang if he be a Chinese, be removed to the central dépôts, and the owner of the estate or establishment shall be liable to the infliction of a fine of $ 500 for each member of the gang, as prescribed in the Order referred to.

The Governor, as well as the Captain of the District where the gang is discovered, shall be suspended, and the intervention of the tribunals shall be resorted to in order that it may be ascertained whether there has been culpable connivance on the part of the officials in question.

> The first paragraph of the Temporary Provision of the Decree of 1871 prohibits working in gangs, adding that a free Chinese can only dispose of his own individual services, and must do so directly to the owner of the plantation or establishment where he works, without the intervention of a third person.

> The Order of 13th May, 1872, refers to the non-observance of the provision of the Decree of the previous year, to the facilities afforded by gangs for the concealment of deserters and non-recontracted Chinese, and declares that all Governors, Lieutenant-Governors and Captains of Districts shall be held strictly responsible for their suppression, whilst the employer shall be liable to a fine of $ 500.

41.—The suppression of these gangs is specially urged upon the Sub-Commissions and Delegates of Colonization. Any residents in the vicinity may also denounce their existence, whilst the Central Commission shall, with the approval of the Colonial Government, issue authorization for the inspection of estates on which the presence is suspected of these assemblages so justly prohibited as offering inducements to flight and affording facilities for the concealment of deserters.

42.—Free Chinese duly registered, who have directly engaged their services at fixed wages or by the day to the owner of a plantation, commercial or industrial establishment or private residence, with the cognizance of the Captain of the District, shall not be held liable to the application of the preceding two clauses; but such Chinese can take part in no work other than that of such plantation or establishment or residence, and their Letters of Domicile and Cedulas shall be subject to any scrutiny ordered on behalf of the Central Commission.

43.—Deserters confined in the central dépôt shall also be delivered to their employers on compliance with the provisions of Article 29, and on payment of the amount specified in Article 3.

44.—After admission of a deserter into the central dépôt, enquiries with the view of discovering his original employer shall be instituted.

The entries of his name and personal appearance shall also be transferred from Registration Table 2 ("Deserters,") to Table 3 ("Deserters detained in dépôts"). The fact of his admission into the central dépôt, together with all the details procurable regarding himself, his employer, and the place of residence of the latter, shall be made public in the official journal of the Central Commission, and the insertion of these details in it shall be repeated every fortnight until he is delivered to his employer.

45.—During the stay of a deserter in the central dépôt, his services shall be utilized in the manner laid down in Article 4; but at the close of 11 months he shall recontract himself for 6 months, as prescribed in Articles 46 to 49 of the Instructions of 1868, and in Articles 13 to 16 of the Regulations of 14th September, 1872.

46.—It is compulsory on all who have engaged, under Articles 4 and 5, gangs of deserters whose previous employers have not been discovered, to permit their inspection in accordance with the provisions of Article 15 of the Regulations of 14th September, 1872.

47.—The authorization of inspection shall be void on the expiration of three months, as laid down in the last paragraph of Article 16 of the Regulations just referred to.

48.—On the expiration of 11 months from the date of admission of a deserter into the central dépôt, he shall be recontracted for the term of 6 months, in accordance with the provisions of Articles 46 to 49 of the Instructions of 1868 and of 13 to 16 of the Regulations of 14th September, 1872. The recontract shall stipulate for the payment of monthly wages of $ 12, of which $ 4 shall be paid to the Chinese and $ 8 shall be retained as revenue by the Central Commission. When applicants for such recontracts are in other respects alike, the preference shall be given to landowners who prove by reference to Registration Table No. 2, that deserters from their service have not been recovered.

49.—Employers shall not resume possession of deserters whom they may discover in the service of others under the provisions of the preceding Article until, on fulfillment of the formalities prescribed in Article 29, the necessary order has been issued by the Central Commission. If this rule is not observed, the Chinese affected shall be brought back to the central dépôt at the cost of the employer, who, together with the recontractor who has permitted the removal, shall be liable to a fine of $ 100.

If, however, deserters hired out according to Article 4 are identified by their employers, they may be removed by the latter on condition of the production by him, within 48 hours after such removal, of the contract with a view to the fulfillment of the provision of Article 29.

50.—In the official journal of the Commission of Colonization shall be published monthly a statement of the deserters who, through having passed 11 months in the central dépôt, are subject to recontracting; and also a statement of such recontracts effected during the month, specifying the name, number by which known in dépôt, antecedents, recontractor and residence of each of the Chinese so recontracted.

51.—A deserter whose name has been retained on the books of the central dépôt for six years, whilst he has been working under the contracts prescribed in the Instructions of 1868 and the Regulations of 14th September, 1872, shall be transferred to the class and dépôt of Chinese who have duly fulfilled their contracts, and shall be at liberty to either quit the island or to recontract for his own benefit, subject to the provisions of the 2nd section of these Regulations, and to those of the Regulations of 14th September, 1872.

ˍᴇᴄᴛɪᴏɴ IV.

Concerning the Internal administration of the Central Dépôts.

52.—The conductor of a Chinese to the central dépôt shall, on delivery of him to that establishment with the necessary reports of the circumstances of the case, be furnished by the Superintendent or employé designated, with a receipt, the ˉproduction of which or of the despatches from the sender advising transmission of the immigrant, shall enable those interested to obtain from the Central Commission the refund of any outlay incurred after due approval of the items of which it consists. The receipt shall specify the number given to the Chinese in the central dépôt, his name, whether he is a deserter or has completed his contract; if the former, the the name of his employer if known, and the locality whence and the authority by whom he was forwarded; and it shall also contain a description of his personal appearance made out according to prescribed forms.

53.—The Superintendent of the central dépôt shall report, according to the prescribed form, the admission of each Chinese to the Central Commission, and this report shall also be sufficient authority for the refunding of outlay referred to in the preceding Article.

54.—The Superintendent of the central dépôt shall enter all admissions on the proper Registration Tables, and he shall also, in the separate record of deserters and of immigrants who have completed contracts, make full notes of each admission, following the prescribed forms.

55.—The Superintendent of the central dépôt shall weekly furnish the Commission with a statement of the admissions and discharges, following the prescribed form, and on this statement shall be based the estimates of the various supplies required.

Accounts of the quantities of these purchased and distributed shall be kept, and a weekly statement for the inspection of the Commission prepared according to prescribed form.

56.—No purchases of supplies of any class for the central dépôt can be effected without the sanction of the President of the Commission.

57.—When a Chinese escapes from a dépôt of any class, the fact shall at once be reported by the Superintendent to the local official, to the Governor of Havana and to the Central Commission.

58.—The dress of deserters detained in the central dépôt shall be different from that of the Chinese who have completed their contracts. The number by which they are distinguished shall also be marked on the back of their outer garment.

59.—Deserters hired out as provided in Article 41 or contracted after the expiration of 11 months, as provided in Article 48, shall only be permitted to leave the central dépôt on presentation of an order made out in the prescribed form.

60.—When delivered over to their new employer, the latter shall acknowledge the fact of delivery at the foot of the order. When deserters are hired out, the agreement shall be prepared and signed by the employer in duplicate, and one copy shall be retained by the latter.

61.—When deserters are contracted, the contract shall be prepared and signed in quadruplicate as prescribed in the Instructions of 1868 and the Regulations of the 14th September, 1872.

62.—All employers hiring out or contracting with Chinese from the central dépôt shall effect their registration before the Authorities of the locality where they are to serve, so that due effect may be given to various provisions of the Decree of 1860 and of the Instructions of 1868. Reports of cases of flight or death shall also be made to both the local officials and the Central Commission.

Any neglect in the observance of this rule shall be punished by the infliction of a fine proportioned to the culpability of the employer or the official.

63.—The Commission shall, in addition to its other records, keep an account current with each employer of deserters hired out from the central dépôt.

64.—Delay in payment of the wages due for the labour of such deserters shall cause their removal back to the central dépôt, and the arrear shall be made good out of any amount deposited in advance by the employer or by the person, if any, who acted as his security.

65.—When Chinese re-enter the central dépôt, although the various formalities of report shall be observed as at the time of first admission, they shall receive the number originally given to them.

Labor Contract, 1866,
and Letter of Domicile, 1869

EMIGRACION CHINA PARA CUBA.

CONTRATA.

Conste por este documento que yo _____ natural del pueblo de _____ en China, de edad de 21 años, he convenido con el Señor **N. TANCO ARMERO**, Agente de los Señores **LOMBILLO, MONTALVO** y **Ca.** de la HABANA en embarcarme para dicho puerto en el buque que se me designe bajo las condiciones siguientes:

1ª.—Me comprometo a trabajar en la Ysla de Cuba á las ordenes de dichos Señores ó de cualquiera otra persona a quien traspase este Contrato, para lo cual doy mi consentimiento.

2ª.—Este Contrato durará ocho años, que principiarán á contarse desde el dia que entre á servir, siempre que el estado de mi salud sea bueno; pero si me hallare enfermo ó imposibilitado para trabajar, entonces no será hasta que pasen ocho dias despues de mi restablecimiento.

3ª.—Trabajaré en todas las faenas que alli se acostumbra ya sea en el campo ó en las poblaciones, ya en casas particulares para el servicio domestico, ó en cualquier establecimiento comercial ó industrial; ya en ingenios, vegas, cafetales, sitios, potreros, estancias, &c. Enfin, me consagraré á cualquiera clase de trabajo urbano ó rural á que me dedique el patrono.

4ª.—Serán de descanso los Domingos que podré emplear en trabajar por mi cuenta si me conviniere, siempre que no sea destinado al servicio domestico en cuyo caso me sujetaré á la costumbre del pais.

5ª.—Las horas de trabajo no podran pasar de 12 por termino medio de las 24 del dia, salvo siempre el servicio domestico y el interior en las casas de campo.

6ª.—Bajo ningun concepto podré durante los ocho años de mi compromiso negar mis servicios á la persona a quien se traspaste ase Contrato ni evadirme de su poder ni siquiera intentarlo por causa alguna, á no ser la de redencion obtenida con arreglo á la ley.

El Señor Dn **N. TANCO ARMERO**, se obliga á su vez a lo siguiente:

I. A que desde el dia en que principien á contarse los ocho años de mi compromiso, principie tambien a correrme el salario de cuatro pesos, al mes, el mismo que dicho Agente me garantiza y asegura por cada mes de los ocho años de mi Contrato.

II. Que se me suministre de alimento cada dia ocho onzas de carne salada, y dos y media libras de boniatos ó de otras viandas sanas y alimenticias.

III. Que durante mis enfermedades se me proporcione en la enfermeria la asistencia que mis males reclamen, asi como los ausilios, medicinas y facultativo que mis dolencias y conservacion ecsijan por cualquier tiempo que duren. Y mis salarios continuarán asi mismo, salvo que mi enfermedad hubiese sido adquirida por mi culpa.

IV. Será de cuenta del mismo Agente ó por la que corresponda el pasage hasta la HABANA y mi manutencion a bordo.

V. Que se me den dos mudas de ropa, una camisa de lana y una frazada anuales.

VI. El mismo Señor me adelantará la cantidad de ocho pesos fuertes en oro ó plata para mi habilitacion en el viage que voi á emprender, la misma que satisfaré en la HABANA á las ordenes de dicho Señor con un peso al mes que se descontará de mi salario por la persona á quien fuese entregado este Contrato, entendiendose que por ningun otro concepto podrá hacerseme descuento alguno.

VII. A darme gratis 3 mudas de ropa y demas utensilios necesarios el dia de mi embarque.

VIII. A que se me conceda la protecion de las leyes que rijan en la Ysla de Cuba.

IX. A que transcurridos los 8 años estipulados en esta Contrata, tendré libertad para disponer de mi trabajo sin que pueda servir de pretesto para prolongar esta Contrata contra mi voluntad, cualquiera deudas, empeños ó compromisos que hubiera contraido.

DECLARO haber recebido en efectivo segun se espresa en la ultima clausula la suma de pesos ocho mencionados que reintegraré en la HABANA en la forma establecida en dicha clausula.

DECLARO tambien que me conformo con el salario estipulado aunque sé y me consta es mucho mayor el que ganan otros jornaleros libres y los esclavos en la Ysla de Cuba; porque esta diferencia la juzgo compensada con las otras ventajas que ha de proporcionarme mi patrono y las que aparecen en este Contrato.

QUEDO impuesto que al concluir el presente Contrato se me conceden 60 dias para volver a mi país de mi cuenta si me conviniere, ó para buscar acomodo con el patrono que me sea mas util y con el mayor salario que se dice en el anterior articulo ganan los trabajadores en Cuba, segun mi capacidad ó aficion al trabajo ú oficio que me pueda proporcionar.

Y en cumplimiento de todo lo espuesto arriba, declaramos ademas ambos contratantes que antes de poner nuestra firma hemos leido por la ultima vez detenidamente todos y cada uno de los articulos anteriores, y que sabemos perfectamente los compromisos que hemos contraido mutuamente, afin de que en ningun tiempo, ni por ningun motivo pueda arguirse ignorancia ni haber lugar a reclamos, escepto en el caso de faltar a cualquiera de las condiciones estipuladas en esta Contrata.

Y en fé de lo cual firmamos ante testigos el presente documento ambos contratantes en MACAO á 5 de Septiembre de 1866.

_____ _____
Agente.

_____
Procurador.

_____
Superintendente da Emigração.

催　合　工　同

立合同催工人　黃安

中國　廣東省　　府　奥山　縣人民年方　歲今與

在亞灣拿埠先翁燕隆美羅蒙打和公司之在澳代辦人先翁燕呢登哥啞美羅蒙說合揩其願定之船前往該埠催工所有條欵開列於左

一言明在亞灣拿催工聽從美羅蒙打和先翁們使用如將合同轉交別人我亦聽從執合同人使令

二催工期限八年自初半身上無病即于開工日起計若身有病俟醫好八日後起計

三所有城內城外無論何工或田畝或村庄或家中使喚或行內催工或磨房或園圃指不盡各項工程我悉聽從力作

四凡遇禮拜即爲停工之日任作工爲已之益倘家常事務此處規矩等事不得藉端不作

五每日二十四點鐘但作工時候不過十二點鐘之外倘家常事務規矩工夫照常要作

六工期八年之內執合同人所有事務我不得藉端不作亦不得圖謀躲避惟照官定奪遵例而行可也

今與代辦人先翁燕呢登哥啞美羅說合自願約定各項開列于後

一工期八年按照合同每日起工每月工銀四員按月照給包我滿期毫無拖欠

二每日發給鹹肉八兩另雜項食物二務半均係好肉可養人之物

三凡遇有病不論何日多寮事必送入醫院令醫生看病施藥病好爲止但其病亞非自作之孽事主不得扣除工銀

四所往亞灣拿一切船隻食用等項均係代辦人自出

五每年給我衣裳二套小衫二件洋氈一張

六該先翁等燕呢登哥啞美羅給我銀八員或金值銀八員以爲預備行李十物以便行船俟到亞灣拿執合同人可于每月工銀內扣銀一員

七下船之日給我食用十物不在扣工銀之內

八我在亞灣拿催工事主務必無得阻攔無得藉端指欠用法事例照應於我

九滿八年工期任我自便經營事主無得阻攔亞灣拿工人價比我更多但我將來照合同必受事主利益不少則工銀雖少亦無岐異今惟依合同所定工銀而已至期滿後事主務必給我六十日在平安開回國以便自備回國若我不欲回國欲將自已本領另尋高着圖得高價如亞灣拿工人無異悉任我便毫無阻擋之處

今訂明日後離知或訪聞亞灣拿工人價

除已上各欵外現文言明二家於未簽名之先業已將合同逐欵究明朗誦因此二家於合同內彼此所許者無不了悉一切日後萬不能推脫不知另生異論等弊若有不遵者離免罰罰懲恐口無憑二家立此合同當中簽名交執爲據

同治　五年　七月　　立　　　日在澳門立合同工人

黃安　收銀八大員

Signal de_____　Está conforme,

Interprete.

Talon número *122*

ISLA
DE
CUBA.

Señas generales.

Edad *61*
Estatura *reg.*
Pelo *natural*
Ojos *pardos*
Nariz *reg.*
Barba *cana*
Cara *—*
Color *trigueña*

Señas particulares.
—

DEL PAGO AÑO de 1869.

DE
ALACRANES — Gobierno de *Matanzas*

CEDULA DE VECINDAD
PARA CABEZA DE FAMILIA

Andres Meléndez Campos natural de *China = Campos* empadronado en *este Partido = Altos* vive en la calle de *Cuatro Unión* número *—*

Matanzas de *Setiembre* de 1869.

El Gobernador.

EL INTERESADO,

VA SIN ENMIENDA.

Pagó 250 milésimas

IMPRENTA DEL GOBIERNO Y CAPITANIA GENERAL POR S. M.

VIGILANCIA PUBLICA

RELATED TITLES IN THE SERIES

Walton Look Lai, *Indentured Labor, Caribbean Sugar: Chinese and Indian Migrants to the British West Indies, 1838–1918*

João José Reis, *Slave Rebellion in Brazil: The Muslim Uprising of 1835 in Bahia*. Translated by Arthur Brakel

Peter Wade, *Blackness and Race Mixture: The Dynamics of Racial Identity in Colombia*

Neville A. T. Hall, *Slave Society in the Danish West Indies: St. Thomas, St. John, and St. Croix*. Edited by Barry Higman

Philip P. Boucher, *Cannibal Encounters: Europeans and Island Caribs, 1492–1763*

Thomas C. Holt, *The Problem of Freedom: Race, Labor, and Politics in Jamaica and Britain, 1832–1938*

Dale W. Tomich, *Slavery in the Circuit of Sugar: Martinique and the World Economy, 1830–1848*

Richard Price, *Alabi's World*

Philippe I. Bourgois, *Ethnicity at Work: Divided Labor on a Central American Banana Plantation*

Michel-Rolph Trouillot, *Peasants and Capital: Dominica in the World Economy*

David Barry Gaspar, *Bondmen and Rebels: A Study of Master-Slave Relations in Antigua, with Implications for Colonial British America*